SCOTS

THE MITHER TONGUE

BILLY KAY

MAINSTREAM
PUBLISHING

EDINBURGH AND LONDON

First published in Great Britain in 1986 by
MAINSTREAM PUBLISHING COMPANY (EDINBURGH) LTD
7 Albany Street
Edinburgh EH1 3UG

ISBN 9781845960521

A catalogue record for this book is available from the British Library

Typeset in Janson Text

Printed in Great Britain by
Clays Ltd, Elcograf S.p.A

15

For ma mither, Anne Adams Kay

1922–1984

'. . . till a' the seas gang dry.'

Acknowledgements

I should like to thank the following people for their help, advice and contribution of material for the book: Iseabail MacLeod; Eleanor Aitken, director of *The Mother Tongue*; Bruce Young, producer of *The Scots Tongue*; Michael Shaw, producer of *Europe of 100 Tongues*, the companion television and radio series broadcast by BBC Scotland; Don Coutts, director of the Channel 4 Schools television series *Haud Yer Tongue*; A.J. Aitken; Carol Craig; J. Derrick McClure; Dr William Donaldson; Keith Williamson; Alexander Law; Dr David Hewitt; David Purves; William Neill; R.D. Clement; W.A.D. Riach; Suzanne Romaine; Nancy C. Dorian; P.H. Scott; Hans Speitel; Tom Leonard; William McIlvanney; Gordon Williams; Walter Elliot; Linde Lunney; Jack McKinney; Ernie Scott of Ulster; John J. Graham and the Sandison family, Shetland; Ian D. Hendry; Duncan Muirden; Ellie McDonald; John Hodgart; Sheena Blackhall; Matthew Fitt; Edwin Morgan; James Robertson; Irvine Welsh; Dr Anne King; Irene McGugan; Rob Gibson and fellow members of the Cross Party Group for Scots at the Scottish Parliament; Bob Fairnie of Scots Tung; John Law; Michael Hance an the guid fowk o the Scots Language Resource Centre in Perth; Emma McCallum; Tim Norwood; Ian Máté; Claire Rose and the staff of Mainstream Publishing; ma wife João, son Euan an dochters Joanna an Catriona for their support; ma late mither an faither, wha gied me Scots an wes aye eident tae mak siccar that their pride in it lowed bricht in me.

Contents

Prolog

Sae come aa ye at hame wi freedom,
Never heed whit the hoodies croak for doom;
In yer hoose aa the bairns o Adam
Will find breid, barley bree an painted room.

I begin with the words of Hamish Henderson's song 'The Freedom Come All Ye', the great anthem of the movement to create a Scottish parliament, which finally achieved its aims on 12 May 1999, when Winnie Ewing uttered the historic words, 'the Scottish Parliament, adjourned on the 25th day of March 1707, is hereby reconvened'. As a trustee of Common Cause, a speaker at Scotland United rallies and an activist in the Artists for Independence movement, I sang the song with smeddum and pride – with thousands at the great Edinburgh Democracy Demonstration in 1992 and with a few fellow-travellers outside Arbroath Abbey before setting off on the Bus Party, which tried to convince the public of the need to vote yes in the devolution referendum of 1997. The song became an anthem because it said so much about the kind of Scotland we wanted – Scots in language, international in perspective, egalitarian in outlook and inclusive of all humanity.

It is part of a wonderful tradition of songs in the Scots tongue, where words and music reach straight tae the hert an gar it lowp – even people who do not understand the language feel its power to communicate something profound in the human condition. Burns' 'Auld Lang Syne' and 'Is There for Honest Poverty' are classic examples of the genre. So when the Scottish Parliament opened with Sheena Wellington's powerful rendition of 'A Man's A Man', it was as if not only the privileged few inside the Parliament were singing along, it seemed to encompass the whole world, 'for aw that an aw that, it's comin yet for aw that, that man tae man the world ower shall brithers be for aw that'. It was a moment of intense emotion for Scots at home and abroad, the kind of experience which makes you agree for a while with the famous words of Andrew Fletcher of Saltoun: 'I knew a very wise man [who believed that] if a man were permitted to make all the ballads, he need not care who should make the laws of a nation.'

Seven years on, I am sure that many members of the ruling executive coalition would love it if we were all content to sing the songs and leave them to the real politics of making laws. Unfortunately for them, those days are past. When we only had recourse to a United Kingdom parliament dominated by the English majority, activists in Scotland accepted the difficulty of fostering native Scottish culture in that context. Now that we have our own parliament, however, our politicians have no excuses, and we expect and demand them to pass legislation which will nurture and promote every aspect of our native culture, including our indigenous languages. Until now, the response to their new responsibilities has been abysmal. It is very much a continuation of the narrow, ultra-unionist focus of both left and right in the old district and city councils most were thirled to before making the step up to what they should regard as a national parliament.

Elsewhere in this book, I compare the Scots situation with that of Catalan. In Catalonia, the new democracy that emerged following the death of General Franco believed that it might take three generations to remove the 'slave mentality' which had evolved over centuries as the native culture was suppressed by Castilian Spanish hegemony. Today, as a member of the Cross-Party Group (CPG) on Scots, having seen our politicians from a closer perspective, I feel that the hostility to and ignorance of ethnic Scottish culture displayed by perhaps the majority in the Parliament means that the struggle to give Scots any status whatsoever will be resisted vigorously.

Indeed, it may take an appeal to Europe to make the Scottish Executive fulfil its responsibility towards Scots. For while a slave mentality existed in Catalonia and certain elites identified with Spanish culture, most Catalans still had a regard for Catalan culture. Many Scottish politicians, however, see Scottish culture as something to be suppressed because it is a dangerous harbinger of nationalist sentiment.

Exaggeration? Here are two examples, comments by Labour ministers related to me by trustworthy sources. In the first, an Education minister is asked why more is not done to promote Scottish studies in the school curriculum. The reply: 'I do not see my role as educating a generation of young nationalists.' In the second, a member of the CPG asks the Culture minister whether he has received an invitation in Scots to come to the next meeting of the group. The reply: 'Oh, that thing, written in the funny writing. Yes, I threw it in the bin.' That is the level of cynicism existing within the Government.

On the Conservative side, the attitude to Scots is little better. In February 2000, there took place a debate as to whether a question on Scots should be included in the 2001 census. Here are extracts from two of the Tory contributions. Jamie McGrigor: 'I am a firm advocate of the protection of the Scots language. Like Gaelic, its history is timeless and is surrounded by romance. I love the poetry of Burns and MacDiarmid and never go anywhere without my nickie-tams.' Brian Monteith: 'In concluding my speech in the debate on a census question on Scots language, I feel that it is only right that we say that we are gaunae no dae that.'

One being a comedian, the other quoting a comedian; hard tae say whit ane wes the biggest scunner but baith certainly gard me grue at the time! Having spent years fighting for a Scottish parliament, it was a salutary experience to thole the fact that at the first opportunity to discuss Scots, elected members and fellow Scots were making a fool of the issue. On such occasions when I feel alienation from my fellow countrymen, I hear Hugh MacDiarmid's humorous response to the same conundrum:

> 'Mercy o Gode, I canna thole
> wi sic an orra mob to roll.'
> *'Wheesht! It's for the guid o your soul.'*

It micht be for the guid o my soul but I dinnae like whit it duis tae my heid!

That debate in the Parliament was instigated by Irene McGugan, the SNP MSP for North-east Scotland. She simply put forward a motion that the census should ask the Scottish people whether or not they were 'able to (a) understand (b) speak (c) read and (d) write Scots (including any local Scots speech form such as Buchan, Glasgow or Shetland dialects)'. Not a difficult question for normal folk, but that is not how it was viewed by the Parliament. Not one single Labour, Liberal or Conservative MSP voted for the motion, even though a few, such as Alex Johnstone and Cathy Peattie, professed a personal interest. I think that those who were sympathetic in these parties were got at by the party whips and brought into line. Nora Radcliffe, Liberal Democrat MSP for Gordon, was the one abstention and at least she was honest enough to acknowledge the personal v. political debate going on within her: 'On the Scots language question, my head hears the difficulties but my heart responded to Irene McGugan's speech. I dinna ken fit tae dee—heid or hert.'

Those who felt embarrassed and guilty for following the party line and voting against the question on Scots had a ready-made 'get out of jail free' card provided by mention of a possible question on Scots in a future, expanded Household Survey. You could see those with their consciences squirming desperately grabbing this as a get-out clause, several mentioning that they looked forward to information on Scots being gathered from that source. Six years on, of course, there has been no Household Survey with a question on Scots.

On the pro-Scots side in the census debate were Robin Harper of the Green Party, the SSP's Tommy Sheridan and the Independent Dennis Canavan, plus all 28 representatives of the Scottish National Party. Scotland's languages should not be the preserve of one political group, and I would love nothing more than to give citations to people from the rest of the parties, but in this debate the only politicians who cared enough to vote in favour of the motion were those situated on the SNP benches. Its speakers were as articulate and passionate as anyone who loves Scots would want them to be. The following extracts give a flavour of what was said.

> **Irene McGugan (SNP, North-east Scotland)**: Many of us were brought up in a country where the major institutions did not recognise our language and culture as valid. Surely our new Scottish democracy must recognise the culture and speech of the mass of the people if it is to approach the ideal of inclusivity which is cherished by all of us who worked for the creation of the Parliament . . .
>
> Scots is still alive and thriving but now needs help and support, such as that given to Ulster Scots as part of the Good Friday Agreement. The proposal is that Ulster Scots will receive £1 million, 75 per cent of which will come from the UK Government, a somewhat larger sum than it has ever given to the parent language, Scots. Currently, only £112,000 per year is given to support Scots, which is almost certainly the worst-funded minority language in Europe . . .

By opposing the question on Scots, this Parliament would effectively be opposing meaningful development of the Scots language and denying equality to one of Scotland's indigenous languages.

Gil Paterson (SNP, Central Scotland): Is it not a sad day when we come to a place called the Scottish Parliament to argue that the Scottish government should agree to have a question on the Scots language in the census? How ungracious of the minister to accept two recommendations out of three from the Equal Opportunities Committee. The one that he cannot swallow – the one that he has rejected – is on the Scots language. What a slap in the face to the vast majority of people who use Scots as their normal everyday way of talking. What is the minister actually saying to them? Is he saying, 'Speak properly'? Or is he saying that the people are second class? . . .

It is not that long ago that Gaelic was derided and frowned upon. However, after a great fight for recognition, it is getting over its trauma. The Scots language has endured the same treatment, having been under attack from a frame of mind that stigmatises it, piling on it large doses of social prejudice. The Parliament is supposed to be committed to a programme of social inclusion. Surely that should include the Scots language.

Until we correct the barriers, hurdles and downright hostility to the people's language – the language of the streets and of homes and workplaces – it will be treated as the ultimate Scottish cringe by those who look to some other place for their vision and their culture.

It would be nothing short of a joke or a farce for this place to call itself the Scottish Parliament while sending out a message that it is OK to humiliate the Scottish people by not recognising their right to speak their own tongue. Ur we no aw Jock Tamson's bairns and should we no be treated like that?

One of the aftermaths of the debate was an illuminating column in the *Paisley Daily Express* by the Labour MSP Hugh Henry, who gave full vent to his feelings about parliamentary time being wasted on irrelevances like language and identity:

There are some who believe that what is described as 'Scots language' should be given the same status as Gaelic . . . In support of this I received an email from, and I quote, the

'Secretair o Scots Tung'. My computer went into overdrive trying to spell-check the email. My brain went numb trying to understand it . . . I would rather ask questions which produce information on whether our society is tackling inequality, poor health, bad housing, low incomes than confuse people with strange words which few would understand.

Paisley, of course, is home to a great tradition of Scots poetry and song produced by the radical weavers of the town, a tradition celebrated throughout Scotland in the songs of Robert Tannahill and extending to the United States through the work of Alexander Wilson. No one but the ignorant could be 'confused' by their 'strange words which few would understand'. What a sad indictment of a society when a prominent figure like Henry can be so removed from the cultural history of his own constituency that he disparages the language at its heart.

There are a number of factors at the core of the Executive's hostility to Scots. Unlike Gaelic, which belongs to a distinct and diminishing community and can be safely supported as long as it is confined to the periphery, Scots is regarded as a nationalist shibboleth, an ethnic step too far into the nationalist unknown for those who adhere to a safe, familiar, unionist world picture. One of the ironies in this is that many of the Labour politicians come from an Irish background where a few generations ago they themselves would have been nationalists and republicans. Now they are entrenched loyalists in the British state. At the same time as the MSPs were rejecting the question on Scots, they were accepting a question on religious affiliation. Because of this political power base in the west of Scotland in particular, newspapers there gave extensive coverage to the demand for a question on religion and almost totally ignored the Scots question. Another factor in Labour hostility is a personal one: many are people who have come from working-class, Scots-speaking backgrounds who have been told that to get on in the world they have to ditch that background, and they have no wish to be reminded of it. A sneaking sense of guilt remains. Then there is the simple fact that to recognise Scots would cost money. If Gaelic, with fewer than 60,000 speakers, has over 8 million pounds invested in it, how much would Scots cost, with projected figures of 1.5 million speakers? Better to adopt what I call the death-wish approach and hope that if Scots is ignored, it will wither and die. Jist mind, though, when ye're mouthin sleekit platitudes and slaiverin radical sangs at yer annual Burns Supper, that the Bard is birlin in his mools aneath ye, scunnert for aye bi the parcel o rogues he kent then an still kens sae weel.

A few weeks after the census debate, Irene McGugan raised the issues of Scots and Gaelic again, when she pointed out that European money would be available to promote the native leids during the forthcoming European Year of Languages. Because this did not require a vote that would have to result in positive action for Scots, the personal rather than the political was more to the fore, with several MSPs making positive noises. Cathy Peattie, the Labour MSP for Falkirk East, said:

> If we take away people's language, we take away their voice . . .
>
> I agree with Irene McGugan – as a Lallans Scots, I want to come into the Parliament and see Scots signage. If people see their Scots language written, they will start to believe that it is their language and that they have every right to use it.
>
> I thank Irene for today's debate, and look forward to strengthening our indigenous languages in many more debates in the Parliament.

The reference to signage in Scots in the new parliament building, supported there by a Labour MSP, was another issue that concerned the CPG over the intervening years – yet another one over which obfuscation and delaying tactics were employed by the Corporate Body until the building went up with the signage in English and Gaelic only.

While some displayed a more enlightened attitude to Scots in the European Year of Languages debate, others reverted to type and came away with one of the old divide-and-rule tactics as an excuse to do nothing. The Liberal Democrat MSP for Caithness, Sutherland and Easter Ross, Jamie Stone, appealed 'against the use of a broad brush. The Scots that is spoken in Caithness is very different from the Scots that Irene McGugan might recognise and includes words such as "scorrie", meaning a seagull, and "semmit", meaning a vest.' Oh dear, Jamie, you really should do your homework before exposing yourself like that; 'semmit' is of course a common Scots word, recognised nationwide. When I was making the Channel 4 Schools television series *Haud Yer Tongue*, it was even chosen by a British Airways stewardess as her favourite Scots word! Looking back at the transcripts of the debate, I came across an exchange which suggests that the anti-Scots hostility on the Labour benches came from the very top, from the First Minister himself, the late Donald Dewar:

Alex Johnstone (Conservative, North-east Scotland): My concern particularly is the attitude, held by a significant number of people in the Parliament, that there is no such language as Scots. When Irene McGugan was making her opening remarks, I heard a chirp coming from my left, where the First Minister was sitting at the time, suggesting that very thing.

Michael Russell (SNP, South of Scotland): Shame.

Alex Johnstone: The member may say 'shame'. I could not criticise that because my culture spokesman, Brian Monteith, might well say the same thing. That is probably one of the few similarities between the First Minister and Brian Monteith. At least, hearing that chirp in my ear, it was nice to have the First Minister back.

I am concerned that we do not make the mistake of treating Gaelic and Scots as two arms of the same policy. Gaelic is a clearly identifiable language. While I believe that there is a Scots language, I do not believe that it is necessarily a single language. A very different language is spoken in Glasgow from what I hear spoken in Buchan. There is more than one culture that needs to be preserved.

Michael Russell: I wonder whether Alex Johnstone will reflect on the same difference in the English language. Perhaps he should go to Newcastle, then Aberdeen, Cornwall, Glasgow and Norwich. His argument is fallacious because in every language there are variations but that does not make them different languages . . . I want to say one thing about Scots. Today we have heard here repeated the calumny that Scots is not one language. That used to be the argument that was made about Gaelic: that there was a Gaelic dialect here and a Gaelic dialect there, that there were words here and words there, but that it should not be treated as a language. Let us lay that calumny to rest here and now. Scots is a language – a language that needs help and assistance.

Mike Russell goes on to say that we have to care for Gaelic and Scots because they are uniquely ours, and no one else's responsibility. One would hope, though, that some of that responsibility would extend to the government of Scotland as well. My experience, however, has been that our legislators are hopelessly out of their depth in this matter. At the CPG, I have witnessed a succession of ministers being astonished by the range, number and quality of the people involved in promoting Scots. They then make bland statements they hope will not come back to haunt them. Caught as they are in the spotlight of their own ignorance, they are desperate to get out, in the hope that they will not be responsible when they are forced to appear again in the future. Chances are they will be correct in this assessment. Thus nothing is done.

The British government's and, since devolution, the Scottish Executive's handling of their responsibilities towards Scots in relation to the European Charter for Regional or Minority Languages have been notable for both prevaricating duplicity and serial ineptitude. When you read the European Committee of Experts' report and their recommendations on how the Scottish and UK authorities should fulfil their responsibilities vis-à-vis Scots, and then read our authorities' response, you quickly realise that the same tactics we have tholed here are being used on the European Committee of Experts. In the latest UK report, there is not even a separate heading for Scots – it is put under the heading 'Scots Gaelic' in the hope that no one will notice that practically nothing is being done for Scots compared to what is being provided for Gaelic. The Europeans see through it, of course, and a sample of their statements gives an idea of what they think of our government's performance:

> The Committee of Experts has been informed of few initiatives undertaken to promote the Scots language.
>
> The Committee of Experts has not received information of any particular measures adopted by the Scottish Executive to facilitate and/or encourage the use of Scots.
>
> The Committee of Experts has been informed that there are no Scots classes in primary or in secondary schools, and, in the few cases where the language is taught, the teaching relies on the initiatives of individual teachers.

The conclusion by the Committee is one that would be endorsed by all who care for Scotland's other indigenous language – the bonnie broukit bairn that is Scots: 'There appears to be less emphasis on minority language policy on the part of the Scottish Executive, even though there is political will to protect the Gaelic language.'

All of the reports from the UK and Europe are thrang with

references to Welsh, Irish, Gaelic and Ulster Scots, for the political settlement of the Good Friday agreement in Ireland left us with the anomaly of Ulster Scots getting recognition and funding from the UK government which are beyond the wildest dreams of the parent Scots language. Because of that, though, the European experts included in their report the following recommendation for the authorities here to implement: 'Create conditions for the use of Scots and Ulster Scots in public life, through the adoption of a language policy and concrete measures, in cooperation with the speakers of the languages.'

As far as Scots is concerned, dinnae haud yer braith for an instant implementation of that or any other recommendation. For it is unlikely that there will ever be a proper language strategy from the Scottish government. There will be plenty of weasel words about how valued Scots is and there will always be projects they can point to as an indicator of their support – help in book and dictionary publishing for example, or support for writers. But nothing will be done to extend the language itself. In a recent edition of *Scots Tung Wittins*, the monthly Scots language newsletter, Bob Fairnie recalled a visit to Scotland by an Australian expert on threatened languages, Professor Joe LoBianco. He pointed out that when a government gives lots of verbal support to a language but then does nothing actively to help it survive, then that government actually does have a language strategy – and that strategy is to kill off the language for ever. As you will see when you read the rest of this book, that has been an Establishment strategy off and on for the best part of 300 years, since the political union of 1707. Now, though, there are European authorities more sympathetic to the interests of lesser-used language groups and ultimately, I feel, we may need to have recourse to them for our linguistic rights to be maintained. The MSP Irene McGugan, like me frustrated by the Scottish Executive's inactivity regarding Scots, suggested in Parliament a scenario that may well be worth exploring if the status quo remains static:

> There is a body of opinion that holds that discrimination against speakers of a language is in breach of international protocols, namely the International Covenant on Civil and Political Rights, the Universal Declaration of the Collective Rights of Peoples and the Oslo recommendations regarding the linguistic rights of national minorities. How embarrassing it would be for the Executive to defend its action or inaction in international courts during the European year of languages.

What, you might ask, has all this politicking to do with language? Everything. For politics determines the way we view language and culture, and in time that influences how we view ourselves. The perceived difference between a language and a dialect, for example, can be summed up succinctly: a language is a dialect wi an army an navy. As we shall see, the Spanish state regarded Galician and Catalan as provincial patois rather than languages. With political autonomy in Galicia and Catalonia, however, both languages are now being 'normalised' to achieve parity with Spanish.

The effects of centuries of stigmatisation and cultural colonisation cannot, of course, be overcome instantly with a new political attitude. The Catalans are a few decades into the recovery of their language but they concede that it will take several generations of confidence building before what they call the 'slave mentality' of their people can be removed. In public perceptions of Scots, we face similar problems and have not even seriously begun the process of recovery. Our equivalent of the slave mentality is the 'Scottish cringe'. I can cite two examples from my own experience in the past few years. A Fife headmaster was asked how much time his school devoted to Scottish studies. He replied, 'Very little. This is not a very Scottish area.' When it was proposed to the education convener of a major Scottish local authority that Scottish studies should become an integral part of his schools' curriculum, he replied, 'Oh, no. We live in a multicultural environment.' Every culture was to be taught, in other words, except the native one. Gin ye didnae laugh, ye wad greet!

Such outrageous statements could be confined to the dustbin of history if we implemented and acted on the recommendations for Scots that have been put forward over the past decade. 'English Language 5–14', the national guidelines for teaching language in our schools, was issued by the Scottish Office Education Department in the early 1990s. There, the importance of recognising and fostering the languages children bring to school and their linguistic heritage is emphasised. As you will see later in the book, much of the same has been stressed in the past. This time, though, the recognition accorded to Scots in the document acted as a catalyst for those who were sympathetic to act and do something concrete in favour of the tongue. More recently, there have been several major studies made on Scots.

While the new parliament disappointed in its debate on a census question for Scots, it did deliver two major contributions to the Scots debate – the *Statement o Principles* produced by members of the Scots CPG, and the Education, Culture and Sport Committee's report on their inquiry into the role of educational and cultural policy in

21

supporting and developing Gaelic, Scots and minority languages in Scotland – contributions which stand available as the basis for a detailed future language strategy, if there ever exists the political will to deliver such a thing. The report begins by starkly placing our indigenous tongues in the context of what is happening to similar languages all over the world:

> Despite its many advantages, globalisation is threatening linguistic diversity. In particular, the future for Scotland's two heritage languages, Scots and Gaelic, could be at risk. In one of the documents of the Nuffield Inquiry on languages in the UK, it is stated that: 'It has been estimated that 90 per cent of the world's languages will either be extinct or doomed to extinction by the end of the next (twenty-first) century. A language – or, rather, its last remaining speaker – dies every two weeks. This language loss is closely associated with a loss of cultural diversity, together with a loss of small communities and their specialised knowledge and social practices. The loss of cultural and linguistic diversity facing the world in the next decades is far greater than the parallel loss in the biological world.'

Drawing on submissions from experts such as Professor Richard Johnstone, the director of the Scottish Centre for Information on Language Teaching and Research (CILT), the report goes on to highlight the strange anomalies of the Scots position, always stressing that a multilingual society is healthier than a narrow, monoglot one:

> From the submissions received, it would appear that not enough is being done to promote and to introduce into mainstream education the notion of bilingualism and multilingualism. Whilst some success has been achieved in the promotion and teaching of Gaelic, Scots and community languages appear to have been, so far, neglected.

The submissions highlighted the need for Scots to be given official status and adequate recognition in public life, as the language is integral to cultural identity. J. Derrick McClure, senior lecturer in the Department of English at the University of Aberdeen, stated:

> The Scots language, traditionally neglected or actively suppressed in the education system, has in recent years enjoyed a quite dramatic reversal in its fortunes. In chronological order,

the following related developments have taken place: a remarkable literary efflorescence, including a corpus of brilliant, inventive and strongly politically motivated poetry; a major improvement in the status of the language as a field of academic research, both in its historical and contemporary forms; the increasing availability of published materials for research and teaching, most notably the two multi-volume dictionaries and their derived works; a vigorous effort to improve its status in the classroom; and finally the proclaimed intention of the new Scottish Parliament to give active encouragement to the language. However, as a counter to this, an abysm of ignorance on both popular and administrative levels has still to be confronted; initiatives have been exercised largely on an individual and piecemeal basis; and the Parliament has so far failed to develop, much less to promote, a coherent and practical policy designed to encourage the language and secure its status as a national language of Scotland.

The details submitted to the report also give a fascinating snapshot of Scots in contemporary education, particularly in the evidence supplied by Matthew Fitt. Matthew is weel kent as the author of the Scots sci-fi novel *But n Ben A-Go-Go* and, along with James Robertson, the energetic director of the Itchy Coo project, which produces excellent books and teaching materials in Scots. These he takes round Scotland's schools, so no one is better placed to know exactly what is happening to the language in the here and now:

This year I have been in primary schools whose names were comprised of some basic Scots words. At Burnbrae, the children (P7) knew neither the word 'burn' or 'brae'; at Bonnyholm Primary, the children (P6–7 composite) did not recognise the word 'bonny'.

In one school I visited, I was told by a P7 boy that the Scots words I was writing on the board were 'bad' and that the English ones were 'good'.

School children, upper primary and lower secondary, refer to Scots words when they see them written down as 'slang' and to English as 'proper'. It is fairly safe to assume that most of these children will have learned, read or recited a Scots poem at least once in their school careers. It is clear that this one-off study of a Scots poem does not provide pupils with a solid enough understanding of what the Scots language is.

In a lot of schools, most pupils are unable to pronounce the velar fricative 'ch' or <x> using instead 'k' – 'lock' for 'loch', etc.

There are, however, exceptions to this. Children in the North-east generally refer to Scots words on seeing them written as 'Doric'. And children who have some longer-term classroom experience of reading, speaking and writing in Scots refer to the language as 'Scots' or 'Scottish' . . .

One headmistress of a Glasgow Catholic primary school told me on a visit to her school that she was 'ragin that I got the Scots beat out of me when I was at school and my weans are not going to miss out on their linguistic heritage'.

The headmaster of another primary in Glasgow said: 'I didn't believe in it before. There didn't seem to be any point in Scots. But if we've got our own parliament, we've surely got to have our own language to go with it. It's just common sense.' . . .

A probationer teacher in Livingston says that he did not know of the language's existence until he went to a teachers' conference organised by Glasgow University. He now wants to be trained properly in how to deliver Scots to his pupils but is having difficulties getting help to develop courses appropriate for his children.

One teacher, again in Glasgow, has gone a step further than most. In my capacity as writer in residence for the Pollok area, I visited Morag McKie's P7 class at Nitshill Primary for five one-hour lessons at the start of 2001. Due to Morag's amazing capacity to assimilate my ideas into strong, effective learning suitable for each of her children in a class of quite varied ability, we were able, after four visits, to begin Scots-medium education. Morag and I led the class through an exercise about alliteration. We spoke in Scots; we gave examples of alliteration in Scots; the children responded in Scots; the children wrote in their jotters in Scots. What was amazing was that the lesson did not involve discussing in English about what Scots is or not; the whole lesson was conducted in Scots. When it was finished, Miss McKie clapped her hands and told the class they were going to do sums and that they were going to speak in English. The class switched for the next hour (and the rest of the day) to English. And they had no problem distinguishing between the two languages.

My own journey round Scotland to make *Haud Yer Tongue* was similar to Matthew's experience in that I had to cope with dramatically different situations. You would literally despair in one place as you were confronted by the moribund nature of the language, then rejoice in another airt, astonished by its vitality among the bairns. The writer Sheena Blackhall has extensive knowledge of the Scots of her native Aberdeen and Aberdeenshire and, in 2000, as part of her M.Litt. course at Aberdeen University, she conducted a survey to find out the current state of Scots among primary school bairns in the region. The complexity of Scotland's linguistic heritage came across forcibly to her when a pupil who was obviously a Doric speaker found it impossible to speak to her in their native dialect because he did not know her personally. In another school, the reaction was the opposite:

> Fin I spakk in Scots at an inner-city schule in Aiberdeen, efter twa meenits the bairns on the fleer instinctively hodged richt up tae ma taes . . . I puzzled ower this. Syne it dawned on me they anely heard Scots at hame an thocht I must be relatit tae them!
>
> On the contrar, fin I sang a waefu wee lullaby oot at Abyne Primary, the pupils stertit tae lauch . . . jist assumin cause it wis Scots, it wis funny.

Sheena was also struck by the differing reactions of the educational hierarchy to Scots. One headmaster refused point-blank to allow her into his school, presumably out of fear of her contaminating the children with knowledge of their native tongue! In contrast, another headmaster told her how he had responded when an English parent made a complaint about his teaching Burns. He replied that as long as he had one child in his class of Scots origin, he was obliged to cater for its ethnic needs!

In education generally, when the policymakers on high dictate to those howking at the coalface what policies they should implement, they are often ignored, if they can be. Despite statements of support for Scots in the past, it always remained an option and, because of the history of cultural colonisation which I outline throughout the book, it is an option that was ignored. That is why it is encouraging to see so many teachers wanting to get involved in reclaiming the language for their pupils. In the 1990s, the education committee of the largest teachers' union, the Educational Institute of Scotland (EIS), produced a policy paper forcefully arguing for Scots to be taught as an integral part of the primary school curriculum. At the launch of the document, the union's general secretary, Jim Martin, expressed a perspective shared by a growing number of teachers:

> Scots has as much claim to be regarded as a separate speech form as the local forms of speech of places like Catalonia and Luxembourg, and it has an equal claim to official recognition and encouragement. However, its long-term survival and development depend on its continuing to be spoken in local communities, in all its geographical diversity. Primary schools can make a strong contribution to this process and we urge them to do so.

Before devolution, and particularly during the Thatcher era, there was a growing consolidation of feeling for the importance of our cultural distinctiveness to act as a focus for resisting values imposed from without and at odds with our traditions. I value greatly the broad subject base enshrined in Scottish education, its concept of the democratic intellect, and its ideals of egalitarianism and access to higher education for all. I regard the Scots tradition in literature as underpinning these values and therefore despaired in the past at the dearth of Scots material in our schools. It is therefore heartening to see these two vital areas come together, as they should in any civilised country. The final recommendation of the Educational Institute's paper expressed this well:

> The EIS defence of the unique character of Scottish education should be developed through giving a higher profile to Scots language and culture as being important features of the system which is being defended and upheld. All children living in Scotland should be kept in touch with the languages and traditions of the country. Such an approach would act as a counterweight to the many centralising and standardising tendencies which are inherent in a general Anglo-American culture pattern. Making children aware of their heritage represents, in fact, the best long-term guarantee for the future identity and well-being of the Scottish educational system.

That is a fact long recognised by the Association for Scottish Literary Studies (ASLS), whose Schools Committee has done much to enhance the status of Scots literature in schools. It must be gratifying for them at last to see their work bear fruit. In many ways, the positive response of education is a direct result of the growing confidence generated by the quality of contemporary literature and drama written in Scots. This in turn is part of a wider commitment to, and confidence in, every aspect of Scottish culture. All of this fed the demand for political change which ultimately gave us our parliament. In the last edition of this book, written before the Parliament was established, I wrote, 'When [a Scottish parliament] does come about, our languages and culture will be given the political support they will need in the increasingly homogenised world of the twenty-first century.' Seven years into our new democratic dawn, I am still waiting and when my patience begins wearing thin, I remember Lewis Grassic Gibbon's use of the old quotation from the Bible, 'the millstones of God grind slowly'. Weel the millstanes o democracy grind even slower . . . but it's comin yet for aw that!

As with the whole movement towards devolution, the politicians were the last to catch up on the mood of the people. Now they are the last to realise that the old doubts they have about our culture are the doubts of a colonised mentality and have to be cast aside, and conditions created for the advance of the unique language we possess. The work is done for them, for a document like *Scots: A Statement o Principles* elegantly states what is required for Scots to thrive in the twenty-first century. Subtitled 'A Road Forrit for the Scots Language in a Multilingual Scotland', it uses the Universal Declaration of Linguistic Rights as the basis for a compelling case for Scots. Significantly, it is also written in a dignified, accessible Scots which could act as a model for such documents in the future. There is not space here to examine each of the principles in detail but it is worth highlighting a few to remind us all of something that should be ingrained in the new inclusive democracy we are trying to create: the language of the people, Scots, should be at the heart of that democracy:

> Scots is a language
> Action maun be taen tae pit an end tae aw prejudice an discrimination agin the Scots language
> The Scots language is integral an essential tae cultural an personal identity in Scotland
> A knowledge o Scots is vital tae a knowledge o Scotland
> Naebody shuid be penalised or pitten doun for speakin Scots

That the ideas contained in those principles are becoming increasingly part of mainstream opinion was endorsed recently, when in 2005 the Culture Commission's major review of cultural strategy was published. Again, Scots was recognised as being at the core of our cultural identity and the Commission's report called for a national indigenous language body and strategy to be set up with urgency: 'We believe that Scotland's indigenous languages, Gaelic and Scots, are national treasures and have a central role to play in the cultural life of Scotland.'

There are many other positives, which I will relate throughout the book, and one that struck me forcibly writing this chapter was the ready availability of Scots material via the Internet. There is now a Scots version of the Scottish Parliament website and from there you can access, for example, both the *Statement o Principles* and the Scots translation of the Education, Culture and Sport Committee report – the first such report to have been published in Scots for several hundred years! To see in Scots official material relating to such a prestigious institution as a parliament would have been unthinkable until comparatively recently. So things are improving; but we can only thole the Executive's inaction for so long. Everything that has been done to advance the status of Scots has been done by the people. We just need the politicians to finally catch up with the people and put all the good work that others have produced into practice. Until then, we keep the faith, encouraged by the advances made, inspired by our literature and pleased that we are at last approaching having an education system which is geared to support the culture and the language which inspires it. For only when the language is accepted as an integral part of our education, our media and our national parliament itself will the ignorance and confusion surrounding Scots finally be dispelled. Many Scots still need to be enlightened. That is why it was important for me to bring out this new edition of *Scots: The Mither Tongue*, the only accessible history of the language available. When the great German writer Goethe was on his deathbed, he is said to have called out for '*mehr Licht*'. According to its detractors, Scots has been on its deathbed for nearhaund fower hunder year! I hope this book sheds mair licht on our lang-a-deein mither tongue and helps illuminate the way to her full and vigorous recovery in the life of the nation.

1

The Mither Tongue?

The guid Scots tongue . . . a slovenly debased dialect . . . the Doric . . .
corrupt English . . . artificial Lallans . . . uncouth gutturals . . . the
National Language . . . an unintelligible dialect of English . . . Braid
Scots . . . coarse slang . . . a language that never existed. Every one of
those terms and epithets has been used to describe the language I was
brought up to speak, Scots. Its sounds are still the ones which rise most
naturally to my lips and therefore haunt the very writing of this book.
The ideas often come in Scots and the previous passage could just as
easily be transcribed as: every ane o thae terms an epithets has been
uised tae describe the language I wes brocht up tae speak, an its soonds
is aye the anes that rise maist natural tae ma lips. Thinking in Scots and
writing in English, switching from Scots to English when the social
situation calls for a change of register, getting into a muddle or puttin
yer fuit in it when the switch is not a clean one and Scots invades the
English – all are part of the linguistic experience of most Scots raised in
the Lowlands, and that covers the great majority of the population. For
many, admittedly, the change from one register to another is not as
dramatic as in my case, where a very rich dialect of Scots prevails. In the
cities, English and Scots have come closer together, though less so than
many would have us believe. In the country and towns, on the other
hand, speech patterns persist which are little changed in structure from
the Scots spoken in the language's golden age in the sixteenth century.
   When Scots speakers use the full range of their dialect, not only
sounds and words vary greatly from the English equivalent, but also

syntax and grammar: 'Afore I gaed ower the brig, the toon nock chappit hauf twa an thir lassies spierit gin I had got lousit shuiner nor I ettled'; 'Before I went over the bridge, the town clock struck half past two and these girls asked if I had stopped work sooner than expected.' Even among older people who speak a much more conservative form of Scots than anyone of my generation, the more usual form of communicating that information would be in a mixture of the two registers, with the balance of the mixture depending on the circumstances. In my own case, the mixture in normal circumstances would be close to the following: 'Afore I went ower the brig, the toon nock chappit hauf twa an thir lassies asked if I had stopped work shuiner than I expected.' Now, all three versions communicate the information equally well but the reaction to the three variations would be as diverse as some of the descriptive epithets used at the beginning of this chapter.

Alongside the Scots of my community, I acquired knowledge of English, as it was the medium of education, the Kirk, the doctor's surgery, and the radio and eventually television which exerted a strong cultural influence on the home environment. English was very much a written medium for me, however, and it was only really when I went to university that I felt the need to communicate for any sustained period in Standard English. Tongue-tied initially, because I doubted my ability to speak fluently in that register, I eventually sat down with tomes of classic English novels by authors such as Thackeray and Austen, and attempted to master their dialect. To this day, my English resounds with words like propensity and impropriety! Having acquired spoken English and feeling confident in my ability to communicate in it, I also made the conscious decision that knowledge of English did not necessitate the eradication of Scots.

One of the most debilitating phenomena of Scottish society is the false notion that to get on you have to get out. English hegemony is so all pervasive in our society that a sign of success and sophistication among some is to attempt to erase signs of Scottishness from their public persona. The implications of such an attitude for Scottish culture are drastic, not to mention wrong-headed. The linguistic tension is often not resolved at one particular time and can be an ongoing choice throughout one's life. Some people pretend to lose their Scots at some stage, then magically regain it later on because their social circumstances or cultural allegiances have altered. I recall an incident at Edinburgh University when at a social gathering someone accused me of putting on unnaturally a Scots dialect, because I used the word 'twa' instead of 'two'. The same gentleman now teaches in a working-class school and uses 'twa' as 'unnaturally' as I do. For me, then, not to continue using Scots would have been tantamount to rejecting the culture of the people I came from and hacking off the cultural roots which gave me the strength of identity I am lucky to possess. Discovering at university, to my great surprise, that the culture I came from had a literature and a history, and its language a pedigree, made me resolved rather to explore and strengthen awareness of the links between the Scottish intellectual tradition and the working-class culture most Scots stem from.

But long before that, I had pride in the Scots of my childhood. That was perhaps influenced by the fact that I had the good fortune to be born in the same dialect area as Robert Burns, Kyle in Ayrshire. Along with Elvis in the '50s and the Beatles and Tamla Motown in the '60s, his songs were part of the popular working-class culture that surrounded me in Galston and I suppose that helped give our dialect a status perhaps lacking in other airts of Scotland. But when you are young, status is far from your mind – Scots was just the way everyone spoke to everyone else. It was through the medium of this speech that the world became organised and controlled, and my relationship to it got definition. So much so that I still have to think hard to come up with the English for many everyday words: the birds of the surrounding countryside are still speugs, whaups, peesies, linties, stuckies an mavies to me. My mother, whose childhood had been spent in Mauchline, moved to Bowhill in West Fife with her father, a miner. She brought back to Ayrshire exotic terms such as 'baffies' for 'slippers' or 'bauch' for 'unwell' and these were absorbed into her family's speech. The family's annual Fair Holiday was spent, or in my father's case tholed, in Bowhill – 'Galston wi pit bings' was an apt description! There, everyone spoke Scots as well, albeit with that sing-song accent of theirs. As Galston and Bowhill were the limits of my childhood experience, I presumed that everyone in Scotland bar the middle classes spoke Scots. This, then, was my everyday speech, fundamental to my family, my local and national identity and an integral part of my sense of selfhood. Like me, I am sure hundreds of thousands of Scots.

It came as an extreme shock to one's sensibilities to discover that speaking the everyday language of home in the classroom was regarded as giving cheek to the teacher. The dialect was permitted once a year, when the Burns Federation was giving out its certificates or the school was organising a Burns Supper. The rest of the time, you would be belted for using his language within the school. Now, if a person's being is expressed through a language which is not recognised as a valid means of communication by the authorities which govern his life, the results can be traumatic. I am convinced that thousands of people from the same background as myself have rejected education because they felt its values totally alien to those of their own environment. I was lucky in that languages came easily to me and I could adapt to the teachers' requirements the few times this was demanded. For others, though, the banning of what for some was their only means of communication obviously led to a taciturn resignation that school was not for them. If using your first language is classed as the equivalent of sticking your tongue out at the teacher, there is little ground for fruitful dialogue. Educationalists often refer to the 'inarticulate Scot' as if it were a hereditary disease, instead of the effect of shackling people to one language when they are much more articulate in another.

The omnipotent standard of having one correct way of speaking colours our society's attitude and results in false value judgements about people. These value judgements are made in every sector of society, not just in education. In 1979, when I began the series of interviews with working-class Scots which led to the creation of the *Odyssey* series on Radio Scotland, a BBC internal report on my progress in the Corporation praised my ability to make inarticulate people talk. In the six months I had been conducting the interviews, I had met nothing but highly articulate characters – the kind of folk that made the series such compelling listening. The report made the typical British error of judging not what was said but how it was said – the surface, not the content. The BBC's policy on language has changed dramatically, but they have missed out on a wealth of human experience because of the narrow linguistic range they accepted for broadcast until fairly recently.

The schools, too, have become more tolerant of local variations of speech but, again, they have a lot to answer for in terms of the numbers they alienated with that attitude in the past. And not just in the distant past. While doing research for the first edition of this book, I was given copies of memos sent to staff by a headmaster of the old guard who subscribed to the myth or death wish that Scots is dead and all that remains is slang. The irony was that the school in question, Auchinleck Academy, was the one Burns would have gone to if he were alive in Mauchline today. Scots is still strong there, as it is among teenagers in my own home town a few miles away. This was written in March 1985:

The Doric

Five of our former pupils have lost their places in offices, under a youth training scheme, because they either could not or would not attempt to speak Standard English on the phone. If you allow the use of the doric by your pupils in your room, you could be a contributor to what can only be described as a sorry state of affairs.

His other reference to Scots comes in the rules for teachers printed in 1983. This is No. 11:

The Doric is quite often used as a form of insolence. Be on the look out for attempts so to abuse it.

The latter suggests that the headmaster would be happy with a pure and chaste Doric in which the proprieties were observed, but his teachers assure me that any form of Scots was banned as cheek.

In schools now, you can have that kind of attitude adhered to in one classroom and the opposite – where articulacy in the dialect is encouraged – operating in the room next door. William McIlvanney recalled for me an incident that occurred when he was a teacher in Kilmarnock. One of his colleagues in the English Department insisted that everyone spoke in Standard English. One wee boy found it difficult to make the switch, constantly referring to 'haun', 'fuit' an 'heid' rather than the equivalent English terms. Eventually, the teacher brought him out to stand in a corner as punishment. He was standing there when the headmaster walked in and, on seeing the boy, said, 'Oh ho, whit's he been daein noo?', in exactly the same dialect the boy was being punished for. This kind of anomaly prevails all over Scotland. It is little wonder, then, that for some children fierce loyalty to the dialect and a refusal to adapt to English are signs of resistance to the rubbishing of their culture that all too many of them experience in school.

Not a few teachers have replied to my criticism of Scottish education's treatment of Scots by saying that my views are rooted in the past and do not reflect the present situation. An article written in Scots by John Hodgart, head of English in Ayrshire's Garnock Academy, and published in *The Herald* in January 1993, suggests that some pro-Scots proselytising within education is still required even after the support recommended in 'English Language 5–14':

If Scots is tae win this kinna support, it still has a gey ruch road tae travel, for it's a road fu o the dubs an mires o neglect an

abuse, as weill as bein paved wi prejudice. We hae tae begin wi
the varieties o demotic/community speech weans bring tae the
schuil that are vital expressions o their ain an their community's
identity, but if the schuil disnae respect an value the speech o aa
oor weans, we will continue tae discriminate against weans that
stey close tae their roots. If oor uniquely Scottish educational
system cannae learn hou tae cope wi educatin oor weans in the
native languages o Scotland, sae that Scots an Scots English
complement ane anither, Scottish teachers will continue tae fail
Scottish culture as they hae duin owre lang.

For me, dialect loyalty did have elements of class and community
solidarity in it, but these were in tandem with a positive love for
language and all its possibilities. This fascination, I am sure, arose
from an awareness of the different potential I discovered in the two
childhood registers. Knowledge of Scots also helped in concrete
instances. Old John Murray was Provost of Galston and a great friend
to me when I was a child. He used to say that the soldiers who came
back from the Great War maintained that the Germans could
understand them if they spoke broad Scots. When, on the first day of
learning German, the school reader said, '*Die Tochter milchte die Kuh*,'
I recalled John's words and translated with ease: 'The dochter milkit
the coo.' French, too, was tackled with the knowledge that behind *le
gigot, une assiette* and *des groseilles* lurked a gigot chop, an ashet for steak
pies and the grozets that gied their name to Killie's annual Grozet
Fair! Foreign languages with strong links with home. I can think of
many other Scots past and present who have the same delight in
language, which runs counter to the general linguistic chauvinism that
prevails south of the border. Along with the Spaniards, the English
have a deserved reputation as the worst linguists in the world.

If our attitude to foreign languages is better than theirs, we have
unfortunately been infected by the natural corollary of their attitude:
that within these islands as without, there is only one 'proper' way of
speaking and that is Standard English with a Home Counties accent;
all other accents, dialects and languages are dismissed as aberrations.
Britain is one of the few countries in the world where being
monolingual is frequently considered preferable to being bilingual in
any of the country's other native languages. Everyone has strong
opinions on language because it affects class, social advancement for
children, regional and national identity, inferiority and superiority,
and ultimately how we see ourselves. Unfortunately, the historic
dearth of Scottish studies in our education system means that many of

the strong opinions voiced on the subject are based on half-truths and prejudices rather than actual knowledge of the history of the Scots language.

No doubt the arguments will continue as long as there is a tension between how people naturally speak and society's attempts to make them speak differently. Of course, that tension exists in English dialect areas too, but what gives the Scots debate its cutting edge is that Scots was once a national language, one which produced, and continues to inspire, a brilliant literary tradition. The dialects of Scots that remain not only express the present but are also the key to a unique world picture of the past. That is why many people resent and resist the erosion of Scots. It is also why the arguments will continue until every aspect of our linguistic inheritance is accorded the same prestige and status as English.

The tension between different parts of our linguistic inheritance is not, however, without its lighter moments. Joe Paterson from Dundee recalled learning English parrot-fashion from the teacher when he was a child in the 1920s. The teacher declaimed the sentence, asked what it meant, then had the bairns repeat in their best accents. One phrase was indelibly etched on Joe's memory: 'The lady forsook the child,' said the teacher, and asked what it meant. Joe was good at language, so the answer came easily: 'She gied the bairn the breist, Miss!'

In a similar vein, a few years ago my sister sold one of my books to a local bodie in the mill shop she runs in Galston. 'Wes that your Billy I saw oan the telly twa week syne?' spiered the bodie. 'Aye,' said my sister, 'but did ye no hear him last nicht, he works on the radio, tae.' 'Excuse me for interrupting,' said another customer, 'but we're from Perth and we overheard you say your brother works on Radio Tay. Who is he?'

When my sister sorted the confusion out, there arose a heated discussion about Scots. The Kays rarely lose these discussions! Anecdotal evidence on the humour arising from Scots speakers attempting to 'correct' their language abounds. Different sets of Scots-speaking parents told me how adverse reaction by teachers had made their young children hypersensitive and wary of their parents' tongue. So when one set of parents referred to the River Tay and another to a friend called Brian Tottie, the children corrected them with the 'proper' pronunciations: the River Toe and Brian Potato!

It is not only the inheritance of dialect speakers in Scotland which comes under threat from the erosion of Scots, for Scots and English were different dialects of the same Old English language, and as a

35

result had a huge body of shared expression. This means that many people in Scotland who consider themselves to be speakers of the purest Standard English use classic Scots, often unwittingly, in their everyday speech. To illustrate what I mean, I have concocted an imaginary telephone conversation between two girls, conducted in what most Scots would consider to be perfect English, but which is in fact thrang with expressions and words whose use in Scotland is quite different from their use in the English of the sister kingdom, if they are used there at all:

> Well, it happened when I was staying in Glasgow. One day, my pal's mum was away doing the messages and I went to clap the dog . . . I didn't want to let on that I was frightened but when it barked, I fell and jagged my pinkie on some broken wood – I got a huge skelf and had a really sore hand. That was the most exciting thing that happened to me then, so you didn't miss yourself. Here, it's half eleven, I'm away to my bed. See you Monday next. Bye.

The verb 'to stay' where the English would use 'to live', 'doing the messages' for 'running errands', the verb 'to clap' for the English 'to pet', 'a skelf' for 'a splinter', 'to let on', 'a sore hand', 'you missed yourself', 'I jagged my pinkie', 'I'm away to my bed' are a few of a thousand expressions native to Scottish English, but foreign to the English of England. Even 'half eleven', the 'my' in 'to my bed' and the meaning of the 'next' in 'Monday next' are peculiar both to Scots and to the distinctive variety of English spoken here.

Scots, then, underpins the everyday speech or vernacular of the vast majority of Scottish people, so knowledge of its range of expression, its history, its vast potential for extending our ability to express ourselves is vital to our own self-awareness. Hugh MacDiarmid, the leading force behind the renaissance in Scots literature last century, summed up the problem succinctly:

> Tae be yersel's – and tae mak' that worth bein'
> Nae harder job tae mortals has been gi'en.

In Scotland, for long the site of a linguistic battle based on myths, class bias and crackpot theories, children find it difficult to be fully themselves when the language of their home environment is criticised and devalued by a system that is supposed to be educating them to be at one with that environment. That in itself is bad enough but when much of the speech that is criticised is not 'bad English' but 'good Scots' – the historic national tongue of the children and the language in which much of their great literature is written – the situation surely becomes untenable. For many of the shibboleths condemned as slang by the ignorant today would have been used by king, courtiers and poets in the golden age of Scots culture in the late fifteenth and early sixteenth centuries. The grammar of Scots often differs from English. Take, for example, the past tense of the verb 'to be', which in Scots is 'ye wes' not 'you were', giving 'when wes ye wont tae be sae sweir' in David Lyndsay's *Ane Satyre of the Thrie Estaitis*. A Glasgow wean would still naturally say 'When wes ye gaun hame?' and not 'When were you going home?' 'I says to him', 'I gaed hame', 'I haena seen her', 'Hou monie gaes there?', 'Thir aipples wes guid', 'them that daes that' are just a few examples of everyday contemporary Scots speech which would give most teachers apoplexy but which have a pedigree going back hundreds of years. Political and social history, then, can determine that the same language at different periods of time can be defined as gutter slang or an aureate tongue.

It is almost a case of 'The people do not speak properly, elect a new people!' After the Second World War, however, the occasional enlightened attitude began to appear within Scottish education itself, and papers and pamphlets were published which recommended tolerance of non-Standard English forms of speech in the classroom. In a Scottish Education Department (SED) report from 1952 entitled 'English in Secondary Schools', the types of speech approved by the schools are listed as 'an exemplar of English generally acceptable to educated Scots' and 'words and phrases of genuine dialect, whether of the Borders or of Buchan'. For most Scottish teachers, however, 'genuine dialect' is never the local one, and this applies from Buchan to the Borders and includes every city, town and village en route. As long as Scots is in the past, in the country, in the literature, anywhere in fact but in the mouths of children who speak it naturally, it is acceptable. But as soon as it has to be confronted locally, it tends to be dismissed. After all, it is spoken mainly by the working class – and their speech could never be accepted as a model. In the late '70s and early '80s, when interest in Scottish culture was on a high because of the intense political debate surrounding the devolution referendum, a number of excellent consultative papers were produced. The best of them, 'Scottish English: The Language Children Bring to School', came to this conclusion:

> In the Scottish primary school teachers will meet children
> using language that ranges from the rural tones of a farming

community to the possibly more abrasive tones of a city street. We cannot regard this language as some kind of personal aberration nor a reflection of the bad speech habits of parents. Regarded at national level the child's language is a continuation, even in an eroded form, of that language through which for centuries people living in Scotland have expressed their awareness of their own individuality and their sense of inhabiting this place, Scotland. At a personal level it is the child's own language through which he carries on the business of living in a community and must be worthy of respect . . . Can Scottish teachers not accept that diversity in language may be a source of strength and not of weakness? Will the pupil who feels secure in school in his own language and in the language of school not have a better opportunity of using the experience he brings to school – and thereby realising his individual potential – than the pupil who may feel he is entering a world where his language, and all the individual and group experience it carries, is not highly regarded? All we have to work with is the language and the embedded experience that a child brings to school. We cannot reject this.

The momentum for a radical change in attitude to Scots did have an effect but, like all things Scottish, it waned in the post-referendum apathy which for a while depressed the Scottish cultural scene in the early 1980s, before it again picked up momentum in the 1990s. More Scottish literature was taught and a good number of teachers, especially in primary schools, implemented such reports' recommendations. But those who did so still felt they were working in a vacuum, 'enthusiastic amateurs trying to support a national culture', as one headmaster put it. The native culture was treated as of peripheral interest, to be taught if the teacher was interested and if time permitted! Despite the growing body of evidence against it, the myth of Scots as a debased form of English prevailed. As we shall see, that myth has a lang and complex pedigree.

What I want to stress in this book, however, is that Scotland is not unique in this, for most of the nation states of Europe have similarly rewritten linguistic history to justify the neglect of the culture of their so-called minority languages. There are close on 50 million people in Europe whose culture is likewise based on the use of two languages. In Spain, for example, the Spanish equivalent of 'talk proper' was *'habla cristiano'* ('speak the language of Christians'), a policy of linguistic genocide executed by the Spanish state but resisted with varying degrees of success by eight million Catalans, two million Basques and three million Galicians.

Scots is a similarly disadvantaged language, broken up into dialects which often express a strong regional rather than national identity; in the North-east, for example, the common term for Scots is 'the Doric', in Shetland it is 'da Shetland tongue' and often town-dwellers refer to the dialect as, say, Selkirk or Kilmarnock rather than giving it the national term, Scots. Linguists attempt to define it variously as a *Halbsprache* or half-language, a deposed language, or a national variety of world English. People who believe in the dominance of a single language dismiss it as just another uncouth regional dialect, like Lancashire or Somerset, desperately trying to think of one internationally respected writer who has enhanced those dialects. All ways of speech should be valued, but there is no equivalent of Scots anywhere else in the English-speaking world; Scots have an identity with and loyalty to Scots which is unparalleled in any other area.

The contrast can be ascertained by simply crossing the River Tweed at Coldstream and Cornhill, where all but the deaf will hear the difference. There is little left of Northumbrian on one side of the border but there is a lot left of Scots on the other. Coldstream bairns have all the words of the English children for use in the classroom but they also have a very different, additional vocabulary for everyday use: lugs and ears, een and eyes, dook and swim, breeks and trousers, etc., etc. They are the perfect example of the case for Scots, for these children's horizons are extended by having the two registers. Curiously, the scene where this fact was illustrated in *The Mother Tongue* was the one that provoked the most delight and the greatest ire. 'A set up', 'an artificial distinction' were typical reactions from the group which cannot bear to think of Scotland and England having separate cultures in any way. The most outrageous response came from a Lancashire minister resident in Scotland. He decided that the scene arose from 'the horrible chauvinism which caused suffering to my children at one time and some difficulties for myself [and] is not to be encouraged. It is unchristian, irrational and reminds me of certain people in brown shirts.' Having heard most of the arguments before, the only part of that insane outburst that got to me was the reference to Brownshirts on the border! As the grandson of two Communist miners, it made me see red in more ways than one.

Interestingly, the border became more and more distinct linguistically as the twentieth century progressed. Because of the historic pull of London on the English Borderers and Edinburgh on the Scots side, the greatest concentration of isoglosses – a term for distinctive linguistic features – in the whole of the English-speaking world is to be found along the length of that border. The originally shared dialect had long developed separate features because of the different political orientation of the two areas, and now these differences are being heightened rather than diminished by the pressures towards standardisation on either side of the border. Features of the English Northern dialects are being eroded at a far faster rate than those of Scots. This is probably due to the national identities of either side influencing the way they regard the dialects. For the Scots, it is one of their distinguishing badges of identity, while for the English, their dialect is increasingly and erroneously perceived as Scots – a linguistic identity they want nothing to do with.

A Swiss linguist, Beat Glauser, undertook exhaustive research into the speech of the area and published his findings in a fascinating book, *The Scottish–English Linguistic Border*, which surveys the survival of traditional dialect in the area. Here are his findings on some of the old plurals once common to Scots and the dialects of Northern England:

> According to my material, the line between kye, shuin, een and cows, shoes, eyes is now practically identical with the border . . . On the English side of the border, instances of the old plural forms are rare. Some informants do remember them when asked, but most of them would not use them any longer. Only towards the south of Northumberland and Cumberland are there a few informants that make use of kye, shoon or een.

Noting that many of his English informants actually referred to the words as Scottish, he sums up as follows:

> The conclusion sounds paradoxical. As far as the old plurals are concerned, Northern England seems to be 'englified' in a southern direction, originating from artificial distinctions between Scottish and English as drawn by the population in the Border area.

The actual border appears to act as a focus for the respective cultural identities of the two nations. The differences are exaggerated there, presumably because of the frontier mentality. Away from the physical border, the English appear happier with their dialect, possibly because they do not think of it as Scots. This was the phenomenon that those gorgeous weans in Cornhill and Coldstream so vividly and endearingly demonstrated. The point was not to show that two different languages existed, but that the Scots bairns were bilingual to a degree that has disappeared from the English children. The positive feature in this is that they all seemed perfectly happy with their lot.

Despite all the pressures, Scots survives. But if it is to resist the threat of erosion posed by the mass media of the twenty-first century, it must be more actively promoted in our media and our schools. The fact of such an important part of the common heritage of Scottish children not being taught would be regarded as unthinkable or at the very least strange in any other civilised nation. Yet, so powerful is English cultural ascendancy in the British Isles, it is the desire to teach Scottish children their heritage which is regarded as so strange that very few even question the matter. Fortunately, most Scots today are happy with their Scottish accents and their Scottish English – so we have progressed from the ludicrous situation of the eighteenth century, although some are still conditioned to look down on the uniquely Scots element in our speech. Yet to deny part of our heritage is to deny part of ourselves and the people we stem from. I am descended from Ayrshire and Fife miners who spoke nothing but Scots, and they are part of an unbroken line which goes back to the Scots of the Makars. English is also part of that heritage and should be valued as a means of communicating with the world.

But our English linguistic heritage seems able to look after itself; it is the other tongues, Scots and Gaelic, we need to promote. If we don't, we are in danger of becoming strangers to the cultural background that made us what we are. Unlike Gaelic and English, Scots and English are closely related. They are complementary – two branches of the same tree which nevertheless express very different world pictures. We can and should be at home with both. It would be a tragedy if Scots children became like the unfortunate deracinated Gaels of the cities who sing Gaelic songs in a native tongue they don't understand. For if we lose Scots, we lose the key to how people have lived, loved, thought and played in our part of the world for many centuries. It leas a gey tuim feelin, the very thocht. It duisnae need tae happen an gin ye ken the history o the leid, ye micht jine the fecht tae mak siccar it never happens.

2

The Beginnings

> Often the Scots writer is quite unaware of this essential
> foreignness in his work; more often, seeking an adequate word
> or phrase, he hears an echo in an alien tongue that would adorn
> his meaning with a richness, a clarity and a conciseness
> impossible in orthodox English. That echo is from Braid Scots,
> from that variation of the Anglo-Saxon speech which was the
> tongue of the great Scots civilisation.

Lewis Grassic Gibbon gives eloquent testimony to the linguistic
duality of most Scots today. He also reminds us of the ancient
pedigree of the Scots language, which is spoken by most of us and
haunts the rest. Champions of a language, like Gibbon, often cite its
antiquity to strengthen its claim to be recognised as the true national
tongue. Well, neither Scots nor Gaelic speakers can claim to speak the
language of the country's distant past. When the Gaels arrived in
Argyll around the fifth century and the Angles in what is now the
eastern Borders in the seventh century, what they found both in the
Pictish north and the Cumbric south were tribes speaking a British
Celtic language, or languages, related to modern Welsh. Indeed,
much early Welsh heroic poetry is set in the regions of Lothian and
Strathclyde. Welsh place names abound all over Scotland: *aber*, a river
mouth, gives Aberdour and Aberdeen; *pen*, a headland or hill, gives
Pencaitland (*pen ced llan*, the enclosure in the wood on the hill).

While Pictish symbol stones give an insight into the art of the Picts,
not a line of their language comes down to us today. However, in

eastern Scotland, north of the Forth, there are over 300 place names with the prefix 'pit-', from *pett*, a share or portion of land. Pitlochry in Perthshire is the stony share, Pitcaple in Aberdeenshire is the horse share, and Pittencrieff in Fife is the share of the tree. They are almost certainly of Pictish origin and although most of the second elements of these 'pit' names are Gaelic, they provide one of the few indications of the extent of Pictish lands in Scotland.

Another piece in the linguistic jigsaw that became Scotland is provided by the Norsemen, whose Scandinavian tongue survives in place names as far apart as Shetland, the Western Isles and Dumfriesshire. The Norse colonisation of the Northern Isles around the year AD 800 and their subsequent expansion into Caithness and the Hebrides gives us, for example, names coined from the Norse word for a farm, *bolstathr*: Norbister in Shetland, Scrabster in Caithness and Leurbost in Lewis. The Scandinavian influence in the south-west of Scotland came later, with settlers from the north-west of England, who had a mixed English/Norse background, and another group of settlers from Ireland with a mixed Gaelic/Norse background. Lockerbie and Denby, from the Old Norse *byr*, a farm, are examples of the former's influence, while Kirkbride and Kirkcudbright, from the Old Norse *kirkja*, a church, are examples of the latter's.

Thus, in tenth-century Scotland, five languages were spoken: the Gaelic of the West Highlands, the Pictish of the North-east, the Norse of the Isles and the extreme South-west, the Welsh of the central and western Lowlands, and the Inglis of the South-east. This Inglis later became known as Scots, and is the ancestor both of the dialects of Scots and of the Scottish English spoken by all Scots today. Norse, Pictish and Welsh have, of course, disappeared from Scotland over the centuries and there are no adult monolingual Gaels left in Scotland today, though thankfully around 60,000 people speak both Gaelic and English. But for Gaelic to survive, it will have to fight against the current of language history in Scotland and indeed Britain, for periods of bilingualism have always been followed by the eventual eradication of the less powerful language. This process is bound up with politics and the prestige that politics confers. It is the same today as it was when Gaelic was devouring Pictish, Norse and Welsh in its aggressive expansion out of its original western settlement.

The impetus behind the rise of Gaelic was provided by both military might and political power, which gave the language social status. Kenneth MacAlpin crushed Pictish resistance in the mid-ninth century and absorbed the Picts into his kingdom of Alba, or Scotland. In the course of the tenth and eleventh centuries, Gaelic continued to spread into Welsh Strathclyde and English Lothian as the power of the different ethnic groups ebbed and flowed in southern Scotland and northern England. In 1018, Malcolm II, King of Scots, united with Owein of Strathclyde to defeat the Earl of Northumbria at Carham and confirm the cession of Lothian to his authority. When Owein died, Malcolm placed his own grandson Duncan on the throne of Strathclyde. Duncan in turn became King of Scots, and he ruled over a land whose borders have changed little since that period. By the eleventh century, then, Gaelic was the language of court and state, of scholarship, of literature and the church. Examples of Gaelic place names exist in almost every corner of the country: *baile*, a hamlet, gives Balmuir in West Lothian and Balgownie in Aberdeenshire; *achadh*, a field, gives Auchinleck in Ayrshire and Achintraid in Ross-shire; *cill*, a cell or church, gives Kilbucho in Peeblesshire and Kilbrandon on Mull.

The language of the Angles, Inglis, brought north from Northumbria into Berwickshire in the seventh century, remained the language of a minority in Scotland; but even when the power of Gaelic was at its height and it was absorbing other linguistic groups, the people of this south-east corner continued speaking Inglis. The area where Inglis was spoken did expand a little in the following centuries, spreading out into East Lothian, along the Solway and to an enclave in Kyle in Ayrshire. Whittinghame in East Lothian tells us the name of one of the early Anglian leaders: *Hwitingaham* – the settlement of Hwita's people. *Tun*, an enclosure, gives Haddington in Midlothian; *wic*, a minor settlement, gives Hawick in Roxburghshire and Fenwick in Ayrshire.

Part of the great northern dialect area of Old English, the Inglis of the settlers was a Germanic language brought to Britain during the folk migrations from northern Germany by Anglo-Saxon tribes around the fifth century AD. The earliest example of their language in Scotland is to be found in the beautifully wrought runic inscriptions on the cross in the kirk at Ruthwell in Dumfriesshire. They depict passages from a poem called 'The Dream of the Rood', written in the Old English of the seventh century:

> ongeredae hinae god almehtig
> tha he walde on galgu gistiga
> modig fore alle menn
> ahof ic ricnae kyninge
> haelda ic ni dorstae

girded him then God Almichty
gin he stepped on the gallows
for aw mankind – strang willed
wiout fear. I held the Heich
Keing, Lord o Heiven.
Bou me doun, I daurna.

If the language of 'The Dream of the Rood' appears distant to modern Scots, it is even further removed from Standard English. Many of the distinctive sounds which characterise Scots and English speech today go back to differences in the dialects of Old English in the sixth century. They may be even older still, as the dialect differences may have arisen before the various tribes left the Continent for Britain. The major dialects of Old English – Kentish, West Saxon, Mercian and Northumbrian – probably reflect the pattern of settlement by Angle, Saxon and Jute, and their respective dialects, in different parts of Britain. Scots is descended from Northumbrian, while Standard English emerged from the East Midland dialect of Mercia. Although markedly different, the Old English dialects did share a common store of vocabulary. Due to the different linguistic developments in the separate states of Scotland and England, however, the language of England lost many old words which are retained in Scots. Examples of these include *dicht* (to wipe), *sweir* (reluctant), *blate* (diffident), *reik* (smoke) and *greet* (to weep). Characteristic Scots sounds, too, such as *coo* and *hoose* for cow and house, or *richt* and *nicht* for right and night, were common to all the Old English dialects but disappeared from Standard English due to sound shifts which occurred in Southern and Midland dialects. If antiquity was any justification for a language's survival, a special case could certainly be made for Scots against Standard English, as guardian of an older form of English.

This Northumbrian Inglis held on to its heartlands in the South-east, while Gaelic made spectacular gains elsewhere in the kingdom until its expansion was arrested at the end of the eleventh century. It was as if Inglis was biding its time until the political moment was right for its star to rise at the expense of Gaelic. The Gaelic kings of Scotland had already turned their back on their western homelands as Scone, not Iona, became their country's spiritual centre. Their choice of capitals – Dunfermline, Stirling and Edinburgh – confirms that the political and cultural balance of the country was moving from the west and north to the south and east; in other words, from Gaeldom to the Inglis Lothians. There the Scottish court was wide open to influences from the south, and political turmoil in England at the end of the eleventh century was to have far-reaching effects on Scotland's subsequent linguistic history. Here we can pinpoint the exact moment when Gaelic began its decline as the language of status in Scotland, to be superseded over the following centuries by the Germanic language called variously Inglis, Scots or English.

Malcolm III or Canmore acceded to the throne in 1058. A Gaelic speaker, he had, however, spent a good deal of his life at the English court of Edward the Confessor. When the Normans overran England in 1066, the English royal family fled to Scotland, and the Princess Margaret later married the widower Malcolm. The couple's sons Edgar, Alexander and David were profoundly influenced by their years spent at an English court 'in the full flush of Normanisation'. Norman culture enjoyed tremendous prestige all over Europe at this time and was instrumental in reorganising ideas of government, laws and literature from Sicily to Scandinavia. To encourage this civilising influence, David I (1124–53) and his successors granted lands in Scotland to Norman noble families who held lands mainly in the north of England – Bruce, Balliol, Grant and Fraser, to name but a few.

These grantees originally spoke Norman French but the mass of the people of lesser rank who accompanied them spoke the northern dialect of English. The same people populated the burghs that were established as centres of royal power all over the Lowland area, from Elgin and Forres in the north to Dumfries and Ayr in the south. The polyglot nature of the early Scottish kingdom is confirmed in the royal charters of the period which are addressed to the king's citizens '*Francis et Anglis, Scotis et Flemmingis*', or French, English, Scots and Flemish. For the incoming settlers, the burghs were a cross between pioneer outposts and new towns, a melting pot in which Inglis became the established lingua franca. The power of the burghs meant that the local population, Gaelic speaking on the whole, had to learn Inglis to participate in the trade the towns generated. The economic benefits to the settlers were considerable, with inducements such as two years' tax-free allowance to build houses and a virtual monopoly for the burgesses in the essentials of local and international commerce. The strict control of the burghs is seen in the Burgh Laws passed by David I. Originally written in Latin, they were later translated into Scots. Number 81 refers to the burgh watchman and reminds us of the fears of pioneer settlers surrounded by a potentially hostile hinterland:

> it is for to wyt of ilke house wythin the burgh in the quhilk thar wonnys ony that in the tym of wakying aw of resoun to cum furth, thar sal ane wachman be holdyn to cum furth quhen that

the wakstaff gais fra dure to dure, quha sall be of eylde and sal gang til his wache wyth tua wapnys at the rynging of the courfeu, and sua gate sal wache wysly and besily til the dawying of the daye. And gif ony hereof failye, he sal pay 1111d, outtane wedous.

(*wonnys* dwells; *of eylde* of age; *sua gate* in this way; *outtane wedous* widowers excepted)

Even more English prestige came with the founding of the great monasteries and the arrival of monks from the north of England. By the fourteenth century, Inglis had become the principal spoken language of all of Lowland Scotland, with the exception of Galloway, where Gaelic survived until the beginning of the eighteenth century.

This Inglis which the settlers brought with them was quite different from the Inglis already long established in the Borders. It could be more accurately called Anglo-Danish, for in the Danelaw, north of the Humber, the Scandinavian tongue held sway from the ninth century and the local variety of English adapted to the language of those in power. Many of the features which distinguish modern Scots from Standard English came as a result of this Danish legacy: *kirk*, *kist* and *breeks* for church, chest and breeches; *brig* and *rig* for bridge and ridge; *lowp* for leap, *ain* for own, *strae* for straw, *skirl* for shrill, *mask* for mash. Many of these Scandinavian words are still in everyday use in Scotland, having died out of the English dialects which originally absorbed them – words such as *flit* (to move house), *graith* (tools or equipment), *frae* (from), *lug* (ear), *nieve* (fist) and *hoast* (cough).

Up till now, I have been looking at the shared inheritance of Scots and the Northern English dialects. But in Scotland, this northern Inglis gradually evolved into the sophisticated language of state of the Stewart kingdom, and it developed separately from its sister tongue across an increasingly hostile border. The vocabulary of Scots was enriched by words borrowed from many different sources.

From the twelfth century onwards, the eastern ports of Scotland traded extensively with the Low Countries, where they established colonies in Bruges, Middelburg and Veere. In turn, the Scots encouraged Flemish craftsmen, particularly *wabsters*, or weavers, to settle in the expanding burghs. Thus we have the surnames Fleming, Bremner and Wyper to describe the immigrants from Flanders, Brabant and Ypres respectively. They influenced the language as well; *pinkie*, *golf*, *scone*, *howff* are in everyday use all over the country, while other terms survive in certain dialects: *bucht* (sheep pen), *cuit* (ankle), *craig* (neck), *pleiter* (mess), *to redd* (to tidy up), *loun* (boy), *hunkers* (haunches) and *doited* (daft).

The other great trading partner and military ally of the Scots was France and the language was influenced both by the Norman French of the twelfth-century settlers and by the Central French of the Auld Alliance, the series of treaties which joined Scotland and France in diplomatic and commercial cooperation from the late thirteenth to the mid-sixteenth century. The administration of the burghs, strongly influenced by the Normans, was carried out by the provost (*prévôt*) and baillie (*bailli*). Anyone walking in the old part of Edinburgh will recognise the French influence on the streets leading off the Grassmarket – West Port (*porte*, gate) and The Vennel (*vennelle*, lane). French culture also had a profound effect on English culture and so both north and south of the border many French words were in common use. However, while we in Scotland still use many of these words, they have become obsolete in England: *jigot* (lamb), *ashet* (deep dish), *douce* (soft or sweet) and *mavis* (a thrush). Other borrowings, mainly from the time of the Auld Alliance, were confined to Scots; of the scores of possible examples, *to fash*, to bother, *affeir*, to pertain to, and *disjune*, breakfast, will suffice to give a flavour of the French influence on Scots life.

Nearer home, the Gaelic language added another distinctive element to the vocabulary of Older Scots. Many words refer to major topographical features: *glen*, *ben*, *loch* and *strath*. Others are more general: *ingle* (hearth), *cranreuch* (frost), *tocher* (dowry), *sonsie* (comely, hearty). The reason why Gaelic did not influence the Lowland tongue to a greater extent lies in the low prestige of Gaelic culture in the rest of Scotland from the Middle Ages onward. Most Lowlanders had Celtic blood in them but as they developed a settled agriculture and established both foreign trade and an urban lifestyle, they began to regard the Gaelic way of life, with its warfare and cattle raiding, as barbaric and despicable. Their attitude has many expressions in Scots verse. Typical is a poem from the late sixteenth century by Alexander Montgomerie in which the poet imagines God creating the first Highlander:

> Quod god to the helandman quhair wilt thou now
> I will down in the lawland lord, and thair steill a cow . . .
> ffy quod sanct peter thow will nevir do weill
> and thow bot new maid sa sone gais to steill
> Umff quod the helandman & swere be yon kirk
> Sa lang as I may geir gett to steill, will I nevir wirk.

(*geir* possessions)

48

Another source from which Scots derived its increasingly distinctive vocabulary was the language of learning all over Europe in the Middle Ages – Latin. Many of the borrowings are still used in Scots law today; *to dispone* (to convey land), *homologate* (ratify), *sederunt* (meeting, e.g. of the Court of Session). As we shall see, the Scots poets, or Makars, used Latin to affect a highly ornate, 'aureate' style in their work, employing 'sugurit termis eloquent' such as *preclair, matutine, celicall, palestrall, celsitude, pulchritude, supern, lucern* and many other exquisitely mellifluous words. Of a more down-to-earth nature were later borrowings, which nevertheless show the continued influence of Latin on Scots right through to the nineteenth century; every product of the Scottish education system knows those three pillars of wisdom the dominie, the dux and the jannie!

Until the end of the fourteenth century, Latin and French were the languages of both scholarship and private correspondence among the few who could write. The Anglo-Norman aristocracy spoke Scots by this time but the prestige of French was such that it continued as the medium of written communication. In England, where the Norman influence on language was more profound, French would continue as the language of the law until the seventeenth century. From about 1380 onwards in Scotland, documents and letters begin to appear which are written in the vernacular of the nation. A good example of the Scots of the period comes in a letter from James Douglas, Warden of the Marches, to King Henry IV of England, dated 26 July 1405. It also gives a vivid insight into the cross-border skirmishing and raiding perpetrated by both sides during what were supposed to be periods of truce. This part of the letter concerns the burning of Berwick by the Scots. It was occupied by the English at the time but, of course, the Scots claimed it as part of their own sovereign territory:

> Anente the qwhilkis Hee and Excellent Prynce, qwhor yhe say yhu mervalys gretly that my men be my will and assent has brennede the town of Berwik, the qwhilk is wythin Scotlande, and other place in Inglande, in brekyng fully of the sayde trewis; I understand that giff yhour hee excellent war clerly enfourmyte of the brennyng, slachtyr and takyng of prisoners and Scottis schippis, that is done be yhour men to Scottys men within the saide trewis in divers places of Scotlande, befor the brynning of Berwike; the qwilk skathis our lege lorde the kyng and his lieges has paciently tholyt in the kepyng of the saide trewis, and chargit me til ask, and gar be askyte be me deputs redress tharof; the qwhilk my deputs has askyt at dayis of

49

marche, and nane has gotyne; methink o resoune, yhe sulde
erar put blame and punitioun to the doarys of the saide trespas,
done agayn the trewis in swilke maner, and callys thaim rather
brekars of the trewis than me that has tholyt sa mikylle injur sa
lang and nane amends gottyn.

(*skath* harm, injury; *tholyt* endured, suffered)

By 1424, the stature of Scots was confirmed when it replaced Latin as
the official language recording the statutes of the Scottish Parliament.
From then on, Scots was the official language of state, the medium
used for all national and local legislation, administration and records.
An Act of Parliament of James II from 1457 gives an example of the
style of the records. It also reveals that our national sporting
obsessions have changed little in the intervening years, though
thankfully we can enjoy them free of the guilty consciences of our
forebears, who really should have been preparing for the defence of
the realm:

> Item, it is decretyt and ordanit that wapinschawingis be haldin
> be the lordis and baronis spirituale and temporale four tymis in
> the yere. And at the fut ball ande the golf be utterly cryit doun
> and nocht usit.

(*wapinschawingis* muster of arms)

Scots was also by now the medium of an emerging literature. The
oldest fragment of poetry which survives dates from the year 1286 but
the version which comes down to us is Andrew of Wyntoun's
transcription from his *Oryginale Cronykil of Scotland* of 1424. The verse
mourns the death of Alexander III and the period of rare plenty which
had blessed his reign. It is also prophetic in an uncannily fey manner,
seeming to predict the approaching chaos of the Wars of
Independence, caused by Alexander's death and his inability to
produce an heir for the throne:

> Quhen Alexander our kynge was dede,
> That Scotlande lede in lauche and le
> Away was sons of alle and brede,
> Of wyne and wax, of gamyn and gle
> Our golde was changit into lede.
> Crist, borne in virgynyte,

Succoure Scotlande, and ramede,
That is stade in perplexite.

(*lauche and le* law and peace; *sons* abundance; *gamyn* mirth;
ramede remedy; *stade* fixed)

The earliest masterpiece written in Scots actually concerns itself with
the events that unknown poet seems to foretell. It is John Barbour's
epic poem *The Brus*, which chronicles Robert the Bruce's campaigns
during the period of the Wars of Independence. Addressing his troops
before the decisive battle of Bannockburn, Bruce exhorts the men,
though terribly outnumbered, to fight with the moral force that lies
with them. Just in case that isn't enough, he reminds them of the
plunder they'll enjoy from the wealthy English should the day go with
them. He lists the factors on the Scots side:

The first is, that we haif the richt;
And for the richt ilk man suld ficht.
The tothir is, thai are cummyn heir,
For lypning in thair gret power,
To seik us in our awne land,
And has broucht heir, richt till our hand,
Richness in-to so gret plentee,
That the pouerest of yow sall be
Baith rych and mychty thar-with-all,
Gif that we wyn, as weill may fall.
The thrid is, that we for our lyvis
And for our childer and our wifis,
And for the fredome of our land,
Ar strenyeit in battale for to stand
And thai for thair mycht anerly . . .

(*lypning* counting on)

The Brus also contains the famous lines on freedom. What they assert
is that the tyranny of the English occupation has bound personal and
national freedom inextricably together:

A, fredome is a noble thing,
Fredome mays man to haiff liking,
Fredome all solace to man giffis;
He levys at es that frely levys.

Considering the diverse ethnic and linguistic mixture that existed in Scotland, her sense of nationhood at this early stage of the development of the idea of a shared national identity is quite astonishing, not to say precocious. Some of Europe's major nation states today, such as Italy and Germany, would wait another 500 years before their people identified with the country rather than the locality. Edward I of England – Malleus Scotorum, or Hammer of the Scots, by dint of his constant aggression – appears not to have hammered the Scots into submission as was his intent; instead, like hammer on steel, he forged disparate groups of people into a nation.

The Declaration of Arbroath of 1320 not only offers a brilliant case for Scottish independence and demands recognition of that autonomy from the papacy, it is also the culmination of the struggle by Bruce, Wallace and, most importantly, the community of Scotland. The nobility of the medieval Latin rhetoric loses a little in translation but the statement is unequivocal:

> For, as long as but a hundred of us remain alive, never will we on any conditions be brought under English rule. It is in truth not for glory, nor riches, nor honours that we are fighting, but for freedom – for that alone which no honest man gives up but with life itself.

That Scots enjoyed being reminded of their heroic past is proven by the success of the other great national epic, *The Actes and Deidis of the Illustre and Vallyeant Campioun Schir William Wallace*, by Blin Hary. Written around 1470, it helped create the legend of Wallace, which was still remarkably potent in Burns' day. Writing to John Moore about the major cultural influences on his life and work, Burns recalled Blin Hary's poem: 'the story of Wallace poured a Scottish prejudice in my veins which will boil along there till the flood-gates of life shut in eternal rest'. *The Wallace* is an action-packed tale, full of direct and gory confrontation where the English baddies inevitably get what's coming to them. Hundreds of them share the fate of Sir John Butler, who is about to light down on Wallace from his charger, sword in hand:

> Till him he stert the courser wondyr wicht,
> Drew out a suerd, so maid hym for to lycht.
> Abowne the kne gud Wallas has him tayne,
> Throw the and brawn in sondyr straik the bayne.
> Derffly to dede the knycht fell on land.

Wallace the hors sone sesyt in his hand,
Ane awkwart straik syne tuk him in that sted.
His crag in twa, thus was the Butler dede.

(*courser* charger; *wicht* brave; *the and brawn* thigh and calf;
derffly violently; *crag* neck)

Wallace then escapes on the horse, determined to avenge the men he
had lost in a previous skirmish. His uncle, Sir John Stewart, wants
Wallace to resign himself to the hopelessness of further resistance,
accept Edward's offer of peace and reap the benefits of siding with the
English. Wallace's reply echoes both the Arbroath Declaration and
The Brus:

'Uncle,' he said, 'off sic wordis no mair.
This is no thing bot eking of my cair.
I lik better to se the Sothren de
Than gold or land that thai can giff to me.
Traistis rycht weill, of war I will nocht ces
Quhill tyme that I bryng Scotland in-to pes,
Or de thairfor, in playne to understand.'

(*eking of* adding to)

Now, although Scottish patriotism flowed through the vernacular
literature, Scots linguistic nationalism did not exist until the end of the
fifteenth century, just after the time that *The Wallace* was written. Up
till then, the language of state had been called Inglis, or, in its modern
form, English, in recognition of its origin and long-established history
in Scotland. In the fourteenth century, in fact, there was very little to
distinguish the Inglis spoken north and south of the border right
down to the Humber. By the end of the fifteenth century, however, the
Inglis of Scotland had developed most of the features which still
characterise the Scots dialects today and distinguish them from the
English of the South. Most of the separate borrowings I mentioned
earlier had taken place, and the language was approaching a national
standard form based on the speech of Lothian and the capital. In
England, the emerging standard language came from the East
Midland dialect and later on the speech of London. Given the
linguistic changes and, perhaps more importantly, the continued
hostility between Scotland and England, it is hardly surprising that the
Scots began giving their national term 'Scottis' to their language, to

separate it from the language of the Inglis, or Southren, as they were also called. The terms 'Inglis' and 'Scottis' existed side by side for a time but 'Scottis' eventually persisted and is still the name we give our language today.

The Spanish ambassador to the court of James IV, Pedro de Ayala, gave an insight into the differences between Tudor English and Stewart Scots when he compared them to Castilian and Aragonese – the dialects which became Spanish and Catalan respectively. It was an apt comparison and a prophetic one, for throughout history there have been many parallels between Catalan and Scots. Both languages have had to define themselves against powerful neighbours whose languages gained ascendency in the Spanish and British nation states which attempted to absorb their cultures. But for Scots, that would be well in the future, and in the late fifteenth and early sixteenth centuries, the 'langage of Scottis natioun', as Gavin Douglas called it, emerged triumphantly not only as the language of the nation but also as the medium of possibly the greatest literature that existed in the Europe of that day.

3

Langage of Scottis Natioun

The hundred years preceding the Reformation was undoubtedly the Golden Age of Scottish literature. It is no accident that the flowering of the country's literature coincided with the period that marked the highest point in the development of the national language. Since that period, geniuses such as Burns in the eighteenth century or MacDiarmid in the twentieth century have engaged in superhuman efforts to revive the native muse and prove that Scots could still be the medium of great literature. For both of them, however, it was necessary to go against the trends of their times to write in Scots and certainly in MacDiarmid's case much of his creative energy was expended in propaganda for the Scots language cause. He had to explain to an increasingly anglicised Scotland what he meant by the rallying cry for his literary renaissance – 'Not Burns, back to Dunbar.' In that *cri de coeur*, MacDiarmid was holding up for scrutiny a period in which Scottish literature was unselfconsciously national and international, drawing from and adding to the European civilisation of the Renaissance. For the great Makars of what we now call Middle Scots, there was no exhausting debate about the status of their language; their creative energy was spent adorning and extending it into the vibrant, flexible, forceful medium which makes their poetry a joy to read today. Concern about the use and prestige of Scots was not common in medieval Lowland Scotland, as it was quite unnecessary. From the King down, everyone spoke, read or wrote Scots, and its supremacy was taken for granted. The Makars were fostered and nourished by a tradition which valued their contribution to national life. There is only room for a flavour of their work here, with examples from four of the greatest of them: Henryson, Dunbar, Douglas and Lyndsay.

The greatest achievement of both Robert Henryson (*c*.1425–*c*.1505) and Gavin Douglas (*c*.1475–1522) lay in their translation or reworking of tales and poetry from classical sources in the Scottish vernacular. Taking a classical theme and improving the telling of it was one of the ideals of medieval writers and, in doing that, they wrought finely honed poetry which stood entirely on its own merits. Thus when Henryson approached the tale of Troilus and Cressida, or Douglas Virgil's *Aeneid*, their aim was not simply direct translation from Greek or Latin into Scots but rather a vigorous re-creation of the spirit of the work in a recognisably Scottish environment.

The God Saturn in Henryson's *The Testament of Cresseid* appears to have been transplanted from the Plains of Troy to the Howe of Fife, an the founeran cauld is getting to him:

> His face fronsit, his lyre was lyke the leid,
> His teith chatterit and cheverit with the chin,
> His ene drowpit, how sonkin in his heid,
> Out of his nois the meldrop fast can rin,
> With lippis bla and cheikis leine and thin
> The ice-schoklis that fra his hair doun hang
> Was wonder greit and as ane speir als lang.
>
> (*fronsit* wrinkled; *lyre* complexion; *cheverit* shivered; *how* hollow;
> *meldrop* mucus; *bla* livid; *ice-schoklis* icicles)

Similarly, when Gavin Douglas transports us to observe the multitude attempting to get the favour of Charon to carry them over the Styx, the ambience is tangibly Northern:

> Thir ryveris and thir watyris kepit war
> By ane Charon, a grisly ferryar,
> Terribil of schap and sluggart of array,
> Apon his chyn feil cannos harys gray,
> Lyart feltrit tatis; with burnand eyn red,
> Lyk twa fyre blesys fixit in his hed;
> Hys smottrit habyt, owr his schulderis lydder,
> Hang pevagely knyt with a knot togiddir.
> Hym self the cobill dyd with hys bolm furth schow,

And, quhen hym list, halit up salys fow.
This ald hasart careis owr fludis hoyt
Spretis and figuris in hys irne hewit boyt,
Allthocht he eildit was or step in age,
Als fery and als swipper als a page;
For in a god the age is fresch and greyn,
Infatigabill and immortal as they meyn.
Thidder to the brae swarmyt all the rowt
Of ded gostis, and stud the bank about,
Baith matronys and thar husbandis all yferis,
Ryal princis, and nobill chevaleris,
Smal childering and yong damysellis onwed
And fair springaldis laitly ded in bed . . .

(*feil* many; *cannos* hoary; *lyart feltrit tatis* withered matted tufts;
smottrit stained; *lydder* slouching; *pevagely* squalidly; *cobill* small
boat; *bolm* pole; *hasart* grey-haired man; *eildit was* was grown
old; *fery* nimble; *swipper* quick; *yferis* in company; *springaldis*
youths)

While using classical sources, the Makars employed verse forms and
poetic devices which were rooted in the native tradition and
complemented the native language. Henryson's versions of Aesop's
fables, for example, are full of alliterative lines which strengthen the
poet's descriptive power. In 'The Taill of the Foxe that begylit the
Wolf in the schadow of the Mone', there is a brilliant depiction of a
sleekit fox slipping out of his dark hiding place: 'Lowrence come
lourand – for he lufit nevir licht.'

William Dunbar (*c*.1460–*c*.1520) was the most technically
accomplished of the medieval Makars, absorbing English, French and
Latin influences yet expressing them in a vigorously Scottish form. He
too is a master of the old alliterative style, which he makes great use of in
his bawdy poem of female sexuality, *The Tretis of the Tua Mariit Wemen
and the Wedo*. This is one of his fair damsels describing her husband:

To see him skart his awin skyn grit scunner I think.
When kisses me that carybald, than kyndyllis all my sorrow
As birs of ane brym bair, his berd is als stiff,
Bot soft and soupill as the silk is his sary lume.

(*skart* scratch; *scunner* revulsion; *carybald* cannibal; *birs* hairs;
brym bair fierce boar; *sary lume* sorry tool)

But if his Scots was capable of gutsy colloquial invective, it was also capable of transforming itself into a highly polished, aureate tongue, which sought to compete with prestigious Latin poetry and rhetoric in elegance of style. In 'Ane Ballat of Our Lady', Latin mells with Scots to dazzling effect:

> Empryce of prys, imperatrice,
> Brycht polist precious stane,
> Victrice of vyce, hie genitrice
> Of Jhesu, lord soverayne:
> Our wys pavys fra enemys
> Agane the feyndis trayne,
> Oratrice, mediatrice, salvatrice,
> To God gret suffragane!
> *Ave Maria, gracia plena!*
> Haile, sterne meridiane!
> Spyce, flour delyce of paradys
> That baire the gloryus grayne.

(*pavys* shield; *feyndis trayne* fiend's followers; *grayne* seed)

That poem shows Dunbar as a virtuoso showing off the glittering artefact he can fashion with words. In an exaggerated form, both poems reveal the range that was available to speakers of Scots in those days: the higher register of the educated few, replete with foreign words and adaptations; the everyday language of the majority, very close to its Anglo-Saxon origins.

This social differentiation in registers of Scots is exploited by Sir David Lyndsay (c.1490–1555) in his play *Ane Satyre of the Thrie Estaitis*. Criticism of the corruption in the Church runs through the play and it can be read as a forewarning of the inevitability of the coming Reformation. Satire against the priests' vices of sexual excess and exploitation of the poor exists in the speeches by both Sensuality and John the Commonweal but the registers of Scots they employ are quite different. This is Sensuality's address to her Goddess, Venus:

> O Venus goddess, unto thy celsitude
> I give laud, gloir, honour and reverence,
> Whilk grantit me sic perfite pulchritude.
> I mak a vow, with humill observance,
> Richt reverently thy temple to visie
> With sacrifice unto thy deitie!

58

To every state I am sa agreabill
That few or nane refuses me at all –
Papes, patriarchs, nor prelates venerabill,
Common people, nor princes temporal,
But subject all to me Dame Sensual!

(*celsitude* majesty)

This is John the Commonweal's complaint of the vicar appropriating the few possessions of the poor. The tone is much more colloquial and, noticeably in this passage, very close to contemporary spoken Scots:

The poor cottar being like to die,
Havand small bairnis twa or three,
And has twa kye withouten mae,
The vicar must have ane of thae,
With the grey coat that haps the bed,
Howbeit the wife be poorly cled!
And if the wife die on the morn,
Thocht all the bairns sould be forlorn,
The other cow he cleeks away,
With the poor coat of raploch grey.
Wald god this custom was put doun
Whilk never was foundit by reasoun!

(*raploch* rough cloth)

For Lyndsay, tutor to James V, the relationship with his royal patron began in the King's infancy. One of his poems recalls the prince playing as a child and the delight of the poet when his name was among the first sounds the infant uttered:

How, as ane chapman beris his pak,
I bure thy grace upon my bak,
And sumtymes, strydlingis on my nek,
Dansand with mony bend and bek.
The first syllabis that thou did mute
Was PA, DA LYN. Upon the lute
Then playit I twenty spryngis.

(*bek* bow)

Dunbar and Lyndsay were professional poets, supported by their positions at court. Both depict the pleasures and pastimes of court life. Lyndsay:

> Off lustie lordis and lufesum ladyis ying,
> Tryumpand tornayis, iustyng, and knychtly game,
> With all pastyme accordyng for ane kyng.

Dunbar:

> Sum singis, sum dances, sum tellis storyis,
> Sum lait at evin bringis in the moryis.

> (*moryis* morris dancers)

The reign of James IV in particular was one of great achievement in Scottish culture. The Education Act of 1496 required elder sons of barons and substantial freeholders to master Latin and to undertake courses of study in arts and law. This led to a great improvement in regional administration. Scotland's third university, King's College, Aberdeen, was founded, giving the country one more seat of higher learning than her wealthier neighbour England. A programme of building was undertaken, influenced by French architects and master masons, who made the Great Hall of Stirling Castle the first Renaissance construction in Scotland. The Chapel Royal was created at Stirling and one of its effects was to promote 'musyck fyne', as courtly music was termed. In Edinburgh, Chepman and Myllar set up the first printing presses. The status and popularity of the national poetry was confirmed when they published a collection by Henryson and Dunbar in 1509, the very first book to come off a Scottish printing press.

A typical Renaissance prince, James encouraged those around him with his love for poetry, architecture, languages and music, bringing foreign artists to settle in Scotland in order to diversify the cultural life of his court. All of this was combined with an impetuous streak which would eventually lead to his ill-starred invasion of England and death at Flodden Field in 1513. Dunbar was one of the many recipients of James's bounty but the court Makar had a guid conceit of his abilities and resented sharing the king's patronage with all the foreign 'mercenaries' at court:

> Soukaris, groukaris, gledaris gunnaris
> Monsouris of France, gud claret cunnaris,

Inopportoun askaris of Yrland kynd,
And meit revaris lyk out of mynd

(*groukar* meaning unknown; *gledaris* mean folk; *cunnaris* tasters)

The close relationship the poet must have enjoyed with the King is revealed in the familiar way he is addressed by Dunbar, who is not scared to come straight to the point when the point is the Makar's lack of ready cash:

> I haif inquyrit in mony a place,
> For help and confort in this cace,
> And all men sayis, My Lord that ye
> Can best remeid for this malice,
> That with sic panis prickillis me.

Dunbar would have been distinctly ill at ease if he had lived through the reign of James V, as 'Monsouris of France' and their culture gained even more prestige and patronage at court. James V married two Frenchwomen, the unfortunate Madeleine de Valois, who died soon after her arrival in Edinburgh, and Marie de Guise, who survived her husband and wielded tremendous pro-French political influence in the years leading up to the Reformation as Regent for her daughter Mary, Queen of Scots. Mary married the Dauphin of France and was Queen of France during his brief reign as François II. There were many French settlers in Scotland at this time and some of them formed a colony in Little France on the outskirts of Edinburgh, an overspill from Craigmillar Castle. More words derived from French were added to the already considerable stock in the language: *vivers* (provisions), *fash* (bother), *dote* (endow) and *howtowdie* (young hen). The period was one of comparative prosperity for Scotland but many regarded the French influence as extravagant in a country whose people had had to be frugal for most of their long history. Bishop Leslie, writing of the 1530s, was to be echoed more and more vociferously by the Protestant Reformers as the century wore on:

> There wes mony new ingynis and devysis, alsweill of bigging of palaces, abilyementis and of banquating, as of men's behaviour, first begun and usit in Scotland at this tyme, eftir the fassioune quhilk they had sene in France. Albeit it semit to be very comlie and beautiful, yit it was moir superfluous and voluptuous nor the substance of the realme of Scotland mycht beir furth or

sustaine . . . [and] remains yit to thir dayis, to the greit hinder and povertie of the hole realme.

(*bigging* building; *abilyementis* fashions, clothes)

The court poets had fewer qualms about the extravagance, provided they were part of it. Sir David Lyndsay's favourite place for enjoying the pleasures of court was Linlithgow:

Lithgow, whose palyce of pleasaunce
mycht be ane pattern in Portingale or Fraunce.

But the court did not simply indulge itself in continental excess, for there the Scottish poets absorbed influences from the other great literary languages of Europe. Villon of France, Ariosto of Italy and Chaucer of England were just a few of the writers whose marks can be traced in the work of the Middle Scots Makars. In addition, as I have already indicated, classical Greek and especially Latin literature was profoundly influential not only on the themes and styles of the poetry but also on the language the poets used. Latin was the language of international learning, the lingua franca of universities all over Europe. Later in the sixteenth century, Scotland produced in George Buchanan the greatest Latin writer in the Europe of the day.

I say this to stress that the Scottish literati of the sixteenth century were part of a European world picture, intellectuals who read several languages and their literatures, and took what they wanted from the diverse sources available to them. Many today, however, can only approach the past from within the confines of the present, totally different Scottish relationship with the world and, because of that, draw erroneous conclusions from the writings of the Makars. This is especially noticeable where the relationship between Scots and English literature and language is concerned. Because Scottish culture has little status in Scotland and the UK today, many presume Scotland has always been a provincial backwater, looking over its shoulder with envy at the glittering culture of the South. This attitude has also been fostered by the imperialism of English medievalist critics who, rather than admit to the superior worth of the Scots Makars, simply appropriated them and relegated them with the ludicrous term 'Scottish Chaucerians'!

As the father of poetry in the vernacular, as opposed to Latin, Chaucer was indeed revered by all of the Makars. Dunbar's lines are typical:

O reverend Chaucere, rose of rethoris all,
As in oure tong ane flour imperiall

Chaucer's prestige was such that the Makars introduced English forms into certain styles of their verse, for example 'quho' for 'quha', 'moste' for 'maist', 'frome' for 'fra', a fashion which increased markedly after the Reformation. But in pre-Reformation Scotland, there was never a slavish copying of English models; the native muse was too vital and wide-ranging to draw from just one tradition. Indeed, if one tradition dominated Scots literature, it was the Latin not the English one. Dunbar's description of Chaucer as 'rose of rhetoric' reminds us of the prestige of the Latin rhetoricians and Dunbar applauds Chaucer's attempt to raise the vernacular up to the exalted standards of the classical language. This has to be remembered when you read the Scots poets apologising for the inadequacy of their language and the necessity of extending it with words from other tongues. This is Gavin Douglas in the Prologue to the first book of his *Aeneid*:

> And yit forsuyth I set my bissy pane
> As that I couth to mak it braid and plane,
> Kepand na sudron bot our awyn langage,
> And spekis as I lernyt quhen I was page.
> Nor yit sa cleyn all sudron I refus,
> Bot sum word I pronunce as nyghtbouris doys:
> Lyke as in Latyn beyn Grew termys sum,
> So me behufyt quhilum or than be dum
> Sum bastard Latyn, French or Inglys oys
> Quhar scant was Scottis – I had nane other choys.

(*Grew* Greek; *quhilum* sometimes)

Many reading those lines today interpret them from the contemporary standpoint of regarding Scots as an inadequate bastardised dialect of English and presume Douglas is admitting much the same there. In fact what he is doing is employing the rhetorical device with which every vernacular writer in Europe preceded his work: an apology for the 'rudeness' and 'barbarity' of their tongue compared to others, especially Latin. This is Chaucer in the Prologue to 'The Franklin's Tale':

At my bigynning first I yow biseche
Have me excused of my rude speche
I lerned nevere rethorik, certeyn;
Thyng that I speke, it moot be bare and pleyn.

Writers using the English language throughout the sixteenth century are extremely disparaging as to its potential for eloquence. Indeed, so virulent are some of the epithets describing English's inadequacy that it would appear that the writers are not simply repeating parrot-fashion the rhetorical denigration, like, for example, their Scottish counterparts, but are actually expressing a deeply felt belief as to the impoverished state of their language compared to others. In the midst of a paean of praise for all things English compared with all things foreign, *The fyrst boke of the Introduction of knowledge* puts a stop to the list at the subject of language: 'The speche of Englande is a base speche to other noble speches, as Italion, Castylion, and Frenche.'

For most of the sixteenth century, English writers have few good words to say about their language and it is only towards the latter part of the century that they begin to have grudging praise for the extension of its potential due to copious borrowing from Latin, Greek or French. Yet the same writers are aware that by the use of foreign terms, they are cutting off the majority of the population from comprehension of their native literature. Most carry on with the borrowings, however, in the hope that eventually the borrowed words will be absorbed into the everyday vocabulary of the people. In *The Arte of English Poesie*, written in 1589 by George Puttenham, the author discusses the fashion for borrowing and the possible detrimental effect it could have. He fears it will leave English a hotchpotch, or, as he terms it, a 'mingle mangle', which occurs 'when we make our speache or writinges of sundry languages using some Italian word, or French, or Spanish, or Dutch, or Scottish, not for the nonce or for any purpose (which were in part excusable) but ignorantly and affectedly'.

A possible explanation for the inferiority complex Englishmen undoubtedly had regarding their mother tongue lies in the fact that historically it had to contend not only with the prestigious classical languages for status but also with another European vernacular language, French. The Norman invasion in the eleventh century had made French the language of the English royal court and the law, the prestigious register of the aristocracy and of a thriving Anglo-Norman literature. John Gower (*c*.1330–1408), for example, is hailed as one of the early exponents of English for literary purposes but the *Balades*, some of his best work, were written in French. In the fourteenth century, Robert of Gloucester stated that for a man to be highly regarded in England, he had to speak French. To all intents and purposes, for over two centuries, English was regarded as the dialect of the lower classes, and it was only after Chaucer had proved that it was capable of being a great literary tongue that its low status slowly changed.

By the end of the fifteenth century, William Caxton apologises not only for his 'rude and comyn englyshe', with its lack of ornate eloquence, but also for his imperfect knowledge of French, which renders his translations from the noble French tongue doubly barbaric. For long after French ceased as an everyday language in England, it continued alongside Latin as the preferred language of, for example, education, parliamentary and local records, and the law. Only after 1450 do we see most English towns changing over from French to English for recording their public transactions. Law French in fact continued to be used in England until the Revolution of 1688, by which time it was very much a debased jargon, with its practitioners divorced from a real grasp of the language. A report on a trial of 1631, for example, could have come out of *Punch*'s 'Franglais' column; there a prisoner is described losing his temper with the judge and proceeding to 'jecte un graund brickbat que narrowly mist'!

The contrast with the Scottish situation is striking. In the period when the English of England was at its lowest ebb and Norman French in the ascendancy – from the late eleventh century to the early fourteenth century – the Inglis of Scotland was engaged in its triumphant rise all over the Lowlands, to become the language of court and state. In Scotland, the Anglo-Norman nobility appear to have deserted their French for Inglis much earlier than in England, so that while French had prestige, it showed itself in the borrowings it gave to Scots, rather than setting itelf up as an alternative to Scots. Latin was the only serious contender to Scots in matters concerning high culture in Scotland, while in England both Latin and French were regarded as more prestigious languages than the native English. I have been looking at the status of English in England in order to compare it with Scots in Scotland in the sixteenth century and to give the general European background to feelings about vernacular languages versus Latin and Greek. This, I feel, is necessary to balance the world picture of the modern reader, who has been conditioned to presume that English always had prestige and Scots never had it, which was patently not the case during the golden age of Scottish culture in the reigns of James IV and V.

When Gavin Douglas augments his Scots with Latin, French and English, he is part of a European phenomenon, as were the English writers who supplemented their language by the same borrowings, and with the same misgivings about its comprehensibility to the ordinary folk. Douglas is adamant to stress that Scottis is 'skant', not in relation to English, which is how many interpret his statement today, but in relation to the style of Virgil's poetry. His language lacks the colours of rhetoric, the sentence and gravity of the original:

> Nocht for our tong is in the selwyn skant
> Bot for that I the fowth of language want
> Quhar as the cullour of his properte
> To kepe the sentence tharto constrenyt me . . .

(*in the selwyn* in itself; *fowth* abundance; *properte* purport, meaning)

Shortly after this conventional statement of modesty, Douglas goes on to show that he in fact has a guid conceit of his ability to use language as a poetic craftsman and turns on what he considers to be the pathetic attempts by William Caxton to translate Virgil into English:

> Thocht Wilyame Caxtoun, of Inglis natioun,
> In proys hes prent ane buke of Inglys gross,
> Clepand it Virgill in Eneados,
> Quhilk that he says of Franch he dyd translait,
> It has na thing ado tharwith, God wait . . .
> So schamefully that story dyd pervert.
> I red his wark with harmys at my hert,
> That syk a buke but sentens or engyne
> Suld be intitillit eftir the poet dyvyne;
> Hys ornate goldyn versis mair than gilt
> I spittit for dispyte to se swa spilt
> With sych a wyght, quhilk trewly be myne intent
> Knew never thre wordis at all quhat Virgill ment . . .

(*but sentens or engyne* without eloquence or ingenuity; *wyght* man)

This is not the tone of one seeking models of excellence in English language and letters! The relationship between Scots and English culture of the fifteenth and sixteenth centuries was a relationship of equals, with the Scots praising or criticising, borrowing or slandering where they saw fit. If Henryson and James I owed a poetical debt to Chaucer, the same was the case with Skelton and Surrey to Dunbar and Douglas. For both nations' poets at this time, the native tradition in either country was much more influential to the development of their art than what was going on north or south of a distant border. That is why the constant comparison with English culture which modern critics seem to dwell on perverts the European dimension the Scots Makars were working within and reduces it to the inappropriate limitations of the British scenario which many cannot see beyond.

The unknown author of *The Complaynt of Scotland* (1548) more typically discusses the use of language purely in terms of the advantages and disadvantages of using Scots as opposed to Latin. He addresses himself to the intellectuals of the country with conventional humility, asking them to excuse the poverty of the writing by remembering the patriotic intent behind the work:

> that procedis fra ane affectiue ardant fauoir that I hef euyr borne touart this affligit realme quhilk is my natiue cuntre. Nou heir i exort al philosophouris, historiographours, & oratours of our scottis natione to support & til excuse my barbir agrest termis; For I thocht it not necessair til haf fardit and lardit this tracteit with exquisite termis, quhilkis ar nocht daly usit, bot rather I hef usit domestic Scottis langage, maist intelligibil for the vlgar pepil.

(*agrest* rural; *fardit* embellished)

The author goes on to ridicule the 'glorius consaits' of past authors, who showed off by using 'thir lang tailit vordis' such as 'conturbabuntur' or 'innumerabilibus'. While criticising verbal extravagance for extravagance's sake, he is aware, like Douglas and other European vernacular writers, that Latin has such a range of rhetorical devices that it is difficult to find equivalents in Scots:

> Ther for it is necessair at sum tyme til myxt oure langage vitht part of termis dreuin fra lateen, be rason that oure scottis tong is nocht sa copeus as in the lateen tong, ande alse ther is diuerse purposis & propositions that occurris in the latyn tong that can nocht be translatit deuly in oure scottis langage: therfor he that is expert in latyn tong suld nocht put reproche to the compilation, quhou beit that he fynd sum purposis translatit in

67

scottis that accords nocht vitht the latyn register: as ve hef
exempil of this propositione, homo est animal. for this term
homo signifeis baytht man ande voman, bot ther is nocht ane
scottis terme that signifeis baytht man and voman.

The author goes on to give other examples where he has kept the
original word rather than change the meaning of it by giving a Scots
word which does not translate the concept exactly. He concludes the
'Prolog to the Redar' by reiterating his earlier statement that he is
writing not for vainglory but 'public necessite'. The book itself consists
largely of translations and adaptations into Scots, mainly from French
sources, in particular Alain Chartier's *Quadrilogue Invectif*. Through the
character of Dame Scotia, the author's complaynt is aimed directly
against English meddling in Scottish affairs and, as we shall see, he fairly
gets going when his dander is up. But the author and Dame Scotia are
at their best when the intent is not propagandist, in penetrating asides
such as this eternal feminist truth: 'Ane man is nocht reput for ane gentil
man in Scotland bot gyf he mak mair expensis on his horse and his
doggis nor he dois on his vyfe and bayrnis.'

There are also a few passages which are strikingly original and
rooted in a natural depiction of the Scottish environment. One of
these involves a scene where country folk gather and have a party,
detailing the kinds of songs, stories, music and dance which were
popular in mid-sixteenth-century Scotland. Another scene not only
paints a vivid picture of the birds and animals which throng the
countryside but also attempts to reproduce exactly the sounds that
they make, employing the old Scots alliterative tradition to good
effect. Here is a short extract:

> The ropeen of the ravynis gart the cran crope, the huddit crauis
> cryit varrok, varrok, quhen the suannis murnit, because the
> gray goul mau pronosticat ane storme. The turtil began for to
> greit, quhen the cuschet youlit. the titlene follouit the gouk,
> and gart her sing guk, guk. The dou croutit hyr sad sang that
> soundit lyk sorrow . . . the laverok maid melody up hie in the
> skyis.
>
> (*goul mau* seagull; *cuschet* wood pigeon; *titlene* meadow pipit;
> *gouk* cuckoo; *dou* dove; *laverok* lark)

Nevertheless, no prose writer in Scots in this period ever achieved the
brilliance of the Makars in poetry. During the Middle Ages and the

Renaissance, creative, imaginative writing tended to be confined to poetry. Prose dominated the realm of practical information to be communicated in as straightforward a manner as possible. Local and national records, Acts of Parliament, the law and accounts of trials were the main uses for vernacular prose. From the mid-fifteenth century on, however, there appear translations from Latin and French sources and original works of a more creative nature, though their aim is usually didactic: Sir Gilbert Hay's *The Buke of Armys* and John of Ireland's *The Meroure of Wysdome* are typically solid but uninspired examples. As writers turned more and more to the vernacular rather than Latin for serious writing, the style of Scots prose gradually progressed. John Bellenden's Scots translation of Hector Boece's *Chronicles of Scotland* in 1533 was the first in a vigorous tradition of Scots historical writing, continued later on in the century by such as Robert Lyndesay of Pitscottie and Father James Dalrymple, the translator of Bishop Leslie's ten-volume Latin *History of Scotland*. Shakespeare did not have to stretch his imagination overmuch – the third scene in Act 1 of *Macbeth* came to him through Holinshed's English version of Bellenden's Scots:

> Quhen Makbeth and Banquho war passand to Fores, quhair King Duncan wes for the tyme thai mett be the gaitt thre weird sisteris or witches, quhilk, come to thame with elrege clething. The first of thame sayid to Makbeth: 'Haill, Thayne of Glammys!' the secund sayid: 'Haill, Thayn of Cawder!' The thrid sayid: 'Haill, Makbeth, that salbe sum tyme King of Scotland!' Than said Banquho: 'Quhat wemen be ye, quhilkis bene sa unmercifull to me and sa propiciant to my companyeoun, gevand him nocht onlie landis and grete rentis bot als triumphand kingdome, and gevis me nocht.' To this ansuerit the first of thir witches: 'We schaw mair feliciteis appering to the than to him; for thocht he happin to be ane king, yit his empyre sall end unhappely, and nane of his blude sall eftir him succede. Be contrair, thou sal neuer be king, bot of the sall cum mony kingis, quhilkis with land and anciant lynage sall reioise the croun of Scotland.' Thir wourdis beand sayid, thai suddanlye evanyst oute of thair sycht.

(*weird* fateful; *elrege* unearthly)

One of the most interesting works of the age follows the conventional format of a wise older man giving sound moral advice to a younger man.

But in Maister Myll's *Spektakle of Luf*, written in St Andrews in 1492, there is more than a suggestion that the author wanted to titillate his audience as well as instructing them against the sin of extramarital sex. The book, republished in the *Bannatyne Miscellany* in the nineteenth century, is divided into chapters containing examples from classical history which the father hopes will convince his son to avoid variously the 'delectatioun of . . . damesillis or young wemen . . . uther mennis wyffis . . . wedowis and agit wemen . . . and [last but certainly not least] . . . The sevynt part schawis that men suld forbeir the delectatioun of wemen of religioun, as nunnis or utheris, with gret examplis allegit tharapon'! The boy originally thinks there could be little harm in the occasional dalliance with any of the women on faither's list but faither soon disabuses him of any such notions. Just one of the numerous stories on wedowis and ancient wemen should be enough to convince any wayward son that celibacy is the only safe existence:

> My Sone, has thow nocht hard that the Quene of Navarre duelt and had hyr mansioun within the toun of Parys, apon the wattir syd of Sayne. This Quene was sa lechorus, that scho desyrit of euery plesand man to have assaye, and sa covatys, that scho wald tak lay meid and proffet tharfor; for the quhilk, als sone as thai had done with hyr at thai mycht, scho wald tak fra thame all thar reches, and a trap within hir chalmer, that was abone the watter, thai war lattyn fall doun, quhar thai war drownyt. And thus mony noble men war myssit, bot nane cuth juge be quhat waye; be the quhilk this Quene grew to sa gret reches of gold that it was mervall, quhill the clerk Prudane persavit this trap, quhar he ordanit his servandis to be in a boit. On the nycht he passit to the Quenis chalmer, and lay with hir to his plesour, and payet the monye; and quhen he had done, he was pelit and cassyn doun at the trap as utheris was done of befor, quhar his servandis in the boite keppit him sone.

(meid reward; *quhill* until; *pelit* robbed)

If medieval Scots prose had few outstanding figures, it did function well in its role as keeper of the nation's records. Public records are not the place for stylists to exhibit their rhetorical skills but realistic portrayals of actual events often provide humorous pictures of our ancestors. The following dialogue could be from the 'Little Stories from the Police Courts' column in D.C. Thomson's *Weekly News*, but in fact they are from a trial recorded in the Kirk Session records of St Andrews in 1560:

'My brother is and salbe vicar of Crayll quhen thow sal thyg thy mait, fals smayk; I sall pul the owt of the pulpot be the luggis and chais the owt of this town.'

'It is schame to yow that ar gentillmen that ye pull hym nocht owt of the pulpot be the luggis.'

(*thyg* beg; *mait* meat; *smayk* rogue; *luggis* ears)

Similarly evocative of the language and the period are the countless inscriptions which adorn the buildings in the old burghs. Many are of a pious nature, such as the following from the Old Town of Edinburgh:

HE.YT.THOLIS.OVERCUMMIS
O.LORD.IN.THE.IS.AL.MY.TRAIST
LUFE.GOD.ABUFE.AL.AN.THY.
NYCHTBOUR.AS.THY.SELF

That can still be seen carved in gold outside the house in the High Street where John Knox is supposed to have lived. Other inscriptions are pithy epigrammatic sayings, such as the one gracing the house in Dunfermline at 21 Marygate:

SENN WORD IS THRALL AND THOCHT IS FRE
KEIP WEILL THY TONGE I COINSELL THE.

The official government and royal records are again more interesting for the political and historical information they contain than for their use of Scots. But as language was profoundly affected by politics, particularly religious politics in the second half of the sixteenth century, the Acts of Parliament take on greater significance for the history of Scots. The following is a short extract from an Act of Marie de Guise in 1558 naturalising French citizens living in Scotland:

Because the maist Christian King of France has granted ane letter of naturalitie for him and his successors to all and sundrie Scotsmen – registered in the Chalmer of Compts – therefore the Queen's Grace, Dowager and Regent of this Realme and the three Estaitis of the samin thinks it guid and agreeable that the like letter of naturalitie be given and granted by the King and Queen of Scotland.

Writers of prose in Scots, like the Makars with their poetic 'flyting' tradition, often appear to derive inspiration from the opportunity to rail against something. One of the favourite targets, then as now, and with much more justification, was the English. English culture was admired north of the border but the English nation in general was regarded with a hostility born of centuries of distrust and warfare. The author of *The Complaynt of Scotland*, a committed supporter of the Catholic and French faction in Scottish affairs, is nowhere more articulate than when he is giein the English laldy:

> Inglis men ar humil quhen thai ar subjeckit be forse and violence, and Scottis men ar furious quhen thai ar violently subjeckit. Inglismen ar cruel quhene thai get victorie, and Scottis men ar merciful quhen thai get victorie. And to conclude, it is onpossibil that Scottis men and Inglis men can remane in concord undir ane monarch or ane prince, because there naturis and conditions ar as indifferent as is the nature of scheip and volvis.

There may be a degree of exaggeration in the analogy of the two peoples being as different as sheep and wolves. But we shall see that as far as the Scots and English languages in the aftermath of the Reformation are concerned, the analogy is not so far fetched.

4

Two Diadems in One

Stewart Scots and Tudor English enjoyed the same kind of relationship as Dutch and German, Portuguese and Spanish, or Danish and Swedish today. In other words, Scots and English were dialects arising from a common root which developed independently due to political rather than linguistic factors. Educated men or women from either country could read the other's language with reasonable ease, though the spoken tongue presented far greater, but not insurmountable, difficulties. People who commented on the languages could emphasise their differences or their similarities, depending on the political purpose it suited. In the period of the Reformation, politics were polarised into two major factions, and both had good reason to adopt a partisan attitude to one or other view of the languages.

The Reforming party in Scotland had always been close to the Reformers in England and they looked south for political help against the Catholic, pro-French faction in Scotland. Closer political union with England, they felt, would guarantee Protestant ascendancy. When Knox and his coreligionists succeeded in establishing Presbyterianism, no complete translation of the Bible into Scots existed. This meant that the first non-Latin Bible available was the Geneva English edition. This was seized upon and came to exercise a tremendous influence on a country besotted with religion. From then on, God spoke English. The Catholic party railed at the anglophile tendencies among the Protestant propagandists, citing their desertion of their native tongue as particularly deplorable. In John Knox, they

73

had a fair target, for the father-figure of the Reformation in Scotland was exceptionally anglicised for that age in his writing. For whatever reasons – his long spells abroad, his stays in England, political motivation to bring Scotland closer to England in language as well as religion, or simply personal predilection – Knox is the first Scot in history known to attempt to conform his writing almost entirely to English models. The Catholic Ninian Winyet, writing from the safety of Paris, it should be noted, tries to get at Knox by citing his aping of English fashion:

> Gif ye, throw curiositie of novatiounis, hes foryet our auld plane Scottis quhilk your mother leirit you, in tymes coming I sall wryte to you my mind in Latin for I am nocht acquent with your Suddrone.

That is very much an ironic dig at the Reformer, not to be taken too literally. But another of the counter-Reformers, Archibald Hamilton, was even more vitriolic in his criticism:

> Giff King James the fyft war alyve, quha hering ane of his subjectis knap suddrone, declarit him ane trateur: quidder vald he declaire you triple traitoris, quha not onlie knappis suddrone in your negative confession, bot also hes causit it to be imprentit in London in contempt of our native language.

> (*knap suddrone* speak English)

There is no trace of James V putting anyone to death for knappin suddrone and Hamilton is undoubtedly exaggerating to make a dramatic point in his argument. The fact remains, though, that these Catholics had a genuine grievance in that the Protestants were initiating a process whereby gradually the English option was preferred to the Scottish one in writing, or, more exactly, printing.

The Reformers are often blamed erroneously for the demise of Scots because they adopted an English Bible and Psalm Book. It must be stressed, however, that their aims were religious rather than linguistic. Historical accident and the human expediency of a readily available English Bible were more important than any pro-Scots or pro-English linguistic identity among the Protestants. In the context of the sixteenth century, it was not necessary for Scots to define the linguistic community they belonged to and this is another reason why when English came in it found little national resistance. The vernacular could be called either Scottis or Inglis, and the choice of term seems to have been arbitrary – they were often used synonymously for the vernacular of Lowland Scotland. An Act of Parliament of 1542, allowing the use of a vernacular Bible, states:

> it salbe lefull to all our souirane ladyis lieges to haif the haly
> write baith the new testament and the auld in the vulgar toung
> in Inglis or scottis of ane gude and trew translatioun and that
> thai incur no crimes for the hefin or reding of the samin.

This could be interpreted as meaning either a Scots or an English version, recognising the differences between the languages but not caring which one is taken up as long as it is in a vernacular the people can understand. But more than likely, it simply means that the terms were interchangeable. The English Bible existed through the quirk of fate that the Reformers in England were ahead of the Scots because of Henry VIII's rift with Rome over his marriage problems. Henry desperately wanted a Protestant ally on his northern border and knew of the growing clamour there for the new teaching. His envoy in Scotland told him in the early 1540s of the demand for vernacular Bibles and psalters, with the words 'if a cartlode [were] sent thither they wolde be bought, every one'. That some of them did get there and were instrumental in fomenting a radical critique of the Church is testified to in Lyndsay's *Ane Satyre of the Thrie Estaitis*, first performed around the year 1540. In one scene, the revelry of the Vices is interrupted by the arrival of Veritie, carrying her Bible. Flatterie is horrified:

> What buik is that, harlot, into thy hand?
> Out! Walloway! This is the New Test'ment,
> In Englisch toung, and printit in England!
> Herisie! Herisie! fire! fire! incontinent.

(*incontinent* immediately)

Veritie is fortunately not burned as a heretic, as Flatterie would like, but truth is nevertheless temporarily suppressed when Veritie is put in the stocks. The feeling abroad in Scotland was that a vernacular Bible was urgently required and it little mattered in which of the national vernaculars, Stewart Scots or Tudor English, it came.

Another feature arising out of the similarities in the two written languages was that Scots could read a text in English yet translate it into their own idiom when speaking it. Thus English could be adapted to Scots, so even those whose identity was bound up with the national language could accept English texts, knowing they would scotticise them for public utterance. A modern parallel may clarify the situation further. Lewis Grassic Gibbon's novel *Sunset Song* can be read as Standard English, and that partly explains the novel's success with non-Scottish readers. However, for those from a Scots-speaking background, it can be rendered broad Scots by simply changing the pronunciation and intonation of the English text. So it must have been with Scots reading the English biblical texts at the time of the Reformation. Indeed, it could not have been otherwise, for at that period the spoken languages were so different that no Scot could have spoken the English of England unless he had spent part of his life there.

There is evidence also that at the time of the Reformation Scots scribes or printers would often reset an English text into a Scots version, based on the way they would pronounce the words themselves. Mairi Robinson, former editor-in-chief of the *Concise Scots Dictionary*, has made a detailed examination of the language used in various editions of *The Scots Confession* of 1560 – 'one of the few indigenous documents of the Reformation in Scotland'. The source of the *Confession* is English, probably Tyndale's New Testament, which had been circulating in Scotland since 1526. The various manuscript editions of the *Confession*, however, adapt the text to more common Scottish features – e.g. 'quhilk' for 'which', 'gif' for 'if', 'lang' for 'long', and past tenses ending in '-it' rather than '-ed'. Here are examples of the alterations – the first extract is from Tyndale's original, the second from one of the most Scots of the various manuscripts:

> And this glad tidinges of the kyngdome shal be preached in all the worlde for a witnes unto all nacions: and then shall the ende come.

> And this glaid tydingis of the kyngdome sall be precheit throwch the haill warld for a witnes unto all natiouns, and than sall the end cum.

One of the manuscripts was completed 20 years after the first *Confession*, but there too there was still no evidence of the scribe going more for the English option available – his text has a similar degree of scotticisation of English to those of his predecessors. This again indicates that the Protestants had no policy of standardising their texts towards English models. Similarly with the printed editions, the normal Scots state of affairs in the sixteenth century, with wide variation in spelling conventions, seems to prevail, rather than the more standardised spelling of the English printing of the period. Robinson suggests that one of the principal printers anglicises his edition of the *Confession* not through intent but through ignorance of the Scots orthographic conventions. When he came back to Scotland, Robert Lekpreuik was a novice at printing in Scots and so abided by the more familiar English models. A few years later, however, he is printing the Acts of Parliament in the correct Scots of the day. If the Reformers had adopted an active policy against Scots, this would have been increasingly reflected in the work of their official printer. That it is not supports the thesis that the anglicisation was part of a wider process, but a process which was undoubtedly precipitated by the adoption of an English Bible.

Strengthening the process was the fact that England was the source of the vast majority of printed books available in Scotland. The few Scottish printing presses in existence copied the technique and language from the English works available as models. The importance of the Bible and the concomitant rise in prestige that English enjoyed resulted in what was initially a slow adaptation of Scots to printing in English becoming a rapid pre-eminence of English over Scots. Thus the final printed edition of the *Confession* of the sixteenth century – Skene's edition of 1597 – is much more English in style than previous printings of the work. Market forces came into play as well, with Scots printers realising that if they anglicised their texts, they could appeal to the much bigger English public. None of this could have happened, however, if the written languages had not been so similar to start with. Indeed, the process of anglicisation is much older than the Reformation, with the Makars introducing English forms to increase their linguisitic options in their poetry in the same way that Burns would rhyme Scots and English words much later, in the eighteenth century.

Of course, it could all have been very different. Protestant writing and parts of a New Testament in Scots had been in existence for a good half-century before the triumph of the Reformers. Over 30 Lollard dissenters were tried in Ayrshire in 1494 and it was a member of that sect, Murdoch Nisbet from Newmilns in my own Irvine Valley, who translated parts of Wycliffe's New Testament into Scots around 1528. This passage is from Matthew 10 and describes Jesus performing miracles:

77

> And, lo, a woman that had the bludy flux xii yere, neirit behind, and tuichet the hemm of his clathe: for scho said within herself, gif I tuiche anly the clathe of him, I salbe saif. And Jesus turnyt and sau hir and said 'Douchtir, have thou traist; thi faith has made the saif.' And the woman was hale fra that hour.

Unfortunately, the Nisbet version remained in manuscript form during the crucial period. If it had been printed, it might have acted as a catalyst for a complete Scots Bible. One of the earliest Scottish statements of the Protestant doctrine was published in Malmø in 1533 by John Gau, a former student of St Andrews who had to leave Scotland because of his heretical opinions. There is no hint of an anglicised Reformation in his vigorously Scots rendering of the Creed:

> I trou in God fader almichtine, maker of heuine and yeird, and in Jesu Christ his sone our onlie Lord, the quhilk wes consawit of the halie Spreit and born of Maria virginem; he sufert onder Poncio Pilat to be crucifeit to de and to be yeirdit; he descendit to the hel, and rais fra deid the thrid day; he ascendit to the heuine, and sittis at almichtine God the fader's richt hand; he is to cum agane to juge quyk and deid; I trou in the halie spreit; I trow that thair is one halie chrissine kirk and ane communione of sanctis; I trou forgiffine of sinis; I trou the resurrectione of the flesch; I trou the euerlastand liff.

> (*yeirdit* buried)

The book, based on the work of a Danish Reformer called Christiern Pedersen, is titled *The Richt Vay to the Kingdom of Heuine*. In his introduction, the author is precise as to whom the book is for and what they will learn from it:

> The richt and chrissine doctrine is heir contenit in this present buyk that al quhilk onderstandis the scotis tung ma haiff with thayme and reid and usz it dailie. That thay may chrissinlie leir and onderstand first quhou thay sall ken thair sins and ar sinful creatures. This thay suld leir of the x commandis of God.

Gau is a Protestant addressing his fellow countrymen in their national language and there he is using the term 'Scots' in the sense that we know it today, differentiating it from the Inglis of England. A similar use is found in an Act of the Lords of Council of 1534, possibly referring to Gau's book. It outlines the sources of the heretical vernacular works coming into Scotland: 'Thir new bukis maid be the said Lutheris secteis baith in Latyne, Scottis, Inglis and Flemys.'

The differences between the languages were such that even the revered English poets, Chaucer, Lydgate and countless unknown authors, rarely appeared in Scottish manuscripts or even early printed books in their original English form. The common practice was to render them Scots for the Scots reading public. The changes in spelling could be easily effected by scribes.

But if the differences in the written languages were rarely commented upon, that is not the case with the spoken tongues. There, the differences were more obvious. Pedro de Ayala was not the only foreigner to recognise that Scots and English were distinct languages. The magistrates of Stockholm as late as 1680 employed one Will Guthrie as interpreter for the English and Scottish tongues. Two Scottish monarchs, separated by over 150 years, passed comment on the foreignness of the English of England. It is recorded in the *Scotichronicon* that the young James I in the early years of his captivity at the English court (1406–24) found it difficult to decipher a tongue he had never heard before: '*etsi linguam quam non noverat audivit.*' Mary, Queen of Scots, also refers to the difficulty of Scots and English communicating. When similarly imprisoned in England in 1581, she endeavoured to procure priests who would set about reconverting her son James VI to Catholicism. When she heard that two English Jesuits had been chosen for the task, she remonstrated both on account of the inbred animosity between the two peoples and, revealingly, because 'they are foreigners and do not understand the language, they could not do much good'. Mary here is not just another Catholic exaggerating the differences for rhetorical effect. She cared passionately about the work the priests were chosen to do and realised that they did not possess the necessary linguistic apparatus to carry it out. Scots and English could be regarded as different dialects of the same language but, where sensitivity and painstaking negotiation were required, the differences between the two were obviously more crucial than their surface similarities.

Of course, it is only now, long after the event, that we can analyse a subject like language change with any degree of objectivity. When the anglicisation of the Scots tongue was beginning through readings from the English Bible, very few people were aware that such a process was in fact taking place. For the majority, of course, it was not taking place – they lived and died monoglot Scots speakers. The fact that I, writing in 2005, was brought up with a full dialect of Scots as my first language says much for the survival of a tongue supposed to have been dealt a death blow in 1560!

In fact, the period during and immediately following the Reformation was one of great richness in Scots language and literature. Printing flourished and a great diversity of books were published. The Register of the Privy Seal in 1559 lists the books published by William Nudry, who was given the privilege of printing and distributing books authorised by the state:

> [Maister William Nudry's] Short Introduction Elementar, degestit into sevin breve taiblis for the commodious expeditioun of thame that are desirous to reid and write the Scottish tongue; Ane Instructioun for bairnis to be lernit in Scottis and Latene; Ane ABC for Scottis men to reid the French toung, with ane exhortatioun to the noblis of Scotland to favour thair ald freinds.

It was worth people's while to master the written Scots of this period, for the disputatious side of the Scottish character was allowed full rein in the intense debate over the religious future of the nation and the prose writing that arose was fired with commitment. Though sometimes alien to our modern sensibility, its native vigour is undiminished across the centuries. This is Knox's gleeful description of the murderers of Cardinal Beaton hanging his body over the wall of his castle at St Andrews to prove the deed to the crowd:

> And so was he brought to the East blokhouse head, and schawen dead ower the wall to the faythless multitude, which wold not beleve befoir it saw: How miserably lay David Betoun, cairfull Cardinall. And so thei departed without Requiem alternam, and Requiescat in pace, song for his saule. Now, becaus the wether was hote (for it was in Maij, as ye have heard) and his funerallis could not suddandly be prepared, it was thowght best, to keap him frome styncking, to geve himn great salt ynewcht, a cope of lead, and a nuk in the boddome of the Sea-toure (a place where many of Goddis childrene had bein empreasoned befoir) to await what exequeis his brethrene the bischopps wold prepare for him. These thingis we wreat merelie.

You will notice from comparing the language of this, from Knox's *History of the Reformation*, with that of other writers of the age that the Reformer's style is much closer to English practice. But even he could jibe at someone who lacked a good command of Scots. Elsewhere in the *History*, he describes one of his enemies: 'He nether had French nor Latyne, and some say his Scottishe toung was nott verray good.' If an anglicised Knox comes as a surprise to those brought up on the myth of the man as the classic dour Scot, the description of his style of preaching by Mr James Melville ties in perfectly with the popular image. Melville's diary of the years 1556–1601 gives a superb insight into the life of the later sixteenth century. Here he recalls Knox at St Andrews:

> when he enterit to application, he maid me sa to grew and tremble that I could nocht hald a pen to wryt . . . I saw him everie day of his doctrine go hulie and fear, with a furring of martriks about his neck, a staff in the ane hand, and guid godly Richart Ballanden his seruand, haldin upe the uther oxter, from the Abbaye to the paroche Kirk, and be the said Richart and another seruant lifted upe to the pulpit, whar he behovit to lean at his first entrie, bot, or he had done with his sermon, he was sa actiue and vigorus, that he was lyk to ding that pulpit in blads and flie out of it.

> (*grew* shudder with fear; *hulie and fear* warily; *furring of martriks* pine marten fur; *ding in blads* smash to pieces)

The foremost historian of the day was Robert Lyndesay of Pitscottie, near Cupar in Fife. His *Historie and Cronicles of Scotland* gives a lively account of events in the country between 1437 and 1575. Here is part of his account of the death of James V and the King hearing the news of the birth of Mary, Queen of Scots. It contains one of the famous sayings of Scottish history:

> Be this the post came out of Lythtgow schawing to the king good tydingis that the quene was deliuerit. The King inquyrit 'wither it was man or woman'. The messenger said 'it was ane fair douchter'. The king ansuerit and said: 'Adew, fair weill, it come witht ane lase, it will pase witht ane lase' . . . He turnit him bak and luikit and beheld all his lordis about him and gaiff ane lytill smyle and lauchter, syne kyssit his hand and offerit the samyn to all his lordis round about him, and thairefter held upe

his handis to God and yeildit the spreit.

Both the strengths and weaknesses of Scots as a national language gradually being undermined by English are revealed in the writings of James VI. The gradual anglicisation of Scots in printing can be seen in three editions of James's book on royal statecraft, *Basilicon Doron* (Kingly Gift), a work originally handwritten in Scots in 1598. Within the space of five years, the language changes from Scots to English and phrases such as 'tak narrow tent' are altered to 'take narrow heede' in printed editions. The first passage is from the original manuscript, the second from the Waldegrave edition of 1603:

> . . . but as ye are cledd uith tua callings sa man ye be alyke cairfull for the dischairge of thaime baith, that as ye are a goode christiane sa ye maye be a goode king dischairging youre office as I sheu before in the pointis of iustice & equitie, quhilke in tua sindrie uayes ye man do.

> But as ye are clothed with two callings, so must ye be alike carefull for the discharge of them both: that as ye are a good Christian, so may ye be a good King, discharging your office (as I shewed before) in the points of justice and aequity: whiche in two sundry waies ye must doe.

The change in the language reflected very much the way the King himself was moving as far as culture and language were concerned. After his court moved to London, of course, James showed little interest in Scotland or things Scottish and projected himself very much as a British king. Before he left Scotland, however, he had been a great champion of the Scots poetic tradition. In his teens, he wrote the first Scottish treatise on the theory of poetry entitled 'Ane Schort Treatise conteining some Reulis and Cautelis to be obseruit and eschewit in Scottis Poesie'. In the preface, he gives as his reasons for undertaking the work the fact that most of the books written are archaic, and also that the difference of language requires different techniques:

> The uther cause is, That as for thame that hes written of it of late, there hes never ane of them written in our language. For albeit sindrie hes written of it in English, quhilk is lykest to our language, yit we differ from thame in sindry reulis of Poesie.

His enthusiasm was not just a passing youthful phase and the last

Scottish court was one in which literature was patronised above all other arts. James's intent, as stated in the 'Reulis', was to promote Scottish vernacular literature by modelling his school of poets on the innovative Pléiade group of writers in France. The new Scottish poetry was to be thoroughly Scots yet also completely European, James inviting poets from France and England, such as du Bellay, du Bartas and Henry Constable, to create the kind of creative intellectual exchange which would help the native muse thrive. The King himself was fluent in French and Italian, and with teachers such as the great Buchanan, his comment on his education is perhaps not surprising: 'They gar me speik Latin ar I could speik Scotis.'

In the cosmopolitan environment of Edinburgh, he gathered around him an impressive group of writers which he termed his 'Castalian Band' – Alexander Montgomerie, John Stewart of Baldynneis, Alexander Hume and Mark Alexander Boyd. All were gifted exponents of the native poetic tradition. In Alexander Montgomerie (c. 1545–c.1610), the most important influence on the rest of the Band, we can recognise someone who is a direct heir of the tradition of Dunbar. The court poet of James VI, like his predecessor at the court of James IV, is concerned in his verse with social criticism, flyting with poetic adversaries and constantly begging for his pension to be renewed by the King. This is him addressing the Lords of Session:

> My Lords, late lads, now leiders of our lauis,
> Except your gouns, some hes not worth a grote.
> Your colblack conscience all the countrey knawis;
> How can ye live, except ye sell your vote?

This is the opening verse of his flyting, or poetic slandering, with Patrick Hume of Polwart which harks back to Dunbar's famous flyting with Walter Kennedy:

> Polwart, yee peip like a mouse amongst thornes;
> Na cunning yee keepe; Polwart, yee peip;
> Yee look like a sheipe, and yee had twa hornes:
> Polwart, ye peip like a mouse amongst thornes.

Finally, here is part of his highly ornate plea to James to restore his patronage. This was written on Montgomerie's return to Scotland after imprisonment in England. James revered Montgomerie as a poet, recalling 'his suggred stile his weightie words divine'. But he was also wary of the poet's Catholic leanings in the charged atmosphere of post-Reformation Scotland. Montgomerie's pleading takes on a rather tragic note when we know it was done in vain. The artificial, 'suggrit' aureate or high style in Scots would die a death when the court moved south and patronage for such poetry disappeared:

> Help, Prince, to whom, on whom not, I complene
> But on, not to, fals Fortun ay my fo
> Quho but, not by, a resone reft me fro
> Quho did, not does, yet suld my self sustene.
> Of crymis, not cairs, since I haif kept me clene
> I thole, not thanks, thame, sir, who served me so
> Quha heght, not held, to me and mony mo
> To help, not hurt, but hes not byding bene:
> Sen will, not wit, too lait – whilk I lament –
> Of sight, not service, shed me from your grace
> With, not without, your warrand yit I went
> In wryt, not words: the papers are in place.
> Sen chance, not change, hes put me to this pane
> Let richt, not reif, my pensioun bring agane.

(*heght* promised; *reif* plunder)

James would have been flattered and pleased by the poem, not just for the craftsmanship of its construction but because it is in sonnet form, a form he personally did much to promote in Scotland.

One of the finest love poems in Scots, also a sonnet, was written at this time by Mark Alexander Boyd. A later member of the Castalian Band, everything else that remains of what he wrote is in Latin:

> Fra banc to banc, fra wod to wod, I rin
> Ourhailit with my feble fantasie,
> Lyc til a leif that fallis from a trie
> Or til a reid ourblawin with the wind.
> Twa gods gyde me; the ane of tham is blind,
> Ye, and a bairn brocht up in vanitie;
> The nixt a wyf ingenrit of the se
> And lichter nor a dauphin with her fin.
>
> Unhappie is the man for evirmaire
> That teils the sand and sawis the aire;
> But twyse unhappier is he, I lairn,
> That feidies in his hairt a mad desyre

84

And follows on a woman throw the fyre,
Led be a blind and teichit be a bairn.

The European dimension of the culture of the last Scottish court has been detailed by David Daiches in his book *Literature and Gentility in Scotland*. There he shows that the inspiration for the above poem came from a sonnet by Pierre de Ronsard which Alexander Montgomerie had already rendered into Scots. A strong French influence prevailed in Scotland long after the golden days of the Auld Alliance were curtailed by the Reformation. The links between French and Scottish literature were intimate and based on personal contact between the poets. Pierre de Ronsard had, of course, visited the Scottish court, when he accompanied James V's first wife Madeleine de Valois to Edinburgh. Montgomerie was in the retinue of Esmé Stuart, Seigneur d'Aubigny, a Franco-Scottish aristocrat who became a favourite at the court of James VI. The court was thus a forcing-house for European culture, but with Scots as its linguistic medium. The poets were encouraged in their art because they identified with each other as a group. Montgomerie begins a poem to an English poet at court 'My best belovit brother of the band' and the King himself addresses them as 'Ye sacred brethren of Castalian band'. With the King's artistic enthusiasm and financial patronage, the writers regarded themselves and their poetry as important, indeed central, to the life of the nation and its cultural identity.

When James and his court moved to London in 1603, both the patronage and the creative ambience disappeared, never to be replaced. From then on, literature in Scots would explode sporadically on an increasingly anglicised scene because of the genius and commitment of individual writers, rather than a group of them. A centre for Scottish artistic life no longer existed. Another result was that the range of Scots literature narrowed. The court poets had exploited the full range of the language, from the earthy and colloquial to the refined and aureate. With their departure, the upper register of Scots – the top end of the market, so to speak – all but disappeared and Scots became more and more associated with the couthy and the country rather than the courtly. Up till then, poets had found within Scots everything they wanted to express; but with the departure of the court, they would subsequently turn to English for their more refined utterances.

A few of the Castalian Band, poets such as William Fowler and Robert Ayton, actually accompanied James on his journey south, adopted English and became tolerable Cavalier poets. Ayton literally left Scots behind as he crossed the Tweed, describing it as:

Faire famous flood which some tyme did devyde
But now conjoyns two Diadems in one.

In a political sense, the poet was right – Scotland and England were now the glittering diadems in James's crown; but in a linguistic sense, the two parts of his realm would remain divided for a long time to come. Indeed, as I have shown, the bridge over the Tweed which joins Coldstream and Cornhill also separates quite different linguistic communities. To this day, the spoken languages there remain to a great extent Scots in the north and English on the south of the river.

In literature, the high ground, so to speak, was given over to English. Poetry joined the elevated tones of the King James version of the Bible as twin pillars of the prestige of the English language in a Scots-speaking country in the seventeenth century. Not only was new poetry written in English but Scots works were increasingly anglicised. An edition of the King's collected works was printed in 1616. It had lost totally the original flavour of the writing. The fashion for things English was taking root at the top. Most expressions of regret for the old language would come much later, when the belief that it was dying had firmly established itself. But there is one poem, in English by a Protestant Scot called Zachary Boyd (1583–1653), which has a fey, wistful quality of nostalgia for a lost past, and criticism for those who follow fashion to the detriment of the native culture. I feel it sums up perfectly the linguistic duality which now prevailed in Scotland:

Words fine before, are banished from the court
And get no roome but with the countrey sorte;
Men's mouthes like trees beare words as leaves that fall
Now greene and good, anon are withered all.
The words which whilom all men did admire
Loath's in a trice may henceforth not appear,
No more than changing French with gallant shews
Could be content to weare the irish trewes;
Our wordes like clothes, such is vain man's condition,
In length of time does all weare out of fashion.
We are like echo which by voice begot
From hollow vales speakes wordes it knoweth not.

5

The Confusion of Union

> It is true that the nations are *unius labii*, and have not the first
> curse of disunion, which was confusion of tongues, whereby
> one understood not the other. But yet, the dialect is differing,
> and it remaineth a mark of distinction. But for that, *tempori
> permittendum*, it is to be left to time. For considering that both
> languages do concur in the principal office and duty of a
> language, which is to make a man's self understood, for the rest
> it is rather to be accounted (as was said) a diversity of dialect
> than of language: and as I said in my first writing it is like to
> bring forth the enriching of one language, by compounding
> and taking in the proper and significant words of either tongue,
> rather than a continuance of two languages.

Francis Bacon's eloquent appraisal of the relationship between the
languages of the two kingdoms, written the year after James's
accession to the English throne, is very much a vision of an ideal
union. There, not one people or their language is to predominate over
the other; instead, their joint culture will be a creative fusion of the
best both has to offer. It never happened! Instead, we begin to witness
the attempt first by the upper classes in Scotland and much later by
the middle classes to divest themselves of all trace of their native
tongue. It was to take them a very long time and was certainly
unsuccessful as far as speech was concerned until wealthy Scots began
sending their sons to be educated at English public schools towards
the end of the eighteenth century.

In the early seventeenth century, however, the elite of the Scottish aristocracy were just beginning to recognise London as the centre of their orbit. It probably came as a great shock to them that language they considered refined was regarded as comic by their peers at court and in high society. In a way, the English reaction was quite natural. Over two centuries later, Lord Cockburn recalled how an English accent was so unusual at the Royal High School in Edinburgh that the arrival of an English pupil sent everyone into paroxysms of laughter whenever the unfortunate boy opened his mouth. The English lad was probably cut to the quick by their cruelty and the Scots aristocrats in London would have felt much the same. However, London was where the action was and if to get a piece of it you had to swallow your pride and adapt to the manners of the southern metropolis, well . . . that would be home from now on. To mak the future siccar, many a Scotsman on the make invested in an English wife – gin faither wes a bittie coorse, weel at least the bairns wad hae the *bon ton*!

Typical of the attitude of the self-styled 'Scoto-Brittanes' who formed James's retinue was that expressed by Sir William Alexander, Earl of Stirling, in an introduction to his poetry published in 1603:

> The language of this Poeme is (as thou seest) mixt of the English and Scottish Dialects; which perhaps may be un-pleasant and irksome to some readers of both nations. But I hope the gentle and Judicious Englishe reader will beare with me, if I retaine some badge of mine owne countrie, by using sometimes words that are peculiar thereunto, especiallie when I finde them propre, and significant. And as for my owne countrymen, they may not justly finde fault with me, if for the more parte I use the English phrase, as worthie to be preferred before oure owne for the elegance and perfection thereof. Yea I am perswaded that both countrie-men will take in good part the mixture of their Dialects, the rather for that the bountiful providence of God doth invite them both to a straiter union and conjunction as well in language, as in other respects.

Inevitably, the content of the mix in writing was increasingly weighted in favour of the English option. Printing, as we have seen, was adapting to English models as early as the sixteenth century and by the seventeenth the process was almost complete, with the old Scots spelling conventions rarely used. In manuscripts, however, the process of anglicisation was more gradual. Keith Williamson has described the change in the seventeenth and early eighteenth centuries as 'a shift from a fairly full Scots through an anglicised Scots to a scotticised English'. Much of the writing concentrated on the continued religious dispute that racked Scotland, and was composed in lofty, biblical English. Other works, particularly the diaries that have come down to us, are in a more colloquial style, often following the writing conventions of the Scots of the previous century. John Nicoll was a Writer to the Signet who recorded events in Edinburgh in the middle years of the century. Here he describes the law's reaction to the *falset* (falsehood) and cheating endemic in God's Kingdom on Earth: 'thair wes daylie hanging, skurging, nailling of luggis, and binding of pepill to the Trone, and booring of tounges; so that it was ane fatall yeir for fals notaris and witnessis.'

Whether as a result of religious and political tension or the dilemma of finding a balance between the two languages, Scottish literature reaches probably its lowest ebb in the seventeenth century. By the eighteenth century, writers appear to have found a workable, at times brilliant, fusion of the two, and the best poetry of Ramsay, Fergusson and Burns is the result. But in the seventeenth century, the creative mix seems to have been beyond the Covenanter and Royalist poets who attempted it. The most successful poetry was very English, as is that of Drummond of Hawthornden, a friend and host to Ben Jonson, or very Scots, as in the case of Robert Sempill of Beltrees. Sempill's famous poem is a mock elegy on the piper from Kilbarchan called Habbie Simpson. It is worth quoting from it, as it illustrates both the type of subject matter and the verse form that would feature even more prominently in the following century. This poem was in fact extremely popular and widely known, so much so that the verse form in which it is written became known as 'Standard Habbie':

> Aye whan he play'd the lasses leugh
> To see him teethless, auld and teugh,
> He wan his pipes besides Barcleugh,
> Withouten dread!
> Which after wan him gear eneugh;
> But now he's dead.

> Aye whan he play'd the gaitlings gethert
> And when he spak the carl blethert
> On Sabbath days his cap was fethert,
> A seemly weid;
> In the kirk-yeard his mare stood tethert
> Where he lies deid.

89

The homely and parochial found ready expression in Scots, while the
'high ground' of art poetry was almost entirely given over to English.
But if the courtly tradition in Scots died a death, there was
considerable compensation in the rise of a great folk literature and its
expression in the ballads of the Borders and the North-east. They
occupy a subtle middle ground between the high and the low, the
universal and the parochial, the aristocratic and the peasant. The
language of the ballads appears to take the best from both English and
Scots. Ballad Scots 'may be said to include English and go beyond it',
as Hamish Henderson describes it. The ballads of the Border lands
especially are a curious mell of directness of speech and action with fey
other-worldliness in ambience. The end of 'Tam Lin', where the
Queen of Fairies addresses Janet, illustrates the style perfectly:

> Out then spak the Queen o Fairies,
> And an angry woman was she:
> 'Shame betide her ill-far'd face,
> And an ill death may she die,
> For she's taen awa the boniest knight
> In a' my companie.'
> 'But had I kend, Tam Lin,' she says,
> 'What now this night I see,
> I wad hae taen out thy twa grey een,
> And put in twa een o tree'

The ballads, of course, evolved in the oral tradition, crafted over many
retellings. We shall never know if there was one original hand at work
on any of them or whether they emerged communally from cultural
exchange between minstrels who wandered the land, bringing news
and entertaining the people. What is perhaps apposite is that in the
period during which the grave doubts many Scots entertain regarding
their native culture were initiated, the country's finest literary
creations were anonymous.

Linguistic anonymity, or the desire to conceal one's Scottishness by
speaking like the English, did not reach bandwagon proportions until
the following century, but its roots were already established in the
seventeenth century. An English visitor to Scotland in 1689, the Revd
Thomas Morer, suggested that the upper classes would have to try
harder, but the will was there:

> They have an unhappy tone, which the gentry and nobles
> cannot overcome, tho' educated in our schools . . . so that we

may discover a Scotchman as soon as we hear him speak: Yet to say truth, our Northern and remote English have the same imperfection.

There are also signs, however, that there still existed among the same upper class a strong lobby which was proud of its speech. The following diarist admits to the provincial imperfection in his writing and his desire to purge it of Scotticisms but he appears to be reasonably content with the way he speaks:

> You know I came to England the last time upon no other account, but to learn the language, and promised to keep correspondence with you upon this condition, that you would make remarks upon my letters, and faithfully Admonish me of all the Scoticisms, or all the words, and Phrases that are not current English therein. I confess I have a great Veneration for our own and the Northern English Language, upon the account of the Anglo-Saxon, to which they are so nearly ally'd; but yet . . . am as ambitious to write modern English, as any Gascon, or Provencal can be to write the modern French.

The feeling of inferior provinciality vis-à-vis the culture of England in general, and its writing and speech in particular, took a stronger and stronger hold on the elite, whose aspirations, whether political or financial, made them look to London. This was a comparatively new phenomenon. Before the unions of the crowns and of the parliaments, Scots compared and contrasted their culture with others from the standpoint of independence. Their scope for self-criticism was international and, with traditional ties to mainland Europe, healthily wide-ranging. Following the unions, English culture came to dominate all others, the only model for artistic and social life. The upper classes and, much later on, the rising middle classes defined themselves not in a Scottish context but in an Anglo-British one. From this perspective, the thriving independent culture of the fifteenth and sixteenth centuries was forgotten and Scotland was regarded as a provincial backwater, rather like East Anglia or Yorkshire. Many individual Scots would continue to assert cultural independence and refuse to style themselves North Britons, but in doing so they were in many ways resisting both current fashion and the general way Scottish society was moving. Scotland could be regarded as both nation and region, the definition, as today, influenced by personal political and cultural aspirations.

In the seventeenth century, however, there were still many who thought Scottish culture had an important and equal role to play in the creation of a shared British culture. Alexander Hume, rector of Edinburgh High School, belonged, like Bacon, to the school of thought that English could benefit from an infusion of Scots. He addressed himself to the problem of devising a grammar for the language of the United Kingdom and tried to interest James VI and I in the project. Most of the pamphlet entitled *Of the Orthographie and Congruitie of the Britain Tongue*, published around 1618, is pretty heavy going but the following passage is of a livelier nature, treating as it does an argument about the nature of the mixture of the two dialects. Interestingly, he begins by criticising Scottish printers, who are abandoning Scots for English conventions, even though the Scots spellings, he feels, more accurately reflect the spoken idiom:

> To clere this point, and alsoe to reform an errour bred in the south, and now usurped by our ignorant printeres, I wil tel quhat befel myself quhen I was in the south with a special gud frende of myne. Ther rease, upon sum accident, quhither quho, quhen, quhat, etc. sould be symbolised with a q or w, a hoat disputation betuene him and me. After manie conflictes (for we ofte encountered), we met be chance, in the citie of Baeth, with a Doctour of divinitie of both our acquentance. He invited us to denner. At table my antagonist, to bring the question on foot amang his awn condisciples, began that I was becum an heretik, and the doctour spering how, ansuered that I denyed quho to be spelled with a w, but with qu. Be quhat reason? quod the Doctour. Here, I beginning to lay my grundes of labial, dental, and guttural soundes and symboles, he snapped me on this hand and he on that, that the doctour had mikle a doe to win me room for a syllogisme. Then (said I) a labial letter cannot symboliz a guttural syllab. But w is a labial letter, quho a guttural sound. And therfoer w can not symboliz quho, nor noe syllab of that nature. Here the doctour staying them again (for al barked at ones), the proposition, said he, I understand; the assumption is Scottish, and the conclusion false. Quherat al laughed, as if I had been dryven from al replye, and I fretted to see a frivolouse jest go for a solid ansuer.

Thus has many a sound Scottish argument been shouted down by force of English numbers since the time of union! Interestingly, the pronunciation he refers to, the 'hw' or 'chw' sound we have in, for

92

example, the word 'whales', is still marked in Scottish speech. Even those Scots who speak what linguists call RP (received pronunciation) and others 'Queen's', 'Oxford' or 'BBC' English will still pronounce 'Wales' and 'whales' differently, unlike RP speakers in England. Hume's pamphlet is also a good illustration of the mixed dialect at work in prose – his style is still recognisably Scots. As the century wore on, though, and the contact and mocking increased, the style becomes less mixed and more English. The balance of the United Kingdom was such that it was the Scots who had to travel to the English capital and impress there. The English had no need or desire to come north and impress the Scots in Scotland – no earthly reason to adapt to their culture. The Scots were the minority in the majority culture and so it was assumed, with the usual arrogance of the larger partner in any union, that the minority should eradicate its differences to accommodate the majority.

Another of the dissenting voices raised in defence of the native tradition was that of Sir George Mackenzie of Rosehaugh, founder of the Advocate's Library and author of numerous works on ethics and Scots law. In 1673, he wrote an impassioned plea for Scots, directed at the English and included in the preface to his book on legal rhetoric entitled *Pleadings*. Note the change in style that half a century has wrought – unlike in Hume, there is little specifically Scots in the writing itself. It does, however, reveal the feelings of a Scots aristocrat of the late seventeenth century, at the same time proud and defensive about his native culture:

> It may seem a paradox to others, but to me it appears undeniable, that the Scottish idiom of the British tongue is more fit for pleading than either the English idiom or the French tongue; for certainly a pleader must use a brisk, smart, and quick way of speaking; whereas the English, who are a grave nation, use a too slow and grave pronunciation, and the French a too soft and effeminate one. And therefore, I think the English is fit for haranguing, the French for complimenting, and the Scots for pleading.
>
> Our pronunciation is like ourselves, fiery, abrupt, sprightly, and bold; their greatest wits being employed at court, have indeed enriched very much their language as to conversation; but all ours bending themselves to study the law, the chief science in repute with us, hath much smoothed our language as to pleading: And when I compare our law with the law of England, I perceive that our law favours more pleading than

theirs does; for their statutes and decisions are so full and authoritative, that scarce any case admits pleading, but (like a hare killed in the seat) 'tis immediately surprised by a decision of statute. Nor can I enough admire why some of the wanton English undervalue so much our idiom, since that of our gentry differs little from theirs; nor do our commons speak so rudely as those of Yorkshire. As to the words wherein the difference lies, ours are for the most part old French words, borrowed during the old league betwixt our nations, as cannel for cinnamon, and servit for napkin, and a thousand of the like stamp; and if the French tongue be at least the equal of the English, I see not why ours should be worse than it. Sometimes also our fiery temper has made us, for haste, express several words into one, as 'stour' for dust in motion; 'sturdy' for an extraordinary giddiness, &c. But generally words significant ex instituto; and therefore one word is hardly better than an other: their language is invented by courtiers, and may be softer, but ours by learned men and men of business, and so must be more massy and significant; and for our pronunciation, besides what I said formerly of its being more fitted to the complexion of our people than the English accent is, I cannot but remember them, that the Scots are thought the nation under heaven who do with most ease learn to pronounce best the French, Spanish and other foreign languages, and all nations acknowledge that they speak the Latin with the most intelligible accent; for which no other reason can be given, but that our accent is natural and has nothing, at least little, in it that is peculiar. I say not this to asperse the English, they are a nation I honour, but to reprove the petulancy and malice of some amongst them who think they do their country good service when they reproach ours.

We must also remember that underlying much of the Englishman's hostility to the Scots in those days was jealousy aroused by the invasion of his capital by thousands of Caledonians decidedly on the make. Both at court in the seventeenth century and at Parliament in the eighteenth century they had tremendous political influence, which they tried to keep among themselves.

The relationship between Dr Johnson and his biographer James Boswell reveals much about the tension between Scots and English identities in London society. In an exaggerated form, their relationship sums up the relative status and the attitudes abroad at the time regarding culture in general and language in particular. Boswell is a typical eighteenth-century Scots aristocrat doing everything he can to ingratiate himself with the London literati and nobility. Dr Johnson is a good example of the elitist Englishman, resentful of the Scots' inordinate influence in every sphere of city life and disdainful of their culture and their attempts to acquire his. Boswell's description of their first meeting encapsulates the ambience of the English capital:

> Mr Davies mentioned my name, and respectfully introduced me to him. I was much agitated; and recollecting his prejudice against the Scotch, of which I had heard much, I said to Davies, 'Don't tell him where I come from.' – 'From Scotland,' cried Davies roguishly. 'Mr Johnson,' said I, 'I do indeed come from Scotland, but I cannot help it.' I am willing to flatter myself that I meant this as a light pleasantry to soothe and conciliate him, and not as an humiliating abasement at the expense of my country. But however that might be, this speech was somewhat unlucky; for he seized the expression 'come from Scotland', which I used in the sense of being of that country; and, as if I had said that I had come away from it, or left it, retorted, 'That, Sir, I find, is what a very great many of your countrymen cannot help.' This stroke stunned me a good deal; and when we had sat down, I felt myself not a little embarrassed, and apprehensive of what might come next.

What came next was that Boswell got the name of being Johnson's 'Scotch cur', becoming – and here I must beg forgiveness of the gracious reader for the impropriety of introducing a Scotticism – the classic sook. The liaison had its reward nevertheless, in the finest biography in the English language. Boswell was prepared to suffer all insults and indignities in order to record the great man's sayings. His near family did not share his enthusiasm. His father, Lord Auchinleck, like many of the Law Lords, continued speaking Scots, which he used to good effect when he heard of his son's attachment to Johnson: 'Jamie has gaen clean gyte . . . whae's tail dae ye think he has preened himsel tae noo? A dominie man! – an auld dominie, wha keepit a schule an caaed it an Acaademy!' Johnson's manners during his tour of Scotland apparently justified the animal imagery frequently used in descriptions of him. Boswell's wife was so put out at the sight of her husband grovelling before the Englishman, she remonstrated that she 'had often seen a bear led by a man, but never till now had she seen a man led by a bear!' An indication of the good doctor's insensitivity and his supercilious dismissal of the notion that the Scots possessed any degree of culture at all is revealed by his remarks, made in obvious wonder and admiration, when he visits an innovative school for the handicapped in Edinburgh:

> It was pleasing to see one of the most desperate of human calamities capable of so much help: whatever enlarges hope will exalt courage; after having seen the deaf taught arithmetick, who would be afraid to cultivate the Hebrides?

Boswell, of course, was so thirled to Johnson and, like many Scots of the age, so in thrall to English culture that he was all but oblivious to the great lexicographer's faults. He was particularly sensitive about his Scottish accent and frequently rails against the speech of his fellow countrymen when he comes across them in London: 'the common style of company and conversation, the coarse jibes of this "hamely" company . . . the Fife tongue and the Niddry's Wynd address were quite hideous.' Contemplating that he may have to go back and live in Scotland in order to inherit his estate fills him with horror; it would be 'like yoking a Newmarket winner to a dung cart'. Given his linguistic insecurity, any praise or hint of approval from his master fell like manna from heaven, and was therefore worthy of note in his diary. The following passage is from 1772:

> On Saturday, 27 March, I introduced to him Sir Alexander Macdonald. Sir Alexander observed, 'I have been correcting several Scotch accents in my friend Boswell. I doubt, Sir, if any Scotchman ever attains to a perfect English pronunciation.'
>
> Johnson. 'Why, Sir, few of them do, because they do not persevere after acquiring a certain degree in it.'
>
> Upon another occasion I talked to him on this subject, having myself taken some pains to improve my pronunciation, by the aid of the late Mr. Love, of Drury Lane theatre, when he was a player at Edinburgh, and also of old Mr. Sheridan. Johnson said to me, 'Sir, your pronunciation is not offensive.' With this concession I was pretty well satisfied; and let me give my countrymen of North Britain an advice not to aim at absolute perfection in this respect. A small intermixture of provincial peculiarities may, perhaps, have an agreeable effect.

The great literary language of the Makars, two centuries on, regarded as a provincial peculiarity! This was how far Scots had sunk in the second half of the eighteenth century. It was to sink even further, to be regarded with odium even by men who did not share Boswell's undiscriminating veneration for the English. David Hume was one of many Scots who felt no personal affinity with the English. He felt at home only in Edinburgh or Paris, where he was fêted by the intelligentsia, and was forever railing against 'the factious barbarians of London, who will hate me because I am a Scotsman and am not a Whig, and despise me because I am a man of letters'. This did not prevent him following blindly the fashion of the age for Augustan refinement, the attainment of which necessitated the rooting out of all trace of Scottishness from one's writing.

With first the aristocracy then the upper and middle classes adopting English manners, there began the slow percolation down through the social ranks of English models of speech. Scots in literary use was deemed appropriate only when dealing with the speech of the lower orders. As we have seen, this process was taking place throughout the century following the Union of the Crowns. But the social downgrading of Scots continued at a more rapid and unchecked pace following the Union of the Parliaments in 1707, when the anglicising tendencies reached obsessive proportions among the upper echelons of society.

The balancing act which the Scots of the eighteenth century performed between Scottish and English culture, in their society and within the individual, produced an almost schizophrenic state of mind in people whose loyalties were constantly stretched in different airts. Allan Ramsay was one of the great poets who revived Scots as a literary language, yet he too was very much a man of his time and sometimes found it difficult to resolve the dichotomy which pulled him in different directions. His son and namesake, Allan Ramsay the painter, helped found the Select Society in 1754. From its ranks sprang the Society for the English Language, the initial aim of which was to promote the correct use of English, and which to that effect engaged a Mr Leigh, 'a person well qualified to teach the pronunciation of the English tongue with propriety and grace'.

Whereas in the previous century the term used to describe the language of the Lowlands alternated between 'English' and 'Scots', as it had done interchangeably since the sixteenth century, there was now a conscious distinction made between the vernaculars of England and Scotland. As late as the first few decades of the eighteenth century, when schools referred to subjects available on their curriculum they would describe the class teaching the vernacular as the 'Scots class' or the 'English class' and the terms would not imply a difference of emphasis in language teaching.

By the middle of the eighteenth century, however, you have schools starting to refer to teaching English 'by the new method', which usually implied that an attempt would be made to teach southern pronunciation. Heriot's school in the seventeenth century claims it will 'teach the bairns to read and write Scots distinctly', while by the time Edinburgh Academy is founded in the early nineteenth century, 'a proper English articulation and accent' is insisted upon 'in order to remedy a defect in the education of boys in Edinburgh who are suffered to neglect the cultivation of their native tongue and literature during the whole time they attend the grammar schools'. As you can see, by this point English has become so all-powerful that it is deemed 'proper' and the 'native tongue', while presumably the indigenous vernacular, the actual native tongue, is dismissed as a defect! We are now beginning to recognise traits ingraining themselves which persist in our own similarly Enlightened Age!

The modern fallacy of Scots as a corruption of English really took root in this Augustan Age of the later eighteenth century. In order to facilitate the well-nigh-impossible acquisition of spoken English, numerous books were published in Scotland which attempted to show by multifarious orthographic devices how English was pronounced in England. Today, English orthography is a minefield for students from foreign countries; the same symbol can represent totally different sounds, e.g. 'gh' in tough and through. If you do not know how the words should be pronounced, you will get little help from the orthography and are therefore prone to making mistakes in your pronunciation. The Scots were in the same position in the eighteenth century. Having little or no contact with native English speakers on a regular basis, their situation was rendered even more difficult because they did not realise that many of the sounds they made were in fact Scots and not English. Among the books published for the help of our forefathers in this their hour of need were: *The Edinburgh New Method of Teaching English* by Godskirk and Hume, in 1750; *Linguae Brittanicae Vera Pronunciato* by James Buchanan, in 1757; *The Pronouncing Dictionary of the English Language* by John Burns, in 1777; and William Scott's *A General View of English Pronunciation*, published in Edinburgh in 1784.

The last attempts systematically to give numbers to the various vowel sounds in English and, by breaking up the words into numbered segments, reveal how they should be pronounced. He also points out common Scottish confusions: 'bliss (made a verb) for bless, rid for red: o short with o long, as lo-ng for long and most for mo-st.' The differentiation of the English sounds in 'not' and 'note', 'clock' and 'cloak', or 'cot' and 'coat' was particularly confusing for Scots speakers and they frequently got it, and still get it, wrong.

While dubbing the commentary, in English, for the television programme *The Mother Tongue*, I used the verb 'forge', pronouncing it with the same sound as 'door' or 'bore'. My unwitting Scotticism was immediately seized upon and I was assured that the correct pronunciation of 'forge' was to rhyme it with 'gorge' or 'George'. However, knowing where such concessions landed our ancestors, I stuck to what came naturally to me and pronounced the word as always, 'foarge'. I use the example to illustrate the survival of Scots in our English pronunciation and also to show how difficult it must have been for the anglicisers. One of the results of the confusion was that many Scots overcompensated and used imagined English pronunciations for words which share the same sound in Scots and English. For example, if 'box' is pronounced 'boax' in Scots but 'box' in English, it follows that 'coach' in Scots must be 'coch' in English and 'pork', pronounced 'poark' in Scots, must needs be 'pawrk' in English. The last sound is still to be heard among 'polite' speakers in Edinburgh today.

The effect of this mixter-maxter must have been gey hilarious at times, as our ancestors frequently pit their fuit in it. The twentieth-century dramatist Robert McLellan portrayed the problem beautifully in his play *The Flouers o Edinburgh*, set in the period in question in an Auld Reekie awash with anglicisation. In this short scene, a Scottish Augustan poet, Mr Dowie, is just being disabused of the notion that he writes English with propriety by young Charles, who has returned from London speaking a strangulated bourach of a pronunciation he insists is London English:

> CHARLES: Here we are, I think. Yes. You are sitting among the skulls, Doctor, addressing Death. You say:
> Thy bony hand lies chill upon my breast.
> Now add my carcase to thy loathsome feast.
> DOWIE: Breist, no breast.
> CHARLES: I know it has to read breist before it rhymes, but an Englishman says breast.
> DOWIE: B-r-e-a-s-t?
> CHARLES: Yes.
> DOWIE: Breist.
> CHARLES: No, breast.
> DOWIE: An Englishman says breast, for b-r-e-a-s-t?
> CHARLES: Yes, Doctor, have you ever been to England?

DOWIE: Na.

CHARLES: I thought so. English as a spoken language is quite foreign to you.

DOWIE: But I read naething else.

CHARLES: I said as a spoken language. You cannot possibly know how English words should sound. You have no right to write English poetry.

DOWIE: Nae richt! Dae they say that in London?

CHARLES: Englishmen say that.

DOWIE: Dear me. A lot o my rhymes are wrang, then?

CHARLES: A considerable number.

DOWIE: Dear me.

Doctor Dowie is racked to the core of his existence by this revelation, but his type persisted and went to even greater lengths to acquire *bon ton*. In the Scottish capital in particular, a roaring trade for those practising the new science of elocution was available. In the 1760s, a horde of out-of-work actors and linguistic eccentrics flocked to Edinburgh to teach English.

Among their pupils were men who in their saner moments were outstanding philosophers, scientists and economists – members of the brilliant coterie of Enlightenment intellectuals who made Edinburgh one of the cultural capitals of Europe at the time. David Hume was so embarrassed by what he considered to be his inability to speak or write perfect English that when he died he is said to have confessed not his sins but his Scotticisms! With Hume, it appears to have been an *idée fixe* to out-English the English. He is said to have sent his manuscripts to such diverse experts as a linen-draper in Bristol and a cobbler in Norwich in order to have any trace of Scotticism weeded out of the text before exposing it to the scrutiny of polite society. This from a man who was proudly Scottish, whose sceptical view of religion enraged large sections of that society and who retained his principles till his dying day.

Hume and his group were susceptible, gullible prey for the teachers who set up shop to give courses throughout the long Edinburgh winters. Advertisements like the following appeared in the newspapers, placed by teachers such as William Noble intent on exploiting upper-class sensibilities: '. . . taking all imaginable care of the quantity, accent and manner of expression, by which he hopes that the barbarisms, so often and so justly complained of here, will be properly guarded against'. That one is taken from the *Caledonian Mercury* of 19 September 1761. Ten years later, in the *Edinburgh*

Evening Courant, a Mr Telfer, 'lately arrived from London', offers classes which will not only promote English but make sure that no other language rears its head:

> Having studied and taught the English language chiefly for several years past, he hopes he shall be able to teach his pupils that pronunciation and accent which are used by the most polite speakers and great care will be taken that no Scotch be spoken in time of school.

Mr Telfer stresses that he has spent some time in London to recommend himself to his charges. As most of the audience hadn't the faintest idea of what London English actually sounded like, scope for gulling private pupils must have been enormous. A London accent, far from being required, was actually quite a rarity among the teachers. Two of the most successful were Masson, an Aberdonian, and Sheridan, a Dubliner. The mind boggles as to what kind of English their pupils came out with. Boswell attended Sheridan's course of lectures and the *Scots Magazine* reports that he was in the company of 300 gentlemen, 'the most eminent in this country for their rank and abilities'. Those few teachers who were native speakers of the required dialect, of course, could score points against those who had learned the right accent. In the preface to his highly successful *Only Sure Guide to the English Tongue; or New Pronouncing Spelling Book* of 1776, one of the English teachers, William Perry, berates 'North British authors like Masson, the late Mr Drummond, etc; some of whom probably never crossed the Tweed'.

Mr Perry undertook a series of lectures in Edinburgh. His advertisement in the *Caledonian Mercury* shows how entertainment and music hall mixed with the serious attempt to teach refinement in speech. Presumably to illustrate the opposite of what he is aiming at and to introduce some burlesque black humour, he promises in the course of his lecture to introduce 'the following characters, viz The Schoolboy, Schoolmaster, Common Reader, Monotonist, Jingler, Stammerer, Word-monger, Clipper, Coiner and Distorter'. Perry was obviously an expert in public relations. In order to cheer up and encourage his audience, he reveals to them that even unto England there are pockets of language practice even more uncouth than Scots, 'specimens of the dialects of several counties of England remarkable for their barbarism and corruption of speech'. One of the elocutionists actually advertised his lecture as 'a new species of literary entertainment' and Edinburgh was that hoatchin wi language teachers one gets the feeling that many were simply jumping on a bandwagon, exploiting a fashion which in fact did not last much longer than a decade.

Perry and the rest of the teachers probably realised that there was little hope of changing the ladies and gentlemen who attended their lectures. They were set in their ways, their ways were Scots and it would be a few generations yet before that would alter. But if you caught them young enough, the children's ways could be set on a different course. A pointer of things to come is indicated in a report in the *Caledonian Mercury* of 6 May 1776 of Mr Perry's visit to a class in Leith:

> What is very remarkable is that the youngest class, some of whom are not four years of age, repeated the different sounds of the vowels and diphthongs from Mr Perry's *New Pronouncing Spelling Book* to an astonishing degree of accuracy.

Another facet of the rush to acquire English was the publication of articles and books which gave detailed lists of 'Scotticisms liable to be mistaken for English in this country'. The first collection was compiled by James Elphinstone and was published, not surprisingly, as an appendix to Hume's *Political Discourses* in 1752. Elphinstone also published a supplementary list in the *Scots Magazine* in 1764. One of the areas he highlights is the problem of Scots stressing words on different syllables from the English. Our countrymen, 'so remote from propriety and unaided by system', naturally got things wrong: they stress, for example, 'April' and 'harass' on the last syllable, 'ally' and 'perverse' on the penultimate syllable, 'clandestine' and 'contribute' on the antepenultimate syllable. When you have worked that lot out, you soon discover that many of these features which were excruciatingly embarassing to the eighteenth-century cognoscenti have since become accepted, pukka RP English!

James Beattie, the poet, and compiler of one of these bestselling volumes, stresses in his introduction that he wants his readers to beware of using expressions which seem English but are in fact the remnant of that huge area in which Scots and English shared the same vocabulary while expressing things in different ways. One can only smile today when one thinks of men of the stature of David Hume and Adam Smith being fashed with trivialities such as the following examples from the book:

SCOTS	ENGLISH
a bit bread	a bit of bread
the better of a sleep	the better for a sleep
on the morn	on the morrow
a sore head	a headache
to my bed	to bed
he has got the cold	he has got a cold
where do you stay?	where do you lodge, live, or dwell?

A glance at the two lists will show that the Scottish options are still in use in Scottish English today, proof of the survival of Scots even among those who don't consider they speak it. The anglicisers were perhaps more successful in the long term with the words that were unique to Scots. Beattie never regarded them as much of a problem: 'With respect to broad Scotch words, I do not think any caution requisite, as they are easily known and the necessity of avoiding them is obvious.'

The tragedy is that the Scots no longer took what they wanted from other cultures to enrich their own, as had been the case in the days of the Makars. They uncritically adopted English fashion and taste, not realising that their attempts to write in the style of Addison, Pope or Shenstone were doomed to the same kind of failure as their attempts to root out their native idiom from their speech.

In his autobiography, which spans the years from 1722 to 1805, Dr Alexander Carlyle of Inveresk relates how he had been taught 'a tolerable accent' of English by his aunt from London, 'an accomplishment which in those days was very rare'. His journal details the life of the Scottish community in London, in particular their frequenting of the British Coffee House, the London Scots' favourite rendezvous. English was desired by the Scots but for many it remained an impenetrable, foreign jargon. In one incident, in 1758, Carlyle asks a fellow Scot, Dr Charles Congalton, what he thinks of the English now that he has been among them for a few months. He replies that he is unable to answer honestly, as he has not really made acquaintance with any of them: 'I never enter into conversation with the John Bulls, for, to tell you the truth, I don't yet well understand what they say.' Carlyle knew personally many of the leading men of the Enlightenment, such as William Robertson, principal of Edinburgh University, who, he recalled, 'spoke broad Scotch in point of pronunciation and accent or tone . . . his was the language of literature and taste, and of an enlightened and liberal mind'. The great geologist James Hutton, Sir Walter Scott and many others continued speaking

Scots as their natural language long after the fashion for Augustan elegance had abated.

In writing, however, prose had become almost completely unscotched by the latter half of the eighteenth century. Yet it had not yet become English. When Lord Mansfield commented to Alexander Carlyle that he felt that he was not reading English in the works of Hume and Robertson, the sage of Inveresk gave this perceptive reply:

> to every man bred in Scotland the English language was in some respects a foreign tongue, the precise value and force of whose phrases he did not understand and therefore was continually endeavouring to word his expressions by additional epithets or circumlocutions which made his writing appear both stiff and redundant.

The Scots literati had as yet mastered only the surface level of English, a detached register devoid of emotional resonance. They wrote English perfectly and with propriety, in the same way as, for example, a German intellectual who had similarly become fluent in the language and mastered its structure and surface would have done. Ironically, this foreignness of English written by Scots, with its painstaking, precise correctness and formality, made it the perfect medium for discussing science and philosophy, in whose various branches the men of the Scottish Enlightenment excelled.

6

The Vernacular Revived?

For work requiring both head and heart, however, in creative literature, this surface grasp of the English language that the Scots writer had was all but useless. The Scots literati, of course, were so in thrall to English taste at the time that they never realised how forgettable their attempts to copy Augustan English in fact were. Indeed, they were blind to literary brilliance on their own doorstep. Henry Mackenzie's important review of Burns' Kilmarnock Edition in the prestigious periodical *The Lounger* is favourable up to a point, but the fashion for English propriety and elegance gets in the way of objective criticism: 'One bar indeed, his birth and education have opposed to his fame, the language in which most of his poems are written.'

Fortunately, Burns was enough of his own man to ignore the advice of the literary elite to write solely in English; otherwise he would have been just another obscure, stilted versifier, like Blacklock or Beattie, instead of one of the world's genuinely popular yet great poets. All the Scots writers engaged in a balancing act between the two cultures; but it was only when the poets Allan Ramsay, Robert Fergusson and Burns wrote in Scots that the balance tilted from precious gentility towards greatness – proof, if any was required, that Scots still held the hearts if not the minds of the intelligentsia of the period.

For, running throughout the eighteenth century, with its obsession to anglicise, there arose the parallel cultural phenomenon of pride in Scots and the vigorous continuation of its tradition as a medium for both literature and speech. The motivations behind this were diverse and often surprising, taking in: notions of national and religious identity; reaction against artificial gentility; a desire to prove that with a sprinkling of Scots a poet need not desert propriety; academic promotion of the Scottish past as a source of pride in Scottishness at a time when that identity was under threat; and the simple conclusion that, in Scots, Scottish people could communicate more effectively and writers write more relevantly of the Scottish experience.

Many of these strands can be traced in the work of the poet who is very much the father-figure of the vernacular revival, Allan Ramsay. In the preface to *The Ever Green*, his collection of Scots poetry from before 1600, he upbraids his fellow writers for their present predilection for setting their works in the classical landscapes of Europe, instead of rooting them, like the Makars, in their native environment. In the ancient poetry, he claims:

> The Morning rises (in the Poets description) as she does in the Scottish Horizon. We are not carried to Greece or Italy for a Shade, a Stream or a Breeze. The Groves rise in our own Valleys; the rivers flow from our own Fountains, and the Winds blow upon our own Hills. I find not Fault with those Things, as they are in Greece or Italy: But with a Northern Poet for fetching his Materials from these places, in a Poem, of which his own Country is the Scene; as our Hymners to the Spring and Makers of Pastorals frequently do.

You will notice that the style of the preface is not uninfluenced by the sententious neo-classical tones of his English contemporaries; indeed, a quotation from Pope is printed on the title page of *The Ever Green*. The preface also goes on to rail against those Scots so thirled to present fashion that they hardly admit to knowledge of their native tongue. This is an early example of the rise of the 'kent his faither' syndrome which bedevils many Scots' views on their native culture and its exponents:

> There is nothing can be heard more silly than one's expressing his Ignorance of his native Language; yet such there are, who can vaunt of acquiring a tolerable Perfection in the French or Italian Tongue, if they have been a Forthnight in Paris or a Month in Rome: But shew them the most elegant Thoughts in a Scots Dress, they as disdainfully as stupidly condemn it as barbarous. But the true Reason is obvious: Every one that is born never so little superior to the Vulgar, would fain distinguish themselves from them by some Manner or other,

and such, it would appear, cannot arrive at a better Method. But this affected Class of fops give no Uneasiness, not being numerous; for the most part of our Gentlemen, who are generally Masters of the most useful and politest Languages, can take Pleasure (for a Change) to speak and read their own.

Those of the provincial cast of mind Ramsay describes in the culturally colonised minority of fops who automatically dismiss their native culture out of hand would unfortunately increase in number over the next 200 years; members of the Establishment and their many imitators gave themselves over almost entirely to English culture. But there was also an important group who, while absorbing English culture, found time and commitment for the native tradition and patriotically fostered this alternative cultural world picture. In Edinburgh, for example, the Episcopalian and Jacobite coterie was a powerful cultural and political force. Ramsay's *The Ever Green* was printed by Thomas Ruddiman, an Episcopalian Jacobite activist and propagandist from the North-east. He printed the Jacobite newspaper the *Caledonian Mercury* and brought out editions of Gavin Douglas and the Latin poet George Buchanan. All of these efforts were tied in with a deliberate attempt to propagate the pre-Reformation humanist tradition in Scottish letters and provide a viable alternative to the Presbyterian version of Scottish culture.

Ruddiman's printing of *The Ever Green* and Ramsay's interest in Scotland's literary past were almost certainly inspired by a product of the other major printing press in Edinburgh in the first quarter of the eighteenth century. James Watson was also a staunch Jacobite and his *Choice Collection of Comic and Serious Scots Poems both ancient and modern* (1706–11) fulfilled a growing demand for knowledge of the glories of the past, especially in a form which has never really ceased to be popular, that of Scots song.

Hamilton of Bangour and Hamilton of Gilbertfield were two of a large group of minor writers who wrote in Scots and contributed songs and poems to the various collections published at this time. Bangour was a romantic charmer who composed poems to seduce the belles of the city. He was out in the '45 Rebellion and was forced to leave his homeland for exile in France after Culloden. His most popular work was the ballad 'The Braes of Yarrow'. The Jacobites apparently combined politics and pleasure in equal measure, their clubs, like The Horn, The Auld Stuarts and The White Cockade, meeting in the steeran howffs o Auld Reekie where songs like 'Awa, Whigs, Awa' or 'The Wee, Wee German Lairdie' were chorused and the toast, in claret, was 'The King ower the water'. Ramsay's friend, Wiliam Hamilton of Gilbertfield, celebrated the non-political activities of the coterie:

> The dull draff-drink maks me sae dowff
> A' I can do's but bark and yowff;
> Yet set me in a claret howff
> Wi' folk that's chancy,
> My muse may len me then a gowff
> To clear my fancy.
>
> Then Bacchus-like I'd bawl and bluster
> And a' the muses 'bout me muster
> Sae merrily I'd squeeze the cluster
> And drink the grape,
> 'T wad gie my verse a brighter lustre,
> And better shape.

(*draff-drink* thin ale; *dowff* weary; *bark and yowff* rant and rave; *gowff* slap)

Hamilton of Gilbertfield also revived Blin Hary's *The Wallace*, translating it, curiously, into English rather than contemporary Scots. It was this version, however, that kindled a fervent patriotism in the young Robert Burns. From the Covenanting west country, Burns was neither Episcopalian nor Jacobite but he shared the same love of Scotland and its culture as his great literary predecessors of the eighteenth century, Allan Ramsay and Robert Fergusson. Like Fergusson, who also belonged to the Episcopalian group, Burns carried on the interest in Scots songs shown by the earlier poets, devoting the last years of his life to their collection and reworking.

But the undoubted commitment and brilliance of the three greatest of the poets was not enough to stem the slow erosion of Scots in life and letters. Lacking the support of the Establishment, the survival of the Scots tradition now depended on individuals going against their socialisation and saving Scots from the imminent death the Establishment wished on the language and, to a lesser extent, its literature. This has been the case from Ramsay through to MacDiarmid.

While the use of Scots was narrowed to reflect the speech of the lower orders, this also had the effect of giving the language a radical irreverent quality, which it has retained ever since. The writers could adopt the persona of the common man, and criticise and satirise society with impunity. When Burns acknowledged his debt to the individual who had gone before him, Robert Fergusson, he also took a swipe at the condescension of the upper classes:

> My curse upon your whunstane hearts
> Ye Enbrugh gentry!
> The tythe o' what ye waste at cartes
> Wad stow'd his pantry!

The different social status of Scots and English determined the kinds of poems written in each register. In English, Burns tends to look over his shoulder to see the reaction of his aristocratic patrons and polite society. In Scots, he attacks with vigorous directness all the ills in his society, from a local quack doctor in 'Death and Doctor Hornbook' to the Kirk satire of 'The Holy Fair' and the swingeing portrait of the failings of an individual Calvinist in 'Holy Willie's Prayer':

> O Thou that in the Heavens dost dwell,
> Wha, as it pleases best Thysel,
> Sends ane to Heaven an' ten to Hell
> A' for thy glory,
> And no for onie guid or ill
> They've done before thee!

The Calvinist belief in the Elect, the chosen few who will go to heaven, is perfectly expressed in that verse. Burns goes on to describe the earthly imperfections of those who see themselves as the Elect, using humour to bring home the point:

> Yet I am here, a chosen sample,
> To show thy grace is great and ample:
> I'm here a pillar o' Thy temple,
> Strong as a rock,
> A guide, a buckler and example
> To a' Thy flock!

> But yet, O Lord! confess I must:
> At times I'm fash'd wi' fleshly lust;
> An' sometimes, too, in warldly trust
> Vile self gets in;
> But Thou remembers we are dust,
> Defiled wi' sin.

O Lord! yestreen, Thou kens, wi' Meg –
Thy pardon I sincerely beg –
O, may't ne'er be a living plague
To my dishonour!
An' I'll ne'er lift a lawless leg
Again upon her.

Besides, I farther maun avow –
Wi' Leezie's lass, three times, I trow –
But, Lord, that Friday I was fou,
When I cam near her,
Or else, Thou kens, Thy servant true
Wad never steer her.

Despite these 'minor' transgressions, Willie feels confident enough in his status as one of the chosen to demand that the Lord bring the full weight of his awesome fury down upon a 'major' transgressor called Aitken of Ayr Presbytery, who has dared ridicule the Auld Licht conservative party that Willie belongs to in the Kirk. Having done his vengeful duty by the Elect, Willie exhorts the Lord to return to his normal role, that of looking after Willie and his kind:

But Lord, remember me and mine
Wi' mercies temporal and divine,
That I for grace an' gear may shine
Excell'd by nane;
And a' the glory shall be Thine –
Amen, Amen!

Burns focuses on the woes of the country and the village, a parochial setting which his poetry, like that of all great artists, transcends and renders universal.

The man he called his 'elder Brother in the Muse', Robert Fergusson, died tragically young, before his 25th birthday. But he left us a gutsy, realistic description of Scottish urban life in the middle of the eighteenth century. While others, such as Ramsay in *The Gentle Shepherd*, indulged in the fashion for pastoral poetry – a vogue for rusticity perfectly suited to the image of Scots as a peasant dialect – it is refreshing to come across Fergusson's starkly naturalistic portrayal of the darker side of street life in the capital city. This passage from 'Hallow Fair' describes police violence by the City Guard, a corps made up, as you can guess from the poet's transcription of their

speech, of Gaelic-speaking Highlanders who had little love for their
Lowland countrymen:

> Jock Bell gaed furth to play his freaks,
>   Great cause he had to rue it,
> For frae a stark Lochaber aix
>   He gat a clamihewit
>   Fu' sair that night.
>
> 'Ohon!' (quo' he), 'I'd rather be
>   By sword or bagnet stickit,
> Than hae my crown or body wi'
>   Sic deadly weapons nicket.'
> Wi' that he gat anither straik
>   Mair weighty than before,
> That gar'd his feckless body aik,
>   An' spew the reikin gore,
>   Fu' red that night.
>
> He pechin on the causey lay,
>   O' kicks and cuffs weel sair'd;
> A Highland aith the serjeant gae,
>   'She maun pe see our guard.'
> Out spak the weirlike corporal,
>   'Pring in ta drunken sot.'
> They trail'd him ben, an' by my saul,
>   He paid his drunken groat,
>   For that neist day.
>
> Guid folk, as ye come frae the fair,
>   Bide yont frae this black squad;
> There's nae sic savages elsewhere
>   Allow'd to wear cockade.
> Than the strong lion's hungry maw,
>   Or tusk o' Russian bear,
> Frae their wanruly fellin paw
>   Mair cause ye hae to fear
>   Your death that day.

(*clamihewit, straik* blow; *weirlike* warlike; *groat* small coin;
wanruly unruly)

The seamier side of city life is also an area which Allan Ramsay excels in portraying. He deliberately goes out of his way to shock genteel society with poems of low-life characters such as the bawd Lucky Spence:

> My bennison come on good doers,
> Who spend their cash on bawds and whores;
> May they ne'er want the wale of cures
> For a sair snout;
> Foul fa' the quacks wha that fire smoors,
> And puts nae out.
>
> My malison light ilka day
> On them that drink and dinna pay,
> But tak' a snack and run away;
> May't be their hap
> Never to want a gonorrhea,
> Or rotten clap.
>
> (*wale* choice; *snout* protuberance; *smoors* smothers, dowses; *snack* bite, short time)

Yet the same Ramsay and his Jacobite patriots read *The Spectator* at every meeting of their gentlemen's club, The Easy Club, in order to perfect their English, so that 'by a Mutual improvement in Conversation they may become more adapted for fellowship with the politer part of mankind'. Success for the poet wigmaker's efforts to write with propriety came with his enormously popular pastoral play *The Gentle Shepherd*. It received the ultimate stamp of approval when Pope expressed himself to be delighted by it when his friend Dr Arbuthnot read and translated it for him at his grotto in Twickenham. This was doubly pleasing for Ramsay because in the play there is a wide range of linguistic styles, reflecting in an idealised way the linguistic identity of the varying classes in Scottish society. It was proof to a patriot that fashion could still be adhered to without deserting Scots.

Burns similarly indulged in both sides of his dual inheritance. At times it is as if he needs to balance Augustan purity with down-to-earth Scots bawdry! In his letters and prose, however, Burns the Augustan is very much to the fore. The dedication which prefaces his Edinburgh Edition of 1787 is addressed to 'the Noblemen and Gentlemen of the Caledonian Hunt'. It is typical of the high rhetorical style fashionable then:

THE VERNACULAR REVIVED?

My Lords and Gentlemen,– A Scottish Bard, proud of the name, and whose highest ambition is to sing in his Country's service – where shall he so properly look for patronage as to the illustrious Names of his native Land; those who bear the honours and inherit the virtues of their Ancestors? The Poetic Genius of my Country found me as the prophetic bard Elijah did Elisha – at the plough, and threw her inspiring mantle over me. She bade me sing the loves, the joys, the rural scenes and rural pleasures of my natal Soil, in my native tongue: I tuned my wild, artless notes, as she inspired. She whispered to me to come to this ancient metropolis of Caledonia, and lay my songs under your honoured protection: I now obey her dictates.

The only extended prose which Burns wrote in Scots is the tour de force of a letter he sent to his friend William Nicol in Edinburgh from Carlisle towards the end of his Border tour. In it, we get an idea of the colloquial spoken Scots Burns was familiar with in his south-west part of the country. We also have a virtuoso performance by a man taking gleeful delight in words and their possibilities. In fack, it's that stowed an thrang wi fouth o guid Scots words wi nae English equivalent, ye'll hae tae owreset it yersels. I wad be faur ower forjesket een tae begin!

Carlisle 1st June 1787 – or
I believe the 39th o' May rather

Kind, honest-hearted Willie,
I'm sitten down here, after seven and forty miles ridin, e'en as forjesket and forniaw'd as a forfoughten cock, to gie you some notion o' my landlowper-like stravaguin sin the sorrowfu' hour that I sheuk hands and parted wi' auld Reekie.
  My auld, ga'd Gleyde o' a meere has huchyall'd up hill and down brae, in Scotland and England, as teugh and birnie as a vera devil wi' me. It's true, she's as poor's a Sang-maker and as hard's a kirk, and tipper-taipers when she taks the gate first like a Lady's gentlewoman in a minuwae, or a hen on a het girdle, but she's a yauld, poutherie Girran for a' that; and has a stomach like Willie Stalker's meere that wad hae digeested tumbler-wheels, for she'll whip me aff her five stimparts o' the best aits at a down-sittin and ne'er fash her thumb. When ance her ringbanes and spavies, her crucks and cramps, are fairly soupl'd, she beets to, and ay the hindmost hour the tightest. I

could wager her price to a thretty pennies that, for twa or three wooks ridin at fifty mile a day, the deil-sticket a five gallopers acqueesh Clyde and Whithorn could cast saut in her tail.

I hae dander'd owre a' the kintra frae Dumbar to Selcraig, and hae forgather'd wi' monie a guid fallow, and monie a weel-far'd hizzie. I met wi' twa dink quines in particlar, ane o' them a sonsie, fine fodgel lass, baith braw and bonie; the tither was a clean-shankit, straught, tight, weel-far'd winch, as blythe's a lintwhite on a flowerie thorn, and as sweet and modest's a new blawn plumrose in a hazle shaw. They were baith bred to mainners by the beuk, and onie ane o' them has as muckle smeddum and rumblegumtion as the half o' some Presbytries that you and I baith ken. They play'd me sik a deevil o' a shavie that I daur say if my harigals were turn'd out, ye wad see twa nicks i' the heart o' me like the mark o' a kail-whittle in a castock.

I was gaun to write you a lang pystle, but, Gude forgie me, I gat myself sae noutouriously bitchify'd the day after kail-time that I can hardly stoiter but and ben.

My best respecks to the guidwife and a' our common friens, especiall Mr & Mrs Cruikshank and the honest Guidman o' Jock's Lodge.

I'll be in Dumfries the morn gif the beast be to the fore and the branks bide hale.

Gude be wi' you, Willie! Amen!

Robt Burns

Interestingly, while many of his nobler contemporaries spoke Scots and wrote English, Burns appears to have been at home speaking both Scots and English, a forerunner of the truly bilingual society that Lowland Scotland was to become. Many of the literati who met him during his Edinburgh period testified to his refined command of English and one commented that David Hume was far broader in speech than the Ayrshire ploughman. To paraphrase another great Ayrshire writer of our own day, William McIlvanney, Burns and the other poets of the vernacular revival inhabited the paradoxes of their cultural milieu, as writers like McIlvanney are still doing successfully today. The dichotomy in Scottish society, in other words, did not produce a clean divide between a pro-Scots and pro-English faction in matters of language, culture and politics; the divide existed within individuals who were now heir to both the Scots and the imported English tradition. For some, the choice of calling oneself Scottish or

North British was an arbitrary one; for others, the assertion of a Scottish identity under threat was of paramount importance. That divide, I would maintain, still exists within the Scottish psyche today.

The Scots of the eighteenth- and nineteenth-century revivalists was a mixed dialect of the two languages. This reflected the prestige of English rather than any great change to the everyday speech of the mass of the population. The way they wrote their Scots was also influenced by the English ascendancy. With little knowledge of the old ways of spelling, apostrophes are used in abundance to suggest the English letter that is 'missing' – *gie* becomes *gi'e*, *o* becomes *o'*, *an* becomes *an'*. This gives the impression that Scots is derived from English and, in those days of ignorance about how languages evolve, this became the accepted myth. In other words, Scots came to be seen as a debased dialect of English rather than the dialect remnants of what was once the national language of Stewart Scotland.

The mixed dialect, however, gave writers a wonderfully flexible medium. Rhymes are a lot easier to master when you have two words, or two pronunciations, to choose from. In *Tam o' Shanter*, for example, Burns uses Scots one minute, English the next in order to get his rhyming couplets to match. Some lines, such as the following, require the English pronunciation for the rhyme to work:

> Gatherin her brows like gathering storm,
> Nursing her wrath to keep it warm

Ayrshire Scots pronounces the 'o' in storm like the 'o' in Scottish Standard English (SSE) 'quorum'. This obviously does not rhyme with 'warm' in its English form, and even less so in its Ayrshire Scots form, where 'warm' is pronounced like SSE 'farm'. Other rhymes require one word to be pronounced in English, the other in Scots to work. The Ayrshire Scots for a well, for example, is pronounced 'wal', with the 'a' pronounced like the SSE 'a' in 'Balham'. In order to make the word rhyme with the Scots 'hersel', however, Burns chooses the English form 'well':

> And near the thorn, aboon the well
> Whare Mungo's mither hang'd hersel

And, of course, there are many examples where both rhymes are Scots, and knowledge of the Scots pronunciation is required to make the rhyme true. For example 'floods' and 'woods' do not rhyme in English, but in Burns' and my own Kyle dialect, the vowel sound in both words is somewhat like that in SSE 'bid', and so the rhyme works for the Scots speaker, though it does not work in English:

> Before him Doon pours all his floods,
> The doubling storm roars thro' the woods

In the hands of a master like Burns, the two languages fuse imperceptibly into a perfect whole, an extension of the potential of both registers. To paraphrase what was said earlier about the language of the Border ballads, Burns' Scots contains English yet goes beyond it, while his English includes Scots and goes beyond it as well. From this fertile fusion emerged many of his greatest lyrics. Burns also proved that this language could express the philosophic concerns of the age as well as Augustan English. But the Scots does it in a more tangible and intimate fashion, as these verses at the beginning and end of 'To a Mouse' surely demonstrate:

> Wee, sleeket, cowran, tim'rous beastie,
> O, what a panic's in thy breastie!
> Thou need na start awa sae hasty
> Wi' bickering brattle!
> I wad be laith to rin an' chase thee,
> Wi' murdering pattle!
>
> I'm truly sorry man's dominion
> Has broken Nature's social union,
> An' justifies that ill opinion
> Which makes thee startle
> At me, thy poor, earth-born companion
> An' fellow mortal!
>
>   * * *
>
> That wee-bit heap o' leaves an' stibble,
> Has cost thee monie a wearie nibble!
> Now thou's turned out, for a' thy trouble,
> But house or hald,
> To thole the winter's sleety dribble,
> An' cranreuch cauld!
>
> But Mousie, thou art no thy lane,
> In proving foresight may be vain:
> The best-laid schemes o' Mice an' Men
> Gang aft agley,

An' lea'e us nocht but grief an pain,
For promis'd joy!

Still thou art blest, compar'd wi' me!
The present only toucheth thee:
But och! I backward cast my e'e,
On prospects drear!
An' forward, tho' I canna see,
I guess an' fear!

(*brattle* sudden rush; *cranreuch* frost; *agley* awry)

This Scots was also the language of the songs he collected or wrote and whose popularity he established all over the world. 'Auld Lang Syne' has versions I'm sure in a hundred languages, most of which are more agreeable to Scots lugs than the Anglo-American adaptation 'Old Long Zyne'! His love songs, such as 'Ae Fond Kiss', or 'Flow Gently, Sweet Afton', again are popular in the English-speaking world for this very reason – they can be read as Scots or English. To Scots speakers, though, they have an extra dimension which knowledge of Burns' native language brings to all his work. Of all the love songs he wrote, there is none greater than his anthem to international brotherhood, in which he again reconciles his native Scots with Augustan English terms to produce a memorable mell of the two:

Then let us pray that come it may
(As come it will for a' that)
That Sense and Worth o'er a' the earth
Shall bear the gree an' a' that!
For a' that, an' a' that,
It's comin yet for a' that,
That man to man the world o'er
Shall brithers be for a' that.

(*bear the gree* win supremacy)

The brilliance of Burns' achievement and the genuine popularity of his work, and that of Fergusson and Ramsay before him, did have some effect on the way Scottish society viewed the language. One of the most curious effects is still with us today, for I came across it often when I travelled the country to make the television series *The*

Mother Tongue for BBC Scotland and *Haud Yer Tongue* for Channel 4. J. Derrick McClure, in a brilliant essay in *Chapman* magazine, identifies it as the Pinkerton Syndrome, after an eighteenth-century Scottish historian, John Pinkerton, who stated the following in a preface to a collection called *Ancient Scottish Poems, never before in print*, published in the same year as the Kilmarnock Edition, 1786:

> none can more sincerely wish a total extinction of the Scottish colloquial dialect than I do, for there are few modern scoticisms which are not barbarisms . . . Yet I believe, no man of either kingdom would wish an extinction of the Scottish dialect in poetry.

In a country which is justifiably proud of a literature which stems directly from the life of its people, this desire to separate the living dialect from the literary medium is a dangerous one in its inevitable consequences: Scots is forced into a ghetto where it is used only for poetry and denied status in any other sphere.

The contemporary equivalent of the Pinkerton Syndrome is a belief among teachers that they are fostering Scots by teaching their wards to perform one or two party-piece poems in the language, usually for public performance on Burns Nicht, while the language is banned as a respected medium of communication inside the classroom 99 per cent of the time the children spend there. In other words, it is all right for a wee *divertissement* but the last thing you want to do is encourage and extend what is, after all, a 'corrupt dialect'! Pinkerton's language is archaic but the belief and the message has emerged from many a schoolmaster's lips in the intervening centuries:

> An heroic or tragic tale, in the pure Buchan dialect, would be very acceptable. But beware the common fault of taking cant phrases for old speech. Use the words of the vulgar, but use ancient and grave idioms and manner. Remember this vulgar speech was once the speech of heroes.

McClure gets to the nub of the Scots and English tension within individuals of then – and, tragically, now – and his conclusion makes a point which is both incisive and depressing for those of us who value the continuation of a Scottish tradition independent of that of England:

The Pinkerton Syndrome is a mode of defence against this uncomfortable fact: an attempt to retain traces of a Scottish identity without disturbing the 'British' status quo. The study of the things that once gave Scotland its distinctive national character but are now safely consigned to the past is permissible or even meritorious; the study of the things that now give it this, and if recognised and cultivated could do so to a much greater extent, is taboo.

McClure's thesis fits many of the Scots literati of the eighteenth century. Some, such as James Thomson and Thomas Campbell, unscotched themselves completely in their writing. Further, they achieved fame by composing those great hymns of British or pan-English nationalism 'Rule Britannia' and 'Ye Mariners of England'. Perhaps even these two committed anglophiles felt pangs of unease on hearing the verse of 'God Save the King' which crows about the crushing of 'rebellious Scots', and sought to establish their song as the new national anthem? But other arch-anglicisers such as Beattie and, astonishingly, Boswell, reveal their desire to retain some Scots as a badge of identity. James Beattie personifies the Pinkerton syndrome perfectly, for, while publishing lists of Scotticisms to be avoided, he still found time to write the occasional verse in Scots himself. The opening of his poem 'To Mr Alexander Ross', an important North-east poet, reveals exactly the parameters of his interest in the language – the past and the peasantry!

> O Ross, thou wale of hearty cocks,
> Sae crouse and canty with thy jokes!
> Thy hamely auldwarl' muse provokes
> Me for awhile
> To ape our guid plain countra' folks
> In verse and stile.

In his journal for 1763, Boswell refers to a fellow Scot in London, Alexander Wedderburne, who had also attended Sheridan's English classes in Edinburgh two years before. His conclusion will be a surprise to many who presume he wanted no trace of his native land to be obvious in his speech:

and though it was too late in life for a Caledonian to acquire the genuine English cadence, yet so successful were Mr. Wedderburne's instructors, and his own unabating endeavours,

119

that he got rid of the coarse part of his Scotch accent, retaining only as much of the 'native wood-note wild,' as to mark his country; which, if any Scotchman should affect to forget, I should heartily despise him.

On a completely different plane from the genteel anglicisers were a large and kenspeckle group of people who continued using Scots, often to spite those going in the opposite direction. The great Law Lords of the eighteenth and early nineteenth centuries, for example, were famous for their pithy use of Scots. The law was probably the most important and prestigious profession open to the scions of the aristocracy in Scotland after the Union. It is significant that its practitioners continued its tradition of linguistic as well as its institutional independence from England. One anecdote concerning John Clerk of Penicuik, later Lord Eldin, relates how the Scot was arguing a Scottish appeal case before the House of Lords. Pleading his client's use of a burn by prescriptive right, Clerk's rich Scots rang out referring to 'the watter haein rin that wey for mair nor forty year'. The Chancellor, bemused by Clerk's pronunciation, interrupted his oration and enquired in a rather condescending tone: 'Mr. Clerk, do you spell water in Scotland with two "t"s?' Clerk, astonished by the man's rudeness, still managed to give better than he got. 'Na, na, my lord,' he replied, 'we dinna spell watter wi twa "t"s, but we spell mainners wi twa "n"s!'

For some of the judges, their use of Scots was a reaction against the fad for precious gentility particularly prevalent in Edinburgh during the fashion for the cult of sensibility, when grown men would weep in public at sentimental, sententious works such as Henry Mackenzie's *The Man of Feeling*. The sensibility of such as the hanging judge Lord Braxfield was of a quite different order. During the deplorable sedition trials at the end of the eighteenth century, the Englishman Maurice Margarot claimed that he and his fellow radicals stood in a long line of noble men who were reformers as well – Jesus Christ himself being one of them. 'Muckle he made o that,' Braxfield replied. 'He was hangit!' The farewell address of the great Enlightenment figure Lord Kames to the Court of Session when he retired from that august institution in his 80s is memorably concise and terse: 'Fare-ye-aa weel, ye bitches.'

Another belief which emerged towards the close of the eighteenth century and has been repeated ever since is that Scots is dying. In some ways, this has been a benevolent myth, for when something is on the point of extinction, preservation societies spring up to defend it. This was true elsewhere in a Europe dominated by the ideas of the Romantic movement, with its vogue for ancient 'peasant' civilisations and threatened traditional ways of life. Burns and later James Hogg were accepted by the literati as they fitted into the fashionable stereotype of the untutored genius rising out of the *Volk* or people. Walter Scott's novels, with their brilliant use of Scots in dialogue, sold all over the world, and he and Burns enjoyed tremendous popularity in translation, especially in Germany and France. The despised dialect was simultaneously the language of the 'natural genius' which European civilisation craved, possibly as an escape from the Industrial Revolution which was destroying the old order.

History was reinterpreted to suit the latest fashion. Henry Mackenzie, who had criticised Burns' use of Scots a few generations before, could look back from the vantage point of old age, conveniently forget about his previous disdain for Scots and write, 'There was a pure classical Scots spoken by genteel people, which I thought very agreeable; it had nothing of the coarseness of the vulgar patois of the lower orders of the people.' Safely in the past, Scots could now be remembered nostalgically by those *à la récherche du temps perdu*. As we shall see, in the nineteenth century, Scots and Romanticism gae haund in haund, and not only among the peasantry. The literati would now recall old aunts and dowager duchesses who spoke vivid Scots, while in their youth they would have disowned them for shame, or certainly would never have boasted of either the fact of their speaking Scots or their being fond personal acquaintances or relatives. For despite all the pressures against the language, the thrawn auld raucle tongue still came naturally to most Scots most of the time at the turn of the century. The working class spoke nothing else, the upper class was now admitting that they had spoken it until very recently, and the only section which now stood as a bulwark against the 'barbaric dialect' was the expanding middle class, who, again, would have spoken Scots against their better wishes. Their feelings about the language are expressed by their champions, the ministers, who from Unst in the north to the Solway in the south compiled that amazing document of Scottish social history, the *Statistical Account* of the late 1790s. The *Account* is chock-full of references to local speech and almost all are unfavourable. The wishful thinking behind the statement of the minister of Peterhead is typical. It depicts the ignorance and extreme naivety of his class on the subject of language and its nature:

Scots: The Mither Tongue

The language spoken in this parish is the broad Buchan dialect of the English, with many Scotticisms, and stands much in need of reformation, which it is hoped will soon happen, from the frequent resort of polite people to the town in summer.

Some hope!

7

The Last Scotch Age?

Two very different patriots from the Scottish aristocracy, Sir Walter Scott and Lord Cockburn, were torn between love for Scottish culture and the feeling that the future lay with ever-closer ties to England. Scott was very much a Tory who revelled in the feudal past, Cockburn a committed Whig whose drafting of the Scottish Reform Bill in 1832 did much to create a more democratic Scotland. Cockburn was convinced the eighteenth century had been 'the last purely Scotch age. Most of what had gone before had been turbulent and political. All that has come after has been English.' Yet neither really made a committed and sustained stand against the erosion of specifically Scottish institutions, such as the law and education, which was going on in their lifetime.

The deep dilemma of their compromised Scottish patriotism is illustrated by an incident described in J.G. Lockhart's *Life of Scott*. Following a debate about reforming the Court of Session on English lines, Scott leaves the Faculty of Advocates with Francis Jeffrey and some of his reforming friends:

> who complimented him on the rhetorical powers he had been displaying, and would willingly have treated the subject-matter of the discussion playfully. But his feeling had been moved to an extent far beyond their apprehension: he exclaimed, 'No, no – 'tis no laughing matter; little by little, whatever your wishes may be, you will destroy and undermine, until nothing of what makes Scotland Scotland shall remain.' And so saying, he

123

turned round to conceal his agitation – but not until Mr Jeffrey saw tears gushing down his cheek – resting his head until he recovered himself on the wall of the Mound. Seldom, if ever, in his more advanced age, did any feelings obtain such mastery.

Language figured prominently in both men's notions of Scottishness. Their contemporaries recall that both spoke broad Scots, and their writings are full of references to their pride in Scots, a pride tinged with their belief that the language is changing.

The same Scottish patriotic feeling was behind the publication of John Jamieson's *Etymological Dictionary of the Scottish Language* in 1808 and the founding of publishing clubs such as the Maitland and Bannatyne, which sought to encourage interest in Scotland's past history and literature. The Scots language was regarded by the type of Scotsman behind these ventures as a national asset under threat. Lockhart recalls Scott's reverence for his aunt, who had spoken 'her native language pure and undiluted, but without the slightest tincture of that vulgarity which now seems almost unavoidable in the oral use of a dialect so long banished from Courts'. In his journal of 11 August 1844, Lord Cockburn wrote:

> English has made no encroachment on me; yet, though I speak more Scotch than English throughout the day, and read Burns aloud, and recommend him, I cannot get even my own children to do more than pick up a queer word of him here and there. Scotch has ceased to be the vernacular language of the upper classes.

What Cockburn does not go on to say is that the reason his sons have little Scots is that he has sent them to the Edinburgh Academy, the first school in Scotland to model itself on English public schools, where Scots was banned and the English of England fostered. Both Scott and Cockburn were founders of the Academy and presumably agreed with its language policy. Their love of Scotland and Scottish culture was romantic rather than practical and would not be allowed to hinder the progress of youth. In this aspect, loyalty to their class is more crucial than loyalty to their culture. For when the Scottish upper classes frequently stated that Scots was dying and revelled in nostalgia for the generation before, when all classes spoke Scots, they were distancing themselves from the fact that Scots was still spoken in an undiluted form by the vast majority of the population. Scott mentions a classical court Scots which survived until recently in the older generation of aristocrats, a language quite different from the vulgar patois of his own day. The language had not really changed, it was simply that, with the upper classes having deserted it, what was considered fine before was now deemed vulgar. In 1857, when Dean Ramsay wrote his *Reminiscences of Scottish Life and Character*, he was anxious to stress of the older generation of ladies, such as Miss Erskine of Dun, that, while speaking 'downright Scotch. Every tone and every syllable was Scotch . . . Many people now would not understand her. She was always *the lady* notwithstanding her dialect, and to none could the epithet vulgar be less appropriately applied.'

Ramsay's book has many examples of Scots as spoken by these daughters of the aristocracy, some of them very amusing: Lady Perth, for example, said to a Frenchman who was boasting of the superiority of French cuisine to Scottish, 'Weel, weel, some fowk like parritch, and some like puddocks.' Interestingly, 100 years after the Miss Erskine of Dun referred to by Ramsay, and by implication the Scots language of her class, had disappeared from the face of the earth, there appeared the brilliant Scots writing of another Miss Erskine of Dun – Violet Jacob, née Kennedy-Erskine. Her work is perfect testimony to the fact that there are exceptions to every rule in something as ultimately personal as language. Her sensitivity to Scots proves that at least some daughters of the aristocracy were not entirely assimilated into English ways.

While the tiny aristocratic and industrial elite of the nineteenth century attempted to educate their children in England or at English schools in Scotland, the mass of working-class and probably middle-class people continued hearing and speaking only Scots. For it was not until after the Scottish Education Act of 1872 that any systematic attempt was made to teach spoken English in Scottish schools. From then on, inspectors were able to institutionalise and enforce attitudes already entrenched in society. Even then, the changes would take a long time to percolate through the system and actually permanently affect the speech of the pupils. State inspection was initiated in Scotland as early as 1845 but very few were employed in that role. One of the earliest inspectors, J. Kerr, wrote up a volume of reminiscences of his early days in the job. This is how he recorded a teacher in the North-east describing his practice in teaching reading:

> Weel, I begin them wi' wee penny bookies; but it's no lang till
> they can mak' something o' the Testament; and when they can
> do that, I chuse easy bits oot o' baith the Auld and New
> Testaments that teaches us our duty to God and man. I dinna

> say that it's maybe the best lesson book; but it's a book they a'
> hae, and ane they should a' read, whether they hae ither books
> or no . . . and when I see them gettin' tired o' their lessons and
> beginning to tak a look about the house, I bid them tak their
> pamphlets and story books. Ye ken, bairns maun like their
> books.

The same teacher, when reading from the Bible or other works in English, would have adopted a very different register – the English he would have heard all his life from the pulpit. He would have tried to instruct his children to read in the same register. But the language of everyday communication, indeed the language of general instruction, was still Scots.

Until the advance of English literature in Scottish universities in the middle of the nineteenth century, Latin and the humanist tradition had dominated Scottish higher education. Latin was the language of learning, Scots the vernacular. Referring to James Melvin, the rector of Aberdeen Grammar School in the 1850s, the historian John Hill Burton spoke of the man's 'shyness of competing in the language of England with Englishmen'. A report from one of the HMIs in 1852 highlighted the fact that most teachers in Lowland Scotland were influenced by

> the Scotch dialects, to whom many of them have been
> accustomed from infancy, and which are still used by the great
> majority of those, with whom they have daily intercourse, and
> who, till lately, derided the conversational use of English in one
> from among themselves, calling him Anglified or pedantic.

As the century wore on, and the inspectors increased in numbers and influence after the 1872 Education Act, the attempt was made to insist that teachers and pupils should communicate in a form of English. Up till then, literacy in English had been the principal aim. If children could read and write English, the teacher would feel he was doing his job. Now, English as a spoken language was to be actively encouraged and the children's Scots, presumably, actively discouraged. This was the beginning of education appearing as an alien imposition to many Scots, as their home language was systematically devalued and banned from the school. The inspectors' reports are full of references to the two-language split of school and playground. Some realise that Scots should be allowed in the junior classes to encourage the pupils and act as a bridge between their everyday language and the new one they have to master in school. Some enlightened inspectors, such as Mr Muir, complained of the emphasis on artificially promoting English by rote learning. His report of 1876 recalled:

> In one school I asked a junior class the meaning of the word 'passenger' in the lesson before them. I was answered readily, 'One who travels by a public conveyance.' 'Quite right,' said I. 'Now what is a public conveyance? Give me an example. Tell me any public conveyance you have ever heard of?' There was a painful silence.
>
> Far preferable to this are the rough and ready explanations in colloquial, or even vernacular speech I sometimes get. Of a history class I asked one day the meaning of the word 'treason'. 'What do you mean by committing treason against the king?' 'Gie'in him impudence,' was the prompt answer of one boy. 'Well, right so far, but tell me a little more accurately, what it is.' 'Speakin back to him.' It is obviously more pleasant to get such answers than answers like those which define 'invasion' as entering a country with hostile intentions.

Mr Muir's type were increasingly in a tiny minority as the anglicising momentum gathered pace and power. More and more, teachers and inspectors hearing children speak Scots would define it as giein impudence to the teacher. With the schools relying on a satisfactory report from the inspector to obtain their state grant, the uniformity insisted on by the inspector in language had to be obeyed, even by those who disagreed with the policy and regarded it as hindering rather than helping a child's articulacy and linguistic development. Literature in the children's native vernacular as well was regarded as inimical to the advance of English. From Inspector King's report of 1904, the ballads were being taught all over the Border area at the turn of the century; but if they took heed of his report, the national literature as well as the language would be confined to what the bairns could pick up at home:

> Excellent as they are in themselves, and most appropriate to Border schools, the study of them should not absorb much of schooltime, although they might very well be learned at home in the winter evenings. The same criticism applies except to a limited extent to the introduction of poems by Burns and Hogg, and to all other writings however fine, which are not written in good modern English. This must be the staple of

instruction, if we are to give the children the fullest possible equipment in words and thought for modern life. The rest is luxury whatever the perfervid nationalist may say.

Many will recognise the contemporary ring to that statement. Indeed it is so common for Establishment figures in Scotland to be agents of cultural genocide that what in fact is a barbaric negation of civilisation and culture is accepted blandly as the norm. Anyone who stands up for Scottish culture is automatically classed a 'perfervid nationalist'. With the home language and culture given no status whatsoever, and the literary and intellectual tradition increasingly ignored within education, it is little wonder that the Scottish identity is a confused blur at times. Perhaps the most astonishing phenomenon is the survival of the language and the identity it expresses, given the pressure to anglicise that runs through this 'internally colonised' country of ours.

For despite the anglicising momentum which got stronger as the century advanced, the nineteenth century was still a period of great achievement in Scots literature; Sir Walter Scott, James Hogg and John Galt were novelists of major stature in the first half of the century, while Robert Louis Stevenson and George Douglas Brown gave the tradition a lift towards the century's close. In addition, there were many less gifted writers such as Susan Ferrier, Margaret Oliphant and the group of 'Kailyard' novelists, all of whom nevertheless contributed to an understanding of Scottish life in a period of great social change.

In all of these writers, the use of Scots in dialogue gives the raciness and vigour of the speech of real people to their work. Contrasted with the anglified or English dialogue of the 'nobler' characters, the novelists are able to exploit Scotland's wide range of linguistic styles to give texture and character to their novels. There is only enough room here to give two short examples. Here is Neil Blane, the landlord of the howff near Drumclog in Scott's *Old Mortality*, giving advice to his daughter on how to handle the Covenanters and royalist soldiers in the pub:

> Aweel, take notice, Jenny, of that dour, stour-looking carle that sits by the cheek of the ingle, and turns his back on a' men. He looks like ane of the hill-folk, for I saw him start a wee when he saw the red-coats, and I jalouse he wad hae liked to hae ridden by, but his horse (it's a guid gelding) was ower sair travailed; he behoved to stop whether he wad or no. Serve him cannily,

Jenny, and with little din, and dinna bring the sodgers on him by speering ony questions at him; but let na him hae a room to himsell, they wad say we were hiding him . . . Aweel when the malt begins to get aboon the meal, they'll begin to speak about government in kirk and state, and then, Jenny, they are like to quarrel – let them be doing – anger's a drouthy passion, and the mair they dispute, the mair ale they'll drink; but ye were best serve them wi' a pint o' the sma' browst, it will heat them less, and they'll never ken the difference.

The next extract is from R.L. Stevenson's short story 'Thrawn Janet', which is unusual in that it is entirely written in Scots, although, as you can see, it is very much the spoken voice written down, rather than a deliberate attempt to sustain a Scots prose:

About the end o' July there cam' a spell o' weather, the like o't never was in that countryside; it was lown an' het an' heartless; the herds couldnae win up the Black Hill, the bairns were ower weariet to play; an' yet it was gousty too, wi' claps o' het wund that rumm'led in the glens, and bits o' shouers that slockened naething. We aye thocht it but to thun'er on the morn; but the morn cam', an' the morn's morning, and it was aye the same uncanny weather, sair on folks and bestial. Of a' that were the waur nane suffered like Mr Soulis; he could neither sleep nor eat, he tauld his elders; an' when he wasnae writin' at his weary book, he wad be stravaguin' ower a' the countryside like a man possessed, when a'body else was blythe to keep caller ben the house.

Stevenson and the Kailyard writers tended to use Scots when dealing with themes set in the country or the small town. This reflected a further narrowing of the range of Scots literature and perhaps a refusal to cope with a rapidly changing Scotland, where people flocked to overcrowded cities and the industrial experience was more typical than the rural idyll depicted in the Kailyard school. The literature became increasingly escapist, the universal in the works of Scott and Burns descending to the parochial in Ian Maclaren and S.R. Crockett. A couthy Scotland was depicted, and lapped up by Scot and foreigner alike. Readers in countries such as America had been raised on the novels of Walter Scott, so the Scots dialogue of the Kailyard writers presented no problems for them; besides, the popularity of Scots songs kept the language alive there, as well.

The nineteenth century was also a time during which thousands of Scots left home to create the Empire and settle in every corner of the globe. They took their language with them and all over the English-speaking world you will find poetry about Canada, Australia, New Zealand, etc. written in Scots. A good example of the genre is the following verses from Charles Murray's poem 'Scotland Our Mither', written in South Africa at the close of the nineteenth century:

> Scotland our Mither – this from your sons abroad,
> Leavin' tracks on virgin veld that never kent a road,
> Trekkin' on wi' weary feet, an' faces turned fae hame,
> But lovin' aye the auld wife across the seas the same.
>
> Scotland our Mither – we've bairns you've never seen –
> Wee things that turn them northwards when they kneel down
>   at e'en;
> They plead in childish whispers the Lord on high will be
> A comfort to the auld wife – their granny o'er the sea.
>
> Scotland our Mither – since first we left your side,
> From Quilimane to Cape Town we've wandered far an' wide;
> Yet aye from mining camp an' town, from koppie an' karoo,
> Your sons richt kindly, auld wife, send hame their love to you.

In 2002, I made a radio series called *The Scottish Mission* and came across fascinating references to the Scots spoken by men and women who risked their lives taking the faith to far-flung corners of the globe. Indeed, in kirks as far apart as Mulanje in Malawi and Calabar in Nigeria, I felt the visceral emotional response of people to my Scots voice, hearing me talking about revered figures like Laws of Livingstonia, David Livingstone and Mary Slessor. All the accounts of the great Mary Slessor refer to her speaking braid Scots and on the veranda of her house at Akpap in the Okoyong, I recalled an incident at the building of it related by her biographers. For among her many talents, Mary became an expert at laying cement floors to keep the fiendish driver ants at bay. When a fellow Scot spiered who had taught her the art of cement-making, she replied, 'Naebody. I just mix it an stir it like porridge. Then I turn it oot, smooth it wi a stick an say, "Lord, here's the cement. If it be Thy will, please set it!" An he aye does!'

Another fascinating outpost of Scottishness was established in 1802 when the Tsar gave the Edinburgh Missionary Society a grant of 18,000 acres of land at Karass in the foothills of the Caucasus – in the hope that they would bring the wild Islamic tribes over to Christianity. The settlers managed to support themselves through farming the land and they extended the community by buying the freedom of local bairns who had been enslaved. They were then brought up by the Scots. The tribes, however, remained hostile and Cossack soldiers were often sent to protect the colony from attack. The Scots never numbered more than 30, many of whom perished, but this adoption of former slave children and the arrival of a colony of German Christians meant that the mission survived for about 30 years, converting a total of 9 hardy souls.

But there is a Scots footnote to the story of the Circassian colony. For a journalist for *The Times*, D. Mackenzie Wallace, travelled the region in the 1870s, totally ignorant that there had been a Scottish presence there some 40 years before. Here is his account of what he found there after stumbling across a reference to a 'Shotlandskaya Koloniya' (Scottish Colony) on the map:

The first inhabitants whom I encountered were unmistakably German, and they professed to know nothing about the existence of Scotsmen in the locality either at the present or in former times. This was disappointing, and I was about to turn away and drive off, when a young man, who proved to be the schoolmaster, came up, and on hearing what I desired, advised me to consult an old Circassian who lived at the end of the village and was well acquainted with local antiquities. On proceeding to the house indicated, I found a venerable old man, with fine, regular features of the Circassian type, coal-black sparkling eyes, and a long grey beard that would have done honour to a patriarch. To him I explained briefly, in Russian, the object of my visit, and asked whether he knew of any Scotsmen in the district.

'And why do you wish to know?' he replied, in the same language, fixing me with his keen, sparkling eyes.

'Because I am myself a Scotsman, and hoped to find fellow-countrymen here.'

Let the reader imagine my astonishment when, in reply to this, he answered, in genuine broad Scotch, 'Od, man, I'm a Scotsman tae! My name is John Abercrombie. Did ye never hear tell o' John Abercrombie, the famous Edinburgh doctor?'

I was fairly puzzled by this extraordinary declaration. Dr Abercrombie's name was familiar to me as that of a medical practitioner and writer on psychology, but I knew that he was long since dead. When I had recovered a little from my surprise, I ventured to remark to the enigmatical personage before me that, though his tongue was certainly Scotch, his face was as certainly Circassian.

'Weel, weel,' he replied, evidently enjoying my look of mystification, 'you're no far wrang. I'm a Circassian Scotsman!'

John Abercrombie had been one of the weans adopted by the missionaries and brought up as a Christian. Who knows, there may still be remnants of the Circassian dialect of Scots somewhere in the Caucasus!

Back at home, by the end of the nineteenth century, Scots and sentimentality went hand in hand. Even George Douglas Brown, who sought to 'stick the Kailyard like pigs' with his vitriolic counterblast to couthy portrayals of small-town life in *The House with the Green Shutters*, sees Scots only in terms of the fey and the other-worldly. The Ayrshire of his time was full of miners and mill workers who spoke a down-to-earth Scots but Brown talks only of 'the Kyle folk's . . . graphic picturesqueness of speech'. In an essay on John Galt's mastery of dialect, he refers to the author's 'habit of queer metaphorical expression'. Brown hated the Kailyard, but he and Stevenson, who both transcended it, were also influenced by it.

Feyness, Scots, sentimentality and death are all contained in this scene from *Beside the Bonnie Brier Bush*, one of the classic Kailyard novels, by Ian Maclaren. Here, George Howe, dying of tuberculosis, offers up a prayer for his unbelieving schoolmaster Domsie:

> Lord Jesus, remember my dear maister, for he's been a kind freend to me and mony a puir laddie in Drumtochty. Bind up his sair heart and give him licht at eventide, and may the maister and his scholars meet some mornin' where the schule never skails, in the Kingdom o' oor Father.

Stevenson, despite using Scots to good effect, indulges in the death wish affecting people's views of the language and culture. Scots was all around him, yet he chose to write of it in this way in 'The Maker To Posterity':

> Few spak it than, an' noo there's nane
> My puir auld sangs lie a' their lane,
> Their sense, that aince was braw an' plain,
> Tint a' thegither,
> Like runes upon a standin' stane
> Amang the heather.

The literature descended to the nostalgic and the provincial, and it would take a world war and a man called Hugh MacDiarmid to haul it back to a literature of national and international concern. Once again, the revival would be in Scots, still MacDiarmid's and most Scots' mither tongue.

Educational reports apart, another strong indicator of the continuation of Scots as the everyday language of the people lies in the burgeoning popular press of the nineteenth century. William Donaldson of Aberdeen University has made an extensive study of Scottish newspapers in this period and has been struck by the amount of Scots printed, in reported speech and letters to the editor as well as in regular features by local characters. If the literature was getting nostalgic, the people could still write Scots as it was spoken, the language of the people, whose often radical world picture was expressed by it. This is 'Maansie o' Slushigarth' giving an alternative view on the arrival of a new steamer service to Lerwick, which, he says, will only benefit the 'jantry' or gentry:

> Diel hae me if da warld be na just gaen gyte! Da Lurick fock shuttin' wi' cannon, an' lightin' a der collies an' caandles an' dennerin' an' drinkin' an' rejoisin' aboot a fule ting o' a stemmer ship itt da Queen is sent ta carry da jantry's letters every ook ta da sooth! Fule moniments itt dey irr! What gude'ill dis stemmer shipp doe ta wiz puir fock? Will shoe mak meal ony shaper? Truggs! am fear'd shoe'll doe nae gude ava' 'cept helpin' wirr jantry ta gaing awa' ta da sooth wi' less spewin'. Na, na, I aye saiditt nae gude wid come o' new faingled tins an it'ill shune come to pass itt dis stemmer i'll mak kye an' sheep an' butter an' eggs an' a' kind o' kyuntry proddick muckle dearer. Forby da scores an' dizzens an' maybe hunders o' idle jaantin' bodies it'll be comin' frae da south just lek da locusts itt cam frae Egypt davoorin da substance o' da laand! An de'll be tellin' wiz itt kens muckle betterit wi' shu'd hae rodds an' packets an' ferryboats an' inns, and muckle mair nonsense, just ta help dem ta rin o'er an' devoor wiz in a shorter time. Deil cut dem aff!

In the heart of the industrial central belt, an edition of the *Hamilton Advertiser* in 1889 contains the following description of the town. There is an awareness of the change in that environment too, but no nostalgia:

There were thae gawsie, gash guidwives, wi' dirty faces and toozie heids, staunin' clatterin' wi' ane anither at every close mooth an' corner, while their weans were tumlin' ower ilk ither in the glaur, and their hooses at hame lyin' in confusion, as if some earthquake frae Sooth America had been gien' them a ca' in the byegaun'. Of coorse it's heartsome tae see sic an increase o' the population, and it's guid for the bakin business – but for my pairt, I wud prefer the bonnie green fields as they used tae be instead o' thae evidences o' the spread o' ceevilization.

The great social changes which took place in Scotland throughout the nineteenth century undoubtedly had an effect on the way people in different areas and different classes spoke. The muckle rich fermtouns of the eastern and north-eastern Lowlands had to a great extent replaced the small farmer with his croft. With their bothies and chalmers thrang with scores of ploughmen, the environment acted as a forcing-house for traditional song and strengthened the status of the Scots of the area.

When Gavin Greig and J.B. Duncan undertook the monumental task of collecting the folk tradition in the Buchan area at the turn of the century, even they were probably astonished at the wealth of the material still sung – over 3,000 songs. The Aberdeenshire songs are marvellously evocative of time and place. My own favourite is 'Mormond Braes', a song of lost love:

Oh there's juist as guid fish in the sea,
That's ever yet been taken,
I'll cast my net an try again,
For I'm only aince forsaken.

So fare-ye-weel ye Mormond Braes,
Where aft times I've been cheery,
Fare-ye-weel ye Mormond Braes,
For it's there I lost my dearie.

Oh there's mony's the horse
Has snappert an fa'n
An risen again fu early,
There's mony's the lass has tint her lad
An gotten anither richt fairly.

If the country areas remained strong in their Scots, it was very much because the way of life was maintained despite the change in the size of the farms – it was very much the same people who inhabited the crofts and the fermtouns. In the industrial cities, social change resulted in a huge influx of thousands of outsiders into areas which had traditionally been Scots speaking. Gaelic- or English-speaking Highlanders and Irish, and English- and Scots-speaking people from Ulster, especially Donegal, were the two main groups of incomers, but the melting pot was stirred by the addition of Italian-, Yiddish- and Lithuanian-speaking immigrants.

What emerged from all this was a lingua franca which had lost some of the distinctive features of the local Scots dialect in order to accommodate the multifarious group of people who now communicated in it. It still remained Scots, for the immigrants adapted the language they came into contact with and, among the workers, that was not Oxford English. Many words we think of as belonging to the Scots of Glasgow are derived from the native tongues of the main immigrant communities: the derogatory term for a Glaswegian, keelie, is from the Scots Gaelic *gille*, a boy, while the Irish word *buachaill*, a lad or herdsman, is the likely source of that descriptive word for a wee roond Glaswegian, a bachle. The erosion of distinctively Scots vocabulary was also set in train but the grammar and structure of the original dialect remained surprisingly intact. This was a double blow for the status of the city dialects: Victorian society dismissed Scots, but antiquarianism allowed that some of the words were expressive. However, the grammatical features of Scots which differed from English, e.g. *we wes* for we were, were condemned outright as slovenly English.

Without the saving grace of the old words but with the so-called 'slovenly English' intact, the town dialects were liked not a bit by the Establishment. As early as 1840, 'a Babylonish dialect, both in idioms and in accent' has resulted in Lochwinnoch, Renfrewshire, and the blame, according to local commentator Andrew Crawfurd, lies with the influx of a 'clanjamfray of Irish [and] Highlanders'. Crawfurd stresses that 'this corruption is alone in the village . . . The country part of the parish exhibits a pattern approaching to the Doric and chaste dialect.' One of the shibboleths which most enraged the Establishment was the glottal stop, which seems to have originated in the Glasgow area and by association spread out over first the towns of the western Lowlands and, in the twentieth century, to most of the towns of Scotland. Whether it came with the Irish immigrants or was a result of the meeting of the immigrants' language and that of the native population is difficult to ascertain. Whatever it was, pronunciations like 'wa'er', 'bu'er' and 'Cel'ic' still cause middle-class matrons to throw up their hands in horror. The reports of the school inspectors are full of negative responses to the town dialects. Typical is this one from Lanarkshire in 1895, which pinpoints the abhorrent details: 'the mutilation of final syllables, and especially the conversion of final d into t; the slurring over of intermediate consonants, and the omission of sibilants'.

Safe in the knowledge that there was no fear of the traditional dialect coming back to the towns, the inspectors and other members of the Establishment began contrasting the corruption of the city with the chasteness of the country dialects; they now felt they could attack from a purist English and Scots attitude. The falseness of their posture is revealed in the fact that in areas where the so-called corruption of the city had not penetrated, the local inspectors were just as hostile to country dialects as their colleagues were to the speech of the cities. An inspector for the northern district – about as far from the glottal stop as you could get – writing in 1895 regretted that teachers could not contribute more to the 'scotching and eradicating of the horrible accent and vernacular in some parts of the North . . . a number of excrescent branches might usefully be lopped off. The tree would be none the worse for the operation.'

The dialect which has long been regarded as the most unaffected, 'chaste' and conservative Scots is that of Aberdeenshire. One of the North-east ministers who contributed to the second *Statistical Account* of 1845 had this to say about the rural dialect spoken there: 'The most common dialect is a mixture of Scotch and English, the Scotch used being of the somewhat vicious kind, known, I believe, by the name of the Aberdeenshire.' In other words, no matter what the local form of Scots is, you can be sure the local Establishment will be hostile to it.

Yet within that Establishment itself there were undoubtedly many different styles of speech, especially in the first half of the century, when many were still in a transitional stage, trying to lose their Scots but not quite getting the hang of the English. The judge Lord Braxfield said of Francis Jeffrey of the *Edinburgh Review*, 'The laddie has clean tint his Scotch, and found nae English.' The anglified Scot obviously found little initial favour among his countrymen, as this snippet from the *Scots Magazine* of 1821 testifies: 'The haill kintra gat begunkit wi an Yinglifiet jargon.' Jeffrey's hybrid speech appears to hae gart baith friend an fae tak a grue at it. His foe, the Tory Lockhart, described his speech as: 'A mixture of provincial English, with undignified Scotch, altogether snappish and offensive, and which would be quite sufficient to render the elocution of a more ordinary man utterly disgusting.'

Jeffrey may well have spoken what later became known as 'Morningsaide' or 'Kelvinsaide', that peculiarly Scottish expression of over-refinement in speech. It is difficult to give an idea of this speech to non-Scots without using phonetic symbols; its most distinctive feature, though, is the attempt to 'raise' broad Scottish vowels such as the 'a' in 'back' to something closer to 'e', giving the sound 'beck'. This phenomenon gave rise to the old joke that sex are what Morningside ladies put their rubbish in! Some linguists believe these accents to be throwbacks to the eighteenth-century period of Scots trying to learn London English; thus Kelvinside may preserve some fossilised aspects of London speech of the 1760s. Whatever it was, even Cockburn, Jeffrey's political ally and friend, lamented the strange, affected hybrid that escaped his lips:

> It would have been better if he had merely got some of the grosser matter rubbed off his vernacular tongue, and left himself, unencumbered both by it and by unattainable English, to his own respectable Scotch, refined by literature and good society, and used plainly and naturally, without shame, and without affected exaggeration.

The feeling of revulsion this Anglo-Scottish hybrid produced among some sections of Scottish society – those who did not in fact speak it – was still strong in 1903. In his monumental work *A Literary History of Scotland*, J.H. Millar followed the above quotation from Cockburn with the words '*dis aliter visum*' (the gods thought otherwise) and the regretful conclusion that:

> Jeffrey has proved to be the ancestor of a numerous progeny, who, in the pulpit, in the law courts, or in private life, talk a mincing and quasi-genteel lingo of their own (the sort of English known in some quarters as 'Princes Street' or 'Kelvinside'), the subtly hideous nuances of which not the most elaborate system of phonetic spelling yet devised would suffice to reproduce.

Kelvinside eventually became the butt of so many jokes that it survives only in patches, among the very old. When Millar was writing, presumably something approaching the Scottish Standard English we recognise today had evolved and become established alongside Oxford

English as an acceptable medium for 'educated' Scots to communicate in. Even it would have its detractors, for it appears that every form of Scottish speech raises the hackles of one section of society or another, be it urban versus rural, Kelvinside versus received pronunciation, or glottal stop versus affectation; it is all part of a feeling of insecurity about the way we speak. If Lowland Scotland had once been a united linguistic commmunity, it was now one rent with prejudice based on class, locality and nationality. Welcome to the modern world.

8

Renaissance and Erosion

The status of Scots at the beginning of the twentieth century derived very much from trends established in the eighteenth century and hardened in the nineteenth century. The language came to be regarded as a working-class patois, despised by the increasingly anglicised upper and middle classes. To them, Scots was fine as a medium for couthy novels, newspaper cartoons and music-hall comedians. When radio, cinema newsreel and television eventually came along, the Scotch stereotypes established in the music halls by Harry Lauder and his like were adopted by a media dominated by Englishmen who cared little about reflecting the real Scotland and less about the cultural sensitivities of her people. Besides, the Scots swallowed the myths and stereotypes themselves.

The upper classes and sections of the upper middle class spoke now in a manner scarcely distinguishable from the English of the Home Counties. Scottish RP speakers may still pronounce the 'wh' in 'whales' to differentiate it from 'Wales' and they may miss out the intrusive 'r' in the Home Counties' 'lawr and order', but to the majority of Scots, they are speaking with an English accent. Edinburgh, with certain of its fee-paying schools specialising in teaching RP, produces more such speakers than any other town. In all the other towns and cities, Standard Scottish English rather than RP tends to be the favoured medium. Coming from the West of Scotland, where an English accent meant that the person was English, it came as a surprise to me at Edinburgh University that some Scots, and some patriotic Scots at that, could sound like Englishmen.

Most culturally anglicised Scots, however, accept and rejoice in their anglicisation, for British society has conferred status on English culture, not Scottish. English is therefore perceived as the language for personal, social and commercial advancement. The resultant state of mind among many Scots is well put by William McIlvanney in his novel *Strange Loyalties:* 'Scottishness may have been a life but Britishness can be a career.' Those who do speak Scots, and even many who speak Scottish English, nevertheless resent the prestige of RP and regard their countrymen who speak it, often erroneously, as cultural quislings. Strong feelings are raised on both sides of the linguistic divide in Scotland. Both the upper-class and bourgeois contempt for Scots and the working-class dislike of 'posh English' are reprehensible, yet they are symptomatic of a country cut off from knowledge of its own cultural and linguistic history. Expressions of both sides' attitudes are easy to find, the former in official education reports, the latter in literature. Nineteenth-century hostility to the vernacular on the part of the education authorities continued and in 1946 a report on primary education described Scots in the following terms:

> the homely, natural and pithy everyday speech of country and small-town folk in Aberdeenshire and adjacent counties, and to a lesser extent in other parts outside the great industrial areas. But it is not the language of 'educated' people anywhere, and could not be described as a suitable medium of education or culture. Elsewhere because of extraneous influences it has sadly degenerated, and become a worthless jumble of slipshod ungrammatical and vulgar forms, still further debased by the intrusion of the less desirable Americanisms of Hollywood . . . Against such unlovely forms of speech masquerading as Scots we recommend that the schools should wage a planned and unrelenting campaign.

The result of this war of attrition, however, has not been an improvement in English, just a confused resentment among those whose culture was the butt of this educational joke. Gordon Williams portrays well the linguistic confusion which the Scottish Education Department has wrought in this extract from his novel *From Scenes Like These*, in which a young Ayrshire boy contemplates the speech of his environment:

> It was very strange how the old man changed accents. Sometimes he spoke to you in broad Scots, sometimes in what the school

teachers called proper English. They were very hot on proper English at the school. Once he'd got a right showing up in the class for accidentally pronouncing butter 'bu'er'. Miss Fitzgerald had gone on (him having to stand in front of the class) about the glottal stop being dead common and very low-class, something that would damn you if you wanted a decent job. A decent job – like a bank! His mother spoke proper English, but then she was hellish keen on proving they were respectable. His father spoke common Kilcaddie, which he knew his mother didn't like. When the Craigs spoke broad it wasn't quite the same as common Kilcaddie – some of their expressions sounded as though they came straight out of Rabbie Burns! Telfer had a Kilcaddie accent, but he pronounced all his words properly, no doubt from seeing too many pictures. McCann spoke very coarse and broad, but there was something false about him, as though he put it on deliberately.

He still spoke the school's idea of proper English, he knew that all right because every time he opened his mouth he could hear himself sounding like a real wee pan-loaf toff. (Maybe that was what annoyed McCann.) Why did auld Craig and Willie change about? Did it depend on what they thought about you? He remembered Nicol the English teacher saying that broad Scots was pronounced very much like Anglo-Saxon or middle English or some such expression. If that was so why did they try and belt you into speaking like some English nancy boy on the wireless? He'd asked Nicol that and Nicol said right or wrong didn't come into it, proper English was what the school had to teach you if you weren't going to be a guttersnipe all your life. Was it being a guttersnipe to talk your own country's language? It would be a lot healthier if folk spoke one way. Sometimes you hear them say 'eight' and sometimes 'eicht', sometimes 'farm' and sometimes 'ferm'. Sometimes 'ye' and sometimes 'youse' and sometimes 'yese' and sometimes 'you'. Sometimes 'half' and sometimes 'hauf'. Was it your faither or your father? Your mither or your mother? He felt he was speaking to his audience again. You see, if school was any use it would teach you things like that, not jump on you for not talking like a Kelvinside nancy boy. Why teach kids that Burns was the great national poet and then tell you his old Scots words were dead common? What sounds better – 'gie your face a dicht wi' a clootie' or 'give your face a wipe with a cloth'? One was Scottish and natural and the other was a lot of toffee-nosed English shite.

If the conclusion is extreme, so are the circumstances which gave rise to the resentment. William McIlvanney explores the theme of identity conflict in his fine novel *Docherty*. In this extract, the boy Conn is brought before the headmaster to be punished for fighting in the playground. The different linguistic identities of master and pupil are central to what ensues:

'What's wrong with your face, Docherty?'
'Skint ma nose, sur.'
'How?'
'Ah fell an' bumped ma heid in the sheuch, sur.'
'I beg your pardon?'
'Ah fell an' bumped ma heid in the sheuch, sur.'
'I beg your pardon?'
In the pause Conn understands the nature of the choice, tremblingly, compulsively, makes it.
'Ah fell an' bumped ma heid in the sheuch, sur.'
The blow is instant. His ear seems to enlarge, is muffed in numbness. But it's only the dread of tears that hurts. Mr Pirrie distends on a lozenge of light that mustn't be allowed to break. It doesn't. Conn hasn't cried.
'That, Docherty, is impertinence. You will translate, please, into the mother-tongue.'
The blow is a mistake, Conn knows. If he tells his father, he will come up to the school. 'Ye'll take whit ye get wi' the strap an' like it. But if onybody takes their hauns tae ye, ye'll let me ken.' He thinks about it. But the problem is his own. It frightens him more to imagine his father coming up.
'I'm waiting, Docherty. What happened?'
'I bumped my head, sir.'
'Where? Where did you bump it, Docherty?'
'In the gutter, sir.'
'Not an inappropriate setting for you, if I may say so.'

Having received six strokes of the tawse, Conn goes back to his desk and works out what the incident means to him:

Relating to it, realignments were already taking place in him . . .
He knew his father's contempt for the way they had to live and his reverence for education. But against that went Conn's sense of the irrelevance of school, its denial of the worth of his father

142

and his family, the falsity of its judgements, the rarified atmosphere of its terminology.

By way of exorcising the pain, Conn compiles a list of words in the way he had seen in the dictionary:

sheuch	gutter
speugh	sparrow
lum	chimny
brace	mantalpiece
bine	tub
coom	soot
coomie	foolish man (Mr Pirrie)
gomeril	another foolish man
spicket	tap
glaur	muck what is in a puddle after the puddle goes away
wabbit	tired
whaup	curloo
tumshie	turnip
breeks	troosers
chanty	po
preuch	anything you can get
I was taigled longer	I was kept back for a more longer
nor I ettled	time than I desired

One side of the paper was filled. He didn't start on the other side because he now wanted to write things that he couldn't find any English for. When something sad had happened and his mother was meaning that there wasn't anything you could do about it, she would say 'ye maun dree yer weird.' When she was busy, she had said she was 'saund-papered to a whuppet.' 'Pit a raker oan the fire.' 'Hand-cuffed to Mackindoe's ghost.' 'A face to follow a flittin'.' If his father had to give him a row but wasn't really angry, he said 'Ah'll skelp yer bum wi' a tea-leaf tae your nose bluids.'

Conn despaired of English. Suddenly, with the desperation of a man trying to amputate his own infected arm, he savagely scored out all the English equivalents.

On his way out of the school, he folded his grubby piece of paper very carefully and put it in his pocket. It was religiously preserved for weeks. By the time he lost it, he didn't need it.

McIlvanney is an acute and articulate observer of Scottish society. The theme of working-class individuals and communities having to define their worth against hostile authorities and forces which have no regard for their culture is central to all his work. As a writer stemming from the people and expressing their culture, he is very much part of a Scottish tradition in literature which is quite different from that of England. There, literature has tended to be the preserve of an elite. The English Romantic poets were interested in the life of the common man, but they saw his culture as outsiders; Burns was from the people and wrote about them in their own tongue. In *The Mother Tongue*, McIlvanney summed up the difference in the two traditions, recalling his study of English literature at Glasgow University:

> When I went to the fabled fortress of learning, [I] realised, in my terms anyway, that what I was offered as literature excluded the majority of the people that I come from . . . it was like a body of evidence in which 98% of the witnesses are never called. And I don't think that's true of Scottish literature, there is a more radical demand throughout Scottish literature to allow the voice of those who may not write themselves to be validly heard.

Sir David Lyndsay in the sixteenth century, Robert Burns in the eighteenth century and numerous novelists, playwrights and poets of the twentieth and twenty-first centuries testify to the radical tradition in Scottish, and specifically Scots, literature which shows no sign of abating.

The man who created the climate for modern literature in Scots was a radical Communist and nationalist called Christopher Murray Grieve, alias Hugh MacDiarmid. Grieve was a native Scots speaker from Langholm near the English border; single-handedly, he dragged Scots out of the couthy Kailyard to re-create it as a medium of poetry of international calibre. His method of doing this was novel: augmenting his native Scots with words from dictionaries, seeking words from different dialects and past ages of the language, and inventing words of his own when all else failed. What he in fact did was little different from Dante's achievement in creating a national tongue out of the welter of Italian dialects at the beginning of the fourteenth century; MacDiarmid's achievement may be recognised in the same terms some day, but for the moment an anglicised Scotland is still getting over the shock of the despised patois being taken seriously internationally once again.

While his long philosophical and political poems such as *The Drunk Man Looks at the Thistle* and *Second Hymn to Lenin* succeeded in raising and expanding the language's capabilities and finally sweeping away the couthiness of the Kailyard, many feel his greatest poetic achievement lies in his early lyric poetry. 'The Watergaw' has the sensual feel and feyness of the great ballads.

> Ae weet forenicht i' the yow-trummle
> I saw yon antrin thing,
> A watergaw wi' its chitterin' licht
> Ayont the on-ding;
> An' I thocht o' the last wild look ye gied
> Afore ye deed!
>
> There was nae reek i' the laverock's hoose
> That nicht – an' nane i' mine;
> But I hae thocht o' that foolish licht
> Ever sin' syne;
> An' I think that mebbe at last I ken
> What your look meant then.

> (*watergaw* indistinct rainbow; *forenicht* early evening; *yow-trummle* cold weather after sheep-shearing [English – ewe tremble]; *antrin* rare; *chitterin'* shivering; *on-ding* onset [of rain]; *reek* smoke; *laverock* lark; *sin' syne* since then)

MacDiarmid's remarkable synthesis of Scots worked brilliantly and he was followed by a strong group of poets including Douglas Young, Sidney Goodsir Smith, Robert Garioch, William Soutar and Alexander Scott, all part of a renaissance which is still influencing writers today. The synthesis – called variously Lallans (an alternative name for Scots used by Burns), plastic Scots and synthetic Scots – provoked tremendous debate and 21 years after the publication of MacDiarmid's first collection *Sangschaw*, the *Glasgow Herald*'s letter pages were still thrang with arguments for and against the Scots of the new makars. The *Herald* tended to patronise or ridicule the movement and fuelled the controversy with comments in its editorial diary such as this one for 9 November 1946:

> It is, of course, much easier to write plastic Scots than to read it, and the art can easily be mastered with the help of a few simple rules . . . Manner is your concern rather than matter.

Your subjects need be few – Hugh MacDiarmid, Glasgow, the
Highlands, the English, love, drink, and Hugh MacDiarmid.
You should write at least one ode to Hugh MacDiarmid: this is
de rigueur. After all, he invented synthetic Scots, from which
the plastic form is derived. It is not necessary for what you write
to have no meaning, but it is vital to conceal your meaning, if
any, as much as possible.

The main objection to Lallans was that it used words which were not
in current usage and therefore the literature produced in it was
artificial. The fact that every writer in the history of literature in any
language has used words not in current usage never entered the heads
of the detractors – bourgeois Scots, in the main, who knew as much
about current usage in Scots as in Japanese. Sidney Goodsir Smith
gave an apt reply to this criticism in his 'Epistle to John Guthrie (who
had blamed the poet for writing in Scots "which no one speaks")':

> We've come intil a gey queer time
> Whan scrievin Scots is near a crime,
> 'There's no one speaks like that,' they fleer,
> – But wha the deil spoke like King Lear?

(*scrievin* writing; *fleer* sneer)

One or two people did write in Scots because it was fashionable for a
while to do so, and, not being native speakers, there is a certain stilted
labouring in their attempts to convince. For the majority of the poets
and playwrights, however, they were extending a language intimately
familiar to them. In a letter to the *Glasgow Herald* dated 13 November
1946, MacDiarmid stresses this very point. Having dismissed the
quality of Scottish poetry in English, he goes on:

> What, then, is the Scottish poet to do but try to extend and
> strengthen his own native language in precisely the way that all
> languages, including English, have extended and strengthened
> themselves – and that is all synthetic Scots has attempted! It is
> not the case that modern Scots poets have invented new words
> to eke out their vocabulary. Nor is it the case that they have had
> undue recourse to Jamieson's Dictionary. Most of them write
> on the solid basis of the speech they first spoke as children and
> were familiar with in their homes – the speech, incidentally, of
> the vast majority of the Scottish working class, still, and,

146

judging by the scant headway made against it by English during
the past two centuries, likely to remain so!

The prejudice against non-current Scots is, I believe, part of the
Establishment's death wish, and it arises in the spoken as well as the
written tongue. No one blinks an eye if you use English, French or
German words you learn from books or dictionaries, yet come out
with a Scots word ye didnae learn at yer mither's knee and you are
accused of using language 'artificially'. Literature has always gone
beyond the everyday language, the nature of poetry especially being to
extend our linguistic experience. Nevertheless, I have often been
surprised to hear words which I presumed MacDiarmid had got out of
the dictionary being used naturally by Scots speakers in different parts
of the country. This supports his contention that most of the
vocabulary he uses was actually current at the time he wrote. Coming
from a fairly strong Scots-speaking area, I presumed that if a word was
not used in my own dialect, it would also have become obsolete
elsewhere. In 'The Watergaw', for example, *forenicht*, *chitterin*, *reek*
and *laverock* were all familiar to me but *yow-trummle*, *antrin* and
watergaw were not. Since I first read the poem, though, I have
discovered that *antrin* is an everyday word in the North-east and *yow-
trummle* is known in the Borders, and when making *The Mother
Tongue*, a girl from my own Irvine Valley related that *watergaw* was a
word her grandmother used. Growing up in the early part of the
twentieth century, before the erosion of Scots vocabulary initiated by
radio and television set in, MacDiarmid must have heard many of
these words, which appear exotic to us, every day in life.

Scots has been fragmented as a language and, with the dearth of
broadcasting in the remaining dialects, very few people have first-
hand experience of the spectrum of Scots which is spoken across the
country. Many subscribe to the Establishment's desire to destroy the
language, unaware that a few miles down the road it is being spoken
in all its vigour and power. For despite the erosion, a remarkable
amount of Scots survives, and in the unlikeliest places. Once, talking
about Scots to a class of teenagers in Pilton, a big housing scheme in
Edinburgh, I was astonished that a number of the kids knew and used
the word *partan* for a crab. It had long disappeared from my own
dialect. The reason for its survival in Pilton was the fact that the kids
frequent Cramond Shore, which is within walking distance, and they
heard the word used by fishermen there. The word *wappenshaw*, a
muster of arms, is another word from medieval Scots, mentioned by
Scott in *Old Mortality*, which one presumes died long ago. Yet it is a

word in common use among the bowling fraternity in the west of Scotland, describing a competition day when one club plays against another.

Having the good fortune to travel around Scotland in my work and, unlike most, deliberately speaking Scots to the people I meet if I jalouse they are Scots speakers, I can testify to the smeddum that's still in the auld leid. I recall Evelyn Crockett of Lossiemouth coming out with classical Scots sentences such as the following in her description of life at the herring gutting: 'We uised tae hain a puckle stanes tae fleg awa the gows' – 'We used to keep a few stones to frighten away the seagulls'. One of the myths cited against Scots is that it cannot cope with modern life. Given the importance of safe sex in the 1990s, I was delighted to hear of a dialogue that took place in an Ayrshire park on a summer's morning betweeen a friend and the chap responsible for reddin the place up. 'That's a sair darg ye've got there, Andra.' 'Is it no juist, Rab. Ah cannae move for aw thir f'n cahootchie padlocks!' In the east of Scotland a 'puggie machine' refers to a one-armed bandit or, by extension, to any automatic dispenser. It was a trendy Glasgow pal, however, who revealed a new extension of the expression's meaning when he went to a bank cashline and complained when he couldnae find his puggie caird! And it isnae just old folk who have a command of Scots; this was how a 16 year old from Ayrshire described the domestic chores her mother asked her to do following the family's tea:

> Well, she'd tell ye tae gae ben the kitchen, an it wad be in a mogre wi aw the creishie cups an dishes. An she'd say, 'Turn on the spicket an synd oot thae dishes, then dicht roon the sink.' I wad breenge aboot tryin tae pit everythin bye . . . an the dog wad be cooerin in the corner, feart in case I skelpit it for gettin in the wye!

Yet so conditioned are we to thinking of Scots as a dying language that, even after hearing concentrated articulate Scots like these examples above, many would still say, 'Oh, that's guid Scots but, ye ken, it's deein oot!' The overriding propaganda against Scots has resulted even in Scots speakers believing and taking part in the death wish the authorities have had for the language for over 200 years. The working class continue speaking Scots and if there is a slow erosion of the distinctive Scots vocabulary with every generation, it still remains very much the spoken language of the people. Because of that fact, the other social classes are intimately familiar with it. How else could this 'dead or dying' language be such a successful medium for the theatre, with the brilliant plays of the '80s and '90s proving that the resurgence of the '70s, led by such as Hector MacMillan and Donald Campbell, was no flash in the pan? The thirst Scottish audiences have for their own culture was shown by my play *They Fairly Mak Ye Work* breaking box-office records at Dundee Rep during two runs there in 1986. Scots may be marginalised in many sections of our society but in the theatre it has achieved parity with English. In terms of creativity, I would put Scots drama ahead of the plays written by Scots in English. In recent years, we have seen several new major writers emerge – Gregory Burke, Peter Arnott and Janet Paisley have all impressed, writing in varieties of modern Scots and tackling difficult contemporary subjects.

We have also seen how Scots translation has continually thrived as a theatrical medium. In the introduction to their book *Serving Twa Maisters: Five Classic Plays in Scots Translation*, John Corbett and Bill Findlay list 30 plays translated into Scots from a classical repertoire that ranges from Aristophanes to Strindberg. Even more revealing is the fact that since the 1980s more than 20 contemporary plays have been translated into Scots and put on the stage. This was not an academic exercise in other words – the plays reached out to contemporary audiences, who thronged in huge numbers to see the best of them. Among these were the translations by Bill Findlay and Martin Bowman of plays such as *The Guid Sisters*, from the Quebec playwright Michel Tremblay's *Les Belle-Soeurs*, while classics included Liz Lochhead's rendition into Scots of Molière's *Tartuffe* and Edwin Morgan's version of *Cyrano de Bergerac*. Both were particularly exciting because they succeed in fusing the contemporary urban idiom with the more classical Scots established by Robert Kemp and Robert McLellan earlier in the twentieth century. It is a fusion that works, proving that modern Glaswegian, for example, can blend with more traditional Scots – the resultant mell extending and enhancing both idioms.

Morgan and Lochhead are both firmly established writers in English, although their poetry has always drawn on real voices and is strongest when performed. Morgan has also written extensively on Scottish culture. This extract from an essay on the Scots/English linguistic duality called 'Registering the Reality of Scotland', published in 1974, comes across almost as a declaration of intent for what he achieves in *Cyrano*:

> I would rather see the mixed state that exists being explored
> and exploited, more truthfully and spontaneously and hence

more seriously than at present, by writers, and by playwrights and novelists in particular. It may be that we have a blessing in disguise. But if we want to uncover it we shall have to use our ears more and our grammar book less.

The stress is on the voice, but the play proves that contemporary Scottish voices speak guid braid Scots as well as streetwise urban demotic, something exploited majestically in Gerry Mulgrew's memorable production of *Cyrano de Bergerac* for Communicado. More recently, at Dundee Rep, Peter Arnott has shown how fluidly German works by Brecht and Dürrenmatt translate into a Scots idiom. What is striking, for me, is that all of this ongoing explosion of theatrical creativity in Scots is going on against a background of people still saying that Scots does not exist, or if it does exist, it is in its death throes! What is going on? Scots plays are performed to packed, appreciative audiences whose response speaks volumes on the myth of incomprehensibility and the myth of the language being obsolete and dying. The people speak it, writers write it, the audience understands it. It's no deid yet! It's time the claith wes pit ower that particular claikin parrot!

Scots literature must retain its intimacy with the people's experience, and its raw, radical political edge if it is to be relevant to future generations. That edge is to be found in the work of certain Glasgow writers such as James Kelman and Tom Leonard. Influenced by the American poet William Carlos Williams, who sought to write in American speech rhythms, Leonard's poetry seeks to express a variety of Glasgow voices. Again, it registers more powerfully when heard rather than read. 'Unrelated Incidents – 3' is an ironic satire on language and power:

> this is thi
> six a clock
> news thi
> man said n
> thi reason
> a talk wia
> BBC accent
> iz coz yi
> widny wahnt
> mi ti talk
> aboot thi
> trooth wia

voice lik
wanna yoo
scruff. If

a toktaboot
thi trooth
lik wanna yoo
scruff yi
widny thingk
it waz troo.
jist wanna yoo
scruff tokn.
thirza right
way ti spell
ana right way
ti tokit. this
is me tokn yir
right way a
spellin. this
is ma trooth.
yooz doant no
thi trooth
yirsellz cawz
yi canny talk
right. this is
the six a clock
nyooz. belt up.

Purists of both the Scots and English languages have criticised the Glasgow dialect and Leonard's reproduction of it – suggesting he should join one side or the other. With his stress on the voice – the actuality of what people say – language prescription of any kind is anathema to him and is given short shrift. In one poem, a man who accepts that 'thi langwij a thi guhtr' is OK for comic poetry but considers it useless for expressing serious concerns symbolically falls down a lift shaft!

The range of registers available to Scottish writers can be seen in the impressive anthology *The New Makars*, edited by Tom Hubbard in 1991. There, 65 living poets from every airt and pairt of the country celebrate the raucle tongue in all its forms. To take just one area, Dundee and Angus, you find poets like Ellie McDonald and Raymond Vettese writing in a more classical literary Scots, while alongside them you have W.N. Herbert and Mathew Fitt concentrating on the urban voice of Dundee. They are, however, all local, national, international and universal in their concerns. This is from 'Stairway Til Heaven', Fitt's adaptation of the Led Zeppelin song:

an ther's a lassie wha dremes
mang the hell o the schemes
wi her bairns whyle her man is oot bevvin
thinks aye oan yon time
in a laan lang sinsyne
whan she stertit the lang road tae heaven

an sei yon tink oan the street
wi nae schuin oan his feet
he's pischt oot his brens an he's stervin
yon carlsberg hero waants mair
o his gudd maister's cair
no juist sweeties an pennies fae heaven

an it maks ye scunner
it's nae bliddy wunner
kin ye heir the thunner

sum bastart's stole awa the sun nou
pit a mukkil hole intil the sky
yon reid reid rose is catchit fyre nou
the rokks aa melled, the seas gane dry

oor heidyins shoot their weans oan sicht nou
smoor truth an televyse thair lies
steil soajirs merch atour the yirth nou
the hert o aahing tynes an dies

The Scots poetic tradition continues with vigour in the work of James Robertson, Liz Niven, Janet Paisley, William Hershaw, Robert Alan Jamieson, Sheena Blackhall, Ron Butlin, Brent Hodgson, Andrew McNeill and many, many others. Poets who use Scots and English to brilliant effect include Robert Crawford and Kathleen Jamie. They, along with Douglas Dunn, have also helped to establish St Andrews University as a focal point for the study of Scottish literature.

Different in style to the poets but sharing their social concerns, the great Scots folk-song revival which took place in the 1950s still affects popular culture today. Writers like Michael Marra have created contemporary classics like 'Hermless', while his collaboration with a Dundonian enigma called St Andrew resulted in a totally original album called *The Word on the Pavey*. Hamish Henderson is one of the major figures of the revival, both for his discovery and recording of great tradition-bearers such as Jeannie Robertson and for the tremendous emotive impact of his Scots lyrics in political songs such as 'The Freedom Come All Ye', which became the anthem of those wanting democracy for their country in the 1990s:

> O come aa ye at hame wi freedom,
> Never heed whit the hoodies croak for doom;
> In yer hoose aa the bairns o Adam
> Will find breid, barley bree an painted room.
> When Maclean meets wi's freens in Springburn
> Aa the roses an geans will turn tae bloom,
> And a black boy frae yont Nyanga
> Dings the fell gallows o the burghers doon.

(*hoodies* crows; *barley bree* whisky; *geans* wild cherries)

Prose writing in an astonishing range and variety of Scots has also undergone a dramatic transformation in the past decade or so. With no tradition of prose in Scots since the seventeenth century to act as a model, writers have until recently been wary of attempting prose in Scots of any length. Initially, the expansion was spurred by the Scots Language Society and its quarterly magazine *Lallans*. Short stories where the narrator is a Scots speaker are certainly the most successful attempts – Robert McLellan's Linmill stories are excellent by any standard. Expository prose was altogether more difficult – with no precedent to prepare one for it, even the Scots speaker initially found lines like the following strange to the eye: '*Lallans* is publisht bi the Scots Language Society, wi the help o siller frae the Scottish Arts Council.'

Now that we are totally used to it, however, the Scots prose of *Lallans* appears quite natural and fluent, and subjects such as a guide to the Internet are tackled with panache by such as Andy Eagle. Alexander Scott, J.K. Annand, Donald Campbell, William Neill and John Law have all contributed tremendous energy to the advancement of the Scots language cause and are to be applauded for their efforts in re-establishing models for prose in the language. J.K. Annand's bairn-rhymes are weel kent, but here is an example of his prose in Scots, the opening paragraph of an obituary he wrote on a fellow makar, printed in *Lallans*, Mairtinmas 1985:

> Robert McLellan was a Lanarkshire callant. His faither was John McLellan, brocht up in Lanark, a prenter to tred, that was merrit on Elizabeth Hannah, dochter of a fritt fermer frae nearby Kirkfieldbank. Whan they set up hous they baid at 14 Ferguson Avenue, Milngavie. Whan her time cam, his mither, as was the wey o't in thae days afore the National Health, gaed hame til her mither for the lyin-in. And sae it cam aboot that Robert McLellan was born at Linmill on the twinty-eicht o Janwar 1907. (The place is spelt Linnmill nouadays, but Robert aye threipit that Linmill was the richt spellin, eftir the lint or flax that was aince wrocht there, and had nocht to dae wi the nearby linns o Clyde.) In his bairnheid he spent a lot o time at Linmill wi his grannie and grandfaither, and the ongauns there were aa grist til his mill whan he cam in later days to scrieve his Linmill stories.

The douce expression of Scots in prose was gantin for a gunk – desperate for a shock – to kickstart it into the twenty-first century. For me, the shock of the new came on discovering the following:

> They goat ays doon and started kicking ays. Ah wis worried cause ah hud a bit ay money ah'd won fae the bandit. Ah wis shitin it in case they'd go through ma poakits. Fifteen quid ah hud taken the bandit for. They just booted intae ays but. Booted ays and she wis screamin:
> – KICK THE CUNT! KILL THE CUNT! OOR FUCKIN ELECTRIC! IT WIS OOR FUCKIN ELECTRICITY! HE'S GOAT MA FUCKIN BAIRN! HIS FUCKIN AULD HOOR AY A MOTHER'S GOAT MA FUCKIN BAIRN! GO BACK TAE YIR MA! LICK YER MA'S FUCKIN PISS-FLAPS YA CUNT!

That is about as far from the Kailyard idyll of *Beside the Bonnie Brier Bush* as you can get – the unmistakable Irvine Welsh giein the urban Embro demotic demonic laldy in the short story 'A Soft Touch', published in *A Tongue in Yer Heid: A Selection of the Best Contemporary Short Stories in Scots*, edited by James Robertson. Welsh exploded onto the scene with *Trainspotting* in 1993 and proved that if the work is powerful enough it will overcome every prejudice against it. Before

Trainspotting, if you had suggested that a novel reproducing the Edinburgh street dialect of the 1980s would become an international bestseller and inspire a film which would become iconic for a generation, you would have been treated as certifiable! Welsh showed what could be done. 'But is it Scots?' some thirled to a more traditional way of writing the language might well ask. I feel it certainly belongs in the radical Scots tradition that is close to the street – and I do not think it could have existed without that tradition to inform the writer. The voice is again at its core, however, and many other fine contemporary writers use a similar narrative technique: Des Dillon in *Me and Ma Gal*, Janet Paisley in *Not For Glory* and Anne Donovan in *Buddha Da* – the latter was also nominated for both the Orange Prize and the Whitbread First Novel award.

Another innovation came from the the Itchy Coo imprint, which published *Double Heider: Twa Novellas in Scots* by Hamish MacDonald and Sheena Blackhall. When you open MacDonald's novella *The Girnin Gates*, it explains, '*Double Heider* is jist that – a twa-heidit book wi twa stories inside it. Turn it tapsalteerie tae read aboot *Loon* by Sheena Blackhall.' Itchy Coo has fulfilled a remarkable role in generating all kinds of new material in Scots – from bairn books like Susan Rennie's *Planet Fankle* to James Robertson's *A Scots Parliament* and Robertson and Matthew Fitt's collections of wee plays in Scots *Tam o Shanter's Big Night Oot*. Since they started in 2002, they have achieved enormous success, publishing over 20 titles and selling over 60,000 books in the process.

Robertson and Fitt have also contributed immensely to contemporary Scottish literature. James Robertson has edited editions of classic novels by the likes of Sir Walter Scott and John Buchan, and in his own historical novels, *The Fanatic* and *Joseph Knight*, you can feel the influence of those who have gone before. In some passages in Scots, especially in *The Fanatic*, you are aware that you are in the presence of a major novelist totally in command of his language. If Robertson's novels belong more to the classical tradition of having dialogue in Scots and narrative in English, Fitt's *But n Ben A-Go-Go* belangs tae nae tradeition ava, in fack it blooters tradeition intae the mirk unkennt airts ayont cyberspace – which is of coorse patrolled by a cyberjanny. A wee glisk intae Fitt's unbonnie Scotland o the future:

> The But n Ben's location had been carefully waled. The dachas
> on the Gorms belanged the ubercless, each ane hoosin a
> paragon o Port douceness an respectability. Diamond Broon's
> cyberpauchler reputation wisna tholed by the ultra-perjink

community on the ither side sae he had wrocht himsel a coorse
den in sicht an lugshot o their quiet untrauchled hames an had
thrawnly keepit a pairty bilin there 24-oor a day for a lang
radge twinty year.

Fitt's novel, entirely written in Scots, had an excellent response and
won over people who were indifferent to Scots – again, the
imaginative quality of the writing attracted even the non-believers.
Other noteworthy advances in the 'normalisation' of prose writing in
Scots in the late 1990s included a series of popular history books about
Bruce and Wallace written by Glenn Telfer, and an academic Scottish
history journal, *Cairn*, published by the Aiberdeen Univairsitie Scots
Leid Quorum, run with admirable enthusiasm by Dauvit Horsbroch
and Steve Murdoch.

Not everyone, though, is happy to see Scots come out of the ghetto.
Even people you would hope would be sympathetic can turn if what is
being proposed does not comply with a very restrictive vision for the
language. When funding for the Itchy Coo project was announced –
one of the very few positive things the Executive has done for the
language in recent years – William McIlvanney wrote a very negative
article in *Scotland on Sunday*, which included the following:

> The truth is that I think this project, funded with £200,000 of
> Lottery money from the Scottish Arts Council, is well-meaning
> and seriously misguided. I think the return on the outlay will be
> minimal for a couple of reasons.
>
> The first is that it is too little too pathetically late. In 17
> years of teaching English in a secondary classroom, where I was
> happy to accept Scots as a co-tenant with English, I came to
> realise that there wasn't much left to accept. Words that had
> been common usage when I was the age of some of my pupils
> had withered into obsolescence in 10 or 15 years. A language
> has to be more than a few gallus Scotticisms scattered over
> standard English as a kind of local seasoning. It has to have its
> own current vocabulary and syntax and style of thought. It
> seemed to me that this necessarily complex structure was
> ruined beyond recall.
>
> I wish them well, though. I suppose this project, if it is very
> lucky, might re-introduce some Scottish words into temporary
> currency. But any serious rehabilitation of the Scots language?
> Forget it.

McIlvanney seems to believe that any attempt to restore Scots today is unnatural and artificial. He is not alone in this view – thousands believe that the three centuries of English hegemony which went before was a totally natural development, and therefore the continuation of a monoglot English policy is the only logical way forward. Personally, though, I find it sad to see a talented writer in Scots become part of the death wish for the language.

In the past few years, fortunately, I have noticed a tremendous increase in unnatural activities, such as people writing letters and emails to me in Scots. One arrived following a radio interview with Edi Stark in which she suggested I had built an empire out of my work with the language. The letter ended 'PS Can I be a sodger in yer empire?' Despite the advances, I'm afraid it's still a gey shoogly empire. No matter what you feel about Scots prose, the fact is that the ongoing renaissance in literature in Scots has undoubtedly helped towards raising the status and prestige of the language, written and spoken. The success of twentieth-century literature in Scots has forced the schools and universities to take Scots seriously once again. This still falls far short of the status an integral part of a national culture should have within education in its native land; but with Scots taught at Aberdeen, Edinburgh and Glasgow universities (the latter having a Chair in Scottish literature), and the literature expanding throughout Scottish education, the language and culture undoubtedly enjoy more prestige today than for many a long year. The Association for Scottish Literary Studies publishes much of the good work going on in the universities in its journals and actively promotes Scottish studies within Scottish society. The literature, and the intellectual debate surrounding it, is vigorously promoted by magazines like *Chapman* and *Cencrastus*. Significantly, Joy Hendry and Raymond Ross, who edit the publications, have both written plays in Scots and have had them performed in the professional theatre. The Linguistic Survey of Scotland, Scottish National Dictionaries, the School of Scottish Studies, the Country Life Archive of the National Museum, the Saltire Society and countless other local organisations all contribute their bit towards creating a climate whereby Scottish culture is slowly gaining the recognition it merits at home and abroad.

Will Scots expand, or will it move closer and closer to English? Either option is possible. There is certainly enough Scots remaining familiar to most of us that, with language planning and the backing of a sympathetic Scottish Executive and SED, there is no philological reason why Scots should not rise, like Icelandic or Norwegian, from being regarded as a provincial dialect to becoming a full-blown national language, regarded as such the world over. If the very idea seems far-fetched, it seemed just that way to millions in countries where languages have been revived. All that is lacking here is the will. For the moment, though, Standard Scots as an official language of Scotland is a million miles away – most of us would settle in the short term for our children being taught Scottish culture one period a week in the schools!

9

Wha's Like Us?

'Here's tae us, wha's like us? Damned few an they're a' deid' runs the Scot's favourite toast to his ain folk. The swagger implicit in the rhetorical question brooks no reply – we are the people and there is nothing and no one remotely like us in all the world! As far as language is concerned, however, there are millions of people like us, in that they too live in states which give only grudging status, if they give any at all, to the language of so-called minorities within their borders. If we could break out of our landlocked British insular mentality and look, as we did in the past, to mainland Europe, we would find parallels to the Scots/English duality in almost every European country. We would also be astonished to discover that in certain geopolitical circumstances the disadvantaged status of Scots is paralleled in languages such as German and French, which appear to us as pillars of the European linguistic Establishment. As I have shown already, one nation's language is another's corrupt dialect if a political border happens to be drawn in the wrong place. Europe, past and present, offers many varying parallels to the situation of Scots in Scotland – some pessimistic and others extremely optimistic.

Ignorance about how language evolves is at the heart of much of the prejudice against languages which differ from the principal standard variety in, for example, Britain, France and Spain. Many speakers of Standard English, French or Castilian Spanish actually believe that their language has existed unchanged as a pillar of perfection for centuries and that Scots, Occitan or Catalan are aberrant corruptions of this perfection, perpetrated by the irrational thrawnness and innate barbarity of those peoples in question. When I visited Barcelona for my radio series *Europe of 100 Tongues*, the distinguished Catalan academic Albert Bastardes highlighted this attitude humorously: 'Many Spaniards believe that we speak Catalan just to annoy them.' That too is part of the metropolitan world-view. I have heard people in France and Iberia come away with the same hoary old chestnuts that you hear in Scotland: 'The people of Catalonia/Occitania do not speak a language but a ragbag of a dialect that takes the worst from French and Spanish and mixes them together in an uncouth manner to create an unintelligible patois which should be consigned to the trash can.' That the *langue d'oc* and *català*, like Scots, have brilliant literary traditions and have been spoken in their homelands for centuries, these people know not and care not a jot. They have a world picture and they are sticking to it, even if it is wrong-headed.

France, of course, has been the most centralised of European states for a long time. Historically there were two major language groups within French: the *langue d'oïl* of the north, and the *langue d'oc* of the south. When political control of a unified French state became centred in Paris, the southern language and those of the Breton, Basque and Catalan people were regarded as inimical to the unity of the country and so the state sought to impose Northern French on all of these areas. As early as 1539, an ordinance of King Francis I declared this French the only official language of the realm. The erosion of the *langue d'oc*, also known as Occitan or Provençal, proceeded apace, much like the erosion of Scots following the Union of the Crowns. At the time of the French Revolution, the majority of people within the French state did not actually speak French. They spoke Flemish, German, Catalan, Basque, Occitan, Corsican or Breton. Napoleon's concept of *liberté, egalité et fraternité* had dire consequences for all the other native languages of France. To be truly *égal*, the Revolution decided, everyone had to share the same cultural identity and speak the same language. The unifying declaration of intent was '*un état, un peuple, une langue*' – one state, one people, one language. The languages of the so-called minorities were to be rooted out and, in tones reminiscent of the Scottish Augustans, they were denounced as '*un reste de barbarie des siècles passés*'. In 1794, the Revolutionary Bertrand Barère summed up the view from Paris: 'Federalism and superstition speak low Breton; emigration and hatred of the Republic speak German; the counter-revolution speaks Italian and fanaticism speaks Basque.'

As it was, the fanaticism mainly belonged to the state and the thoroughness of its methods of internal colonisation. In Brittany, for example, the local equivalent of the Welsh Not was *le symbole* – a humiliating symbol or token of peasant culture such as a wooden clog hung round the neck of a pupil discovered speaking Breton in class. That child then became the agent of the state and passed it on to the next cheuchter who lapsed into his or her mother tongue. The bairn with the mark at the end of the day was severely punished. It is little wonder that a legacy of bitterness remains. As late as 1972, President Pompidou dismissed the Alsatians' claim for recognition for their language with imperial disdain: 'There is no room for regional languages in a France destined to mark Europe with its seal.' The 'regional language' thus dismissed is, of course, German. The advantage of speaking two community languages fluently is not lost on the *Elsässer*, but to maximise their advantage, they have had to loosen the restrictive straitjacket of linguistic conformity imposed by the French state.

Many of the lesser-used languages of France have parallels with Scots. In the south, for example, the people who speak dialects descended from the Provençal of the troubadours have been indoctrinated by the state to regard their speech as a corruption of French. There as in Scotland, however, an intermittently brilliant literature in the Occitan language has continued and the Provençal equivalent of Hugh MacDiarmid was the poet Frédéric Mistral (1830–1914). He re-created the dialects into a vibrant literary language and initiated a renaissance in the culture of the south of France. There also arose a parallel autonomist political movement, as was the case with most of the deposed linguistic and national groups in Europe. Today, in the area of the *langue d'oc* there is a population of thirteen million, of whom roughly six million have some knowledge of Occitan and two million, mainly in the rural areas, use it as their everyday language of communication. Like those who speak a full canon of Scots, all Occitan speakers are able to switch to their language of education, the *langue d'oil*, or Standard French, with comparative ease.

European linguistic boundaries predate political borders. Political borders are extremely fluid and the twentieth century has witnessed several radical changes in the map of Europe as a result of two world wars and the break-ups of the USSR and Yugoslavia. Linguistic communities tend to have roots in their native regions which go back hundreds of years and, although political change can suddenly affect the fortunes of a language, the change in the native spoken vernacular tends to be slow.

In the case of long-established political borders which run through a distinctive linguistic community, the effect is rather on the status of the language on either side of the national frontier. The northern border of Portugal with Spain provides graphic illustration of the effect of politics on the status and prestige of language. The people to the south and north of the River Minho speak the same language. In the south, it is called Portuguese and has the prestige and kudos of a national and international language spoken from Lisbon to Luanda in Angola, from Rio de Janeiro in Brazil to Timor in the East Indies. In the north, it is called Galician and was regarded until recently as a provincial dialect or 'bad Spanish' by the Spanish state, which imposed its own standard *castellano* as the medium of education and the media. Because of the erosion that inevitably follows from such policies, Galician did not evolve to cope with the demands of modern society like her sister language Portuguese. Because of that, however, it retains many older features which have died out in Portuguese, like Scots in relation to Old English. For the Galician people, though, it is still a powerful focus for their strong Celtic identity and a vehicle for their best poetry and song. Before the recent revival, Galician was in the same kind of condition as Scots, and politics could so easily have placed Portuguese in the same precarious position. For at the time Scots came under threat towards the end of the sixteenth century, Portuguese came under political threat as the Spanish occupied the country for 60 years and began to impose their culture. If the Portuguese had not succeded in kicking out the occupying power, Portugal would have been like Catalonia or Galicia today, its language regarded by the world as corrupt Spanish.

Catalonia is a nation in the north-eastern corner of Iberia. Her language, Catalan, spills over into the French province of Roussillon and is spoken in Valencia and the Balearic Islands, with enclaves of the tongue found in far-flung places such as Sardinia in Italy. Despite suppression and banning by the Spanish authorities at various times in its history, especially during the Franco years, Catalan is still the language of over six million people of all social classes in both town and country. The term 'minority language' is one invented by the nation state which wants to diminish the status of a language. In the public mind, it conjures up images of peasants talking to their stirks in a quaint patois up some sleepy hollow where time stands still. Nothing could be further from the truth as far as Catalan is concerned; it is spoken by intellectuals, industrialists, artists and artisans in one of the most sophisticated and cultured cities of Europe, Barcelona. Catalan gives living testimony to the importance of the survival of a language among the people whose culture it expresses.

The higher echelons of Catalan society had turned to Castilian as the language of court as early as the fifteenth century, and much of the best writing was in Castilian – a parallel to the Scots situation following the Union of the Crowns. In the aftermath of Catalonia's military defeat in the War of the Spanish Succession, Phillip V of Spain determined to destroy Catalan nationalism once and for all, by incorporating the country completely into a centralised Spanish state modelled on France. His *Decreto de Nueva Planta*, or new ground plan, for the country of 1716 was inspired by Castilian nationalism and its desire to root out the identity of, or, as they would term it, grant 'civilisation' to, their neighbours. A memorandum to the King from the Council of Castile stated:

> It is necessary to abolish, efface and to suspend in their entirety the *fueros*, usages and customs of his Principality and to impose the laws of Castile . . . to employ the Castilian language . . . so that books in Catalan must be forbidden, nor must it be spoken or written in schools and instruction in Christian doctrine must be in Castilian.

The language, naturally, suffered and became more restricted in its uses. Like Scots, it enjoyed literary and cultural revivals followed by periods when it appeared to be moribund and the country succumbing more and more to Spanish influence. It may have been the suppression of the culture itself that made the language a symbol of resistance and gave the people a focus for retaining it. Franco's victory in 1936 led to the banning of it in public and until comparatively recently it was not even taught at Barcelona University. But the popular resistance was such that today, with autonomy, the Catalans have their own Catalan television service and the language is represented at every level of the area's life. According to the Spanish government of a few decades ago, Catalan did not exist.

The buzz word used in Catalonia, Galicia and other areas attempting to restore previously suppressed languages today is 'normalisation'. This is a deliberate policy of exposing and using the language in areas of formal life which have traditionally been the preserve of the language of state. So long has the usage of the formal language of state been embedded in the people's conditioning that it has become a fixed state of mind, where use of the native language is unthinkable. Galician, for example, survived strongest, like Scots, in the small towns and in the country. When Galician speakers came to the city, they would automatically switch to Castilian Spanish, for fear of ridicule and, in Franco's era, persecution. In Catalonia during the Franco years, Catalan was very much confined to the hearth and home, for any public use of it would provoke Castilian nationalists into uttering the famous put-down '*Habla cristiano*' (Speak the language of Christians) while public buildings proclaimed '*Habla el idioma del imperio*' (Speak the language of Empire). Many people in positions of power in Catalonia today recall the childhood scars of being thus shamed and chastised in public in Barcelona in the 1960s.

Ironically, Castilian Spanish arrogance and disdain for other languages has helped the process of normalisation in the vital area of television. Unlike neighbouring Portugal, which broadcasts foreign films and programmes in the original language with subtitles, Spain has always dubbed foreign-language soundtracks with the voices of Spanish actors and actresses. Thus everyone from Sean Connery to Angelina Jolie, everything from *ER* to *The Simpsons* sounds as if it is set in a suburb of Madrid. Suddenly, with the advent of Galician and Catalan television, the setting switched to the country areas around Vigo or the Rambla of Barcelona! 'It sounds artificial' was the main complaint at first when middle-class Galicians in the cities suddenly heard the language of the country and the working class coming out of the mouths of television presenters and Hollywood stars. Thirty years on, people have got used to it. Not only that, they turn first to the Galician channels for their news; they feel they will be told the truth in their own language. Jaume Santacana of TV3 in Barcelona recalled his own reaction when they first broadcast films dubbed in Catalan: 'Of course the first time I saw a film with John Wayne or Laurence Olivier speaking Catalan . . . everybody was surprised. Not now, that does not exist. I think it is another sign of normalisation. You can see *EastEnders*, for instance, in Catalan and nobody is surprised now.' Puir sowels!

The programme of linguistic normalisation in Catalonia is an attempt at social engineering on a scale almost beyond the dreams of protagonists of other lesser-used languages. Before the 1992 Olympic Games, for example, groups of linguists were at work publishing handbooks for broadcasters in Catalan. The vocabulary adopted for the finer moves in many sports had been Spanish and although most of the terms are close to the Catalan equivalent, the determination was to establish native terms for everything and where possible expunge the language of Castilianisms. Over 300 people were employed full time in the linguistic normalisation process and the autonomous government devoted 7 million pounds per annum to the language. The results are already impressive. Before autonomy was achieved in

1979, only 30 per cent of the population was literate in its mother tongue. Now, with it firmly established in education, literacy figures are higher than 65 per cent, rising to 85 per cent for the younger generation who have been educated in the language and use it in a full range of circumstances previously the domain of Spanish.

Even more important is the fact that, a few decades on, it is firmly established as the language of prestige and social advancement. The huge Spanish-speaking population of Barcelona is happy to see its children become fully bilingual and integrated into the new order which has developed. Mostly on the extreme right, of course, there are still many Spanish nationalists who see the whole process as an aberration, but they are becoming increasingly marginalised. Important spheres where Spanish is still dominant include the judiciary, the state police (both sources of tension between the Catalan and Spanish governments), the press, and areas of commerce and advertising; but, with time, these last bastions will be catalanised as well.

As I have stated elsewhere, politics is fundamental to the way we perceive languages and what happens to them. The dramatic success of the Catalan revival in Catalonia is contrasted with the fortunes of the same language south of the border in the province of Valencia (whose capital was once the cultural centre for the language) and north of the border in the French province of Roussillon. Fearing pan-Catalanism, the Spanish right in Valencia has engaged in a vigorous and partly successful campaign to create the mistaken idea that Valencian is not Catalan but a separate language. This serves to deflect the influence of the dynamic Catalanist movement coming over from Catalonia itself and weakens its chances for recovery in Valencia. They are helped in this by the fact that the Valencian urban bourgeoisie, for the same reasons as their Scottish counterparts, have shifted away from Catalan to the language of state, Spanish. They have little sense of identity with the local vernacular, nor do they give a jot for what it is called. In French Roussillon, years of politically motivated persecution and neglect provide an even more graphic example of the effect of politics on language. There, the only group of people who today speak fully the area's historic language are the gypsies. Catalan survives among the most stigmatised group at the bottom of the social scale.

The indivisible link that European states have established between themselves and their principal languages is one that belies the complexity of the continent's linguistic heritage. Rather than accepting cultural diversity as a source of vitality and strength, nation states have continuously attempted to deny the existence of the multiplicity of ethnic languages and dialects within their territories. Their thinking has conditioned us all: the word 'language' is frequently associated with the speech of a sovereign national state, while the word 'dialect' is associated with a regional variation of the national language. Yet all languages are dialects, all dialects language! All speech is part of a continuum determined often by the settlement of linguistic groups in a defined area many hundreds of years ago. Some of these dialects, that of the Paris basin or the East Midlands in England, for example, evolved into their national standard, but not because they were in any way superior to the other dialects surrounding them. The prestige of dialects has always been determined by political status – and historical accident.

The connection between language survival and political power is seen clearly when you examine the fate of the languages of the great nation states where they happen to find themselves separated from the fatherland which nurtures them. Suddenly, the giants of Europe's linguistic map come under threat, classified as remote provincial patois which run counter to the drive for national unity. This was the case in the twentieth century with the French and German languages within the Italian state. The French-speaking Val d'Aosta and German-speaking South Tyrol were historically part of the Alpine provinces of French Savoie and Austrian Tyrol respectively.

The Aosta Valley was joined to Italy in 1860. The new Italian Republic was to be *una ed indivisibile* and set about banning the native French, first from schools in 1879 and then from the law courts in 1880. Mussolini's Fascists prohibited the use of French in any sector of public life, including newspapers, speeches, place names and even personal names. With the advent of industry and tourism, Italians flooded into the area as permanent settlers. Rather like 'white settlers' in the Scottish *Gaidhealtachd*, the incomers exercised tremendous influence on the communities they 'invaded' and, with the backing of state propaganda, helped erode linguistic confidence in the native population. Since regional differences were recognised, on paper at least, by the Italian authorities in 1948, there has been a softening of attitude and the schools teach French. But the process of italianisation proceeds unchecked. In 1901, in a population of 83,500 only 6,700 were Italian speakers. Today, half of the population speaks only Italian.

The story is similar in South Tyrol, which was part of the German-speaking world for 14 centuries until its annexation by Italy following the Treaty of St-Germain in 1919. The fate of the language during the

Fascist years was graphically described for me by a former MEP for the province, Joachim d'Alsass:

> Well, speaking the German language was prohibited. The German schools were taken over by Italy. The kindergartens were also dispossessed and then closed down. They were made illegal. German lessons in the primary schools were suspended and it went so far under the Fascist regime that private German lessons became illegal too. At that time, in order to preserve the German language, we established *Katakomben* – catacomb schools, or schools in hidden places. We felt like the Christians in Rome, who had to hide so that they could go on living in their Christian faith. Teachers were arrested and banned. They tried everything to deprive us of our language.

Previously, the province had approximately 233,000 German speakers and 7,000 Italian speakers. Because of the promotion of Italian at the expense of German, today the balance is rather different, with Italian speakers numbering just under a third of a total population of 476,000. Since the Autonomy Statute of 1972, however, the native population has finally gained some degree of control over its destiny and for the first time there appears to be creative cooperation between province and state. Recently, a language act was passed giving equal status to German and requiring all public officials to be bilingual. For the first time since 1919, this will positively discriminate in favour of the native population, who are all bilingual. For most of the twentieth century, only about 20 per cent of the Italian-speaking population bothered to learn German.

The Germans of South Tyrol are now in political control of their destiny again and looking forward to being a region of Europe with a lot more confidence than their experience of being a region of the Italian state has taught them. Yet if universal bilingualism can be created there, South Tyrol may still show Europe the strengths of a multicultural approach to the needs of her minorities. As European nation states bind themselves closer politically, the resistance to other cultures within the states should soften and *l'Europe des cent drapeaux* become a reality. Then perhaps all of Europe's deposed nations can enjoy the status of equality with the language and culture of the dominant group within those nation states.

All languages, from deposed national tongues like Catalan and Scots to politically 'misplaced' languages like French and German, can come under threat if the government decides that their continuation is inimical to the cultural solidarity of the state. It would, however, be naive to think that national autonomy for the deposed language groups would automatically lead to the full restoration of the tongue to its original glory. Few nationalist movements bound themselves so closely to the restoration of their native language as did the Irish in the twentieth century. Since 1919 and the creation of the Free State, Irish Gaelic has been granted the status of 'the first official language' and the compulsory teaching of Gaelic in school has resulted in the expansion of the numbers who have some command of the language, with as many as 1,570,894 claiming to speak it in 2004. For the vast majority of these people, however, their knowledge of Irish is similar to the average Scot's knowledge of the French he was taught at school – no very guid. The actual number of people who use Irish as their everyday medium of communication is probably no more than 30,000, concentrated in the far west of the country in the government-funded official *Gaeltacht*. There, despite financial support, subsidised industry and successful local radio stations broadcasting in the language, the actual number of Irish speakers is rapidly declining. For the linguistic anglicisation of Ireland has had its own inbuilt momentum for four centuries and the people's association of the language with poverty and backwardness has not been eradicated with the alternative world picture on offer from Dublin. Irish Gaelic is in an even more perilous position than Scottish Gaelic today, despite their very different status within their respective countries.

If the failure to re-establish Irish on the same level as English offers a salutary lesson to the wishful-thinking nationalist, there exist nevertheless spectacular examples of language revival against all the odds. At the end of the nineteenth century, when the first wave of Zionist immigrants were arriving in Palestine to put down the roots which developed into the State of Israel, Hebrew was an all but dead language. Its use, like Latin in the Catholic Church, was confined to religious worship, while the Jewish people spoke mainly Yiddish or the vernacular of the various European countries which had been their homelands for centuries.

One of the first Jewish settlers in Palestine was a Lithuanian philologist born Eliezer Perlman. On his arrival in the promised land in 1882, Perlman changed his name to Ben-Yehuda and, probably to the consternation of his wife and family, refused to speak anything but Hebrew. He helped reinvent the language, coining new words and preparing a moribund tongue for the modern world. By the 1890s, this 'new' Hebrew was being taught in Jewish schools. Today, it is the language of all Israelis. Now, admittedly, few ethnic groups have been galvanised by terrible adversity like the Jews and there is nothing typical about their experience. What the story does demonstrate, though, is that if the will is there, even dead languages will revive and thrive. Scots is far from being a dead language.

The parallels between Scots, Hebrew and Irish, however, are not as relevant as those between Scots and Catalan or Occitan. The closeness and similarity of Scots to English, Catalan to Castilian Spanish and Occitan to French has been a source of weakness and a potential source of strength. The erosion of Scots is more subtle and gradual because, with so much being already shared with English, many are unaware where Scots stops and English starts. The style-switching and style-drifting that most Scots engage in show just how easy it is to adapt from one language to the other. If the will existed to expand and extend Scots, in other words, this would not present any great difficulty to the majority of the population. All they would have to overcome would be their social prejudices. On the other hand, up till now the decline of completely separate languages, for example Breton in France, Gaelic in Britain, Basque in Spain and Irish in Ireland, has had a final and possibly irrevocable nature. These languages die out where they come into contact with the major language, then gradually the erosion eats into the heartland – the situation in the *Gaeltacht* of Ireland today. Catalan, Galician and Occitan have not died. As J. Derrick McClure put it, like Scots, they have 'merely been pushed into a limbo of confusion and prejudice' at various points in their history.

The same could be said of Low German, today regarded as a provincial dialect of Northern Germany but once the distinctive lingua franca of the Hanseatic League. High German replaced it as the formal language of the area in a manner not unlike the advance of English against Scots. In some aspects, Scots has fared better than Low German, with its more vibrant literature and with writers such as Burns and Scott who have made the language known in the rest of Britain and the world. Low German literature has never travelled beyond its linguistic province, and has generally been ignored in the rest of Germany. Speakers of Low German, on the other hand, are a lot less self-conscious about using their tongue in public; it is in common use in the church, for example. The Germans have never regarded a strong dialect as standing in opposition to a strong national standard. This is borne out even more forcefully in the case of Swiss German. To the ears of those raised on High German, Swiss German sounds rather like Buchan Doric to a lady from the Home Counties. Backed by their government, media and strong sense of national identity, however, the Swiss are completely at home with their national form of German. They are taught to read and write in High German and can speak it to communicate with foreigners, but they see no earthly reason to abandon their native tongue for the 'foreign' standard one.

Luxembourg has a similar attitude vis-á-vis German and French, the languages of administration in the Grand Duchy. All its citizens are educated to be fluent and literate in those languages, but the local Frankish dialect of German, Lëtzebuergesh, continues to be the everyday medium of oral communication and is the vernacular learned by immigrant groups like the Portuguese. Since the German occupation during the Second World War, linguistic nationalism has increased and more and more young people are using the language for written communication as well. In February 1984, its status as the national language was confirmed by law.

Happy as I am for the Luxemburgers, I could not help but notice the stark anomalies of the Scottish and the Scots language situation when I saw 'Merry Christmas and a Happy New Year' in Lëtzebuergesh up in lights above Edinburgh's George Street during the European Summit there in 1992. Wee totie Luxembourg with a population of 360,000 and a newly declared national language with a sparse literary history were in at the centre of things and fully represented. Scotland, one of Europe's most ancient and distinctive nations with a population of 5 million and a language which has been the medium of a glittering literary tradition was not. We provided the waiters, and the demonstration. Merry Christmas.

Like Swiss or Austrian German, Scots English could be described as a national form of a world language. But when you add the historical Scots elements to any equation with other European linguistic dualities, more valid comparisons present themselves. The German philologist Manfred Görlach, in a paper comparing the fates of Scots and Low German, states:

> Scots was and is more removed from English than is the case with modern pairs such as Czech and Slovak, Serbian and Croatian, Bulgarian and Macedonian, or Swedish, Danish and Norwegian – all of which are considered independent languages by their speakers and, in consequence, by linguists.

Scandinavia has long been held up by Scottish nationalists as a model for what the British Isles could be: a confederation of sovereign nations mutually bound together through common historical and

170

cultural ties. The linguistic situation in Scandinavia also provides stimulating parallels to the Scots/English situation in Britain. Danish, Norwegian, Swedish, Icelandic and Faeroese form a language continuum and, with a modicum of good will, each can understand the other's language. At one time, Norwegian, Icelandic and Faeroese were regarded as dialects of Danish in the same way that Scots is mistakenly regarded as a dialect of English today. From the middle of the fifteenth century onwards, Danish came to dominate Norwegian society. No Bible was produced in Norwegian and, as in Scotland, this led to the decline of the native vernacular as a written and eventually as a spoken medium among the upper classes. Even after Norway gained independence from Denmark in 1814, Danish continued unquestioned as the written and spoken language of power and authority. During its long history in Norway, however, the language adapted somewhat to local circumstances, and *bokmål*, the name the Norwegians give this Dano-Norwegian language, is in a similar position to Scottish Standard English today.

However, while *bokmål* became the language of the elite and eventually of the cities, the country districts held on to their traditional Norwegian dialects. These dialects were the basis of Ivar Aasen's remarkable attempt to intervene in the erosion of the native vernacular. Through language planning and concern for the native culture, he succeeded in creating an alternative national language, *landsmål*. The same phenomenon occurred at different times in Iceland and the Faeroes, where philologists rebuilt a standard language for the country out of the historical native vernacular. In Iceland and the Faeroes, the attempt was entirely successful and both countries have vibrant, thriving cultures in languages that at one time were under the same threat that English poses for Scots.

In Norway, the establishment of *landsmål*, also known as *nynorsk*, as an alternative national standard has only been partly successful. It has had a set grammar from 1864 and has enjoyed official status in the country since 1885. Communities can choose which of the national standards they prefer. In the populous east of the country and in the cities, the prestige of *bokmål* has remained unchanged. In the west and midlands of the country, where the traditional dialects had been strongest, *landsmål* is the preferred standard for all aspects of life. Under a sixth of Norwegian schoolchildren are taught in the language today. Although a minority tongue, it has a thriving literature and is understood perfectly and comprehensively by those who use *bokmål*. There is, however, an element of snobbery attached to the 'higher, foreign' register and the writer Magde Oftedal's remarks are also

171

relevant to some English speakers' attitude to Scots in Scotland: 'If some *bokmål* people claim not to understand *nynorsk*, it is only pretence. It is the usual expedient of making a virtue out of ignorance, with the added ingredient that in this case the ignorance is not even genuine.' *Landsmål*, because of the status it has enjoyed, has also influenced *bokmål* irrevocably, revitalising it with the vigour of native speech.

Scots could be revived on a similar basis to *landsmål*, if the will existed. As we have seen with *landsmål*, the extension of the native dialects into a codified standard was good not only for the native language but for the dominant language itself. I feel there could be the same kind of fertile fusion between Scots and English. But another important effect of all this linguistic activity in countries like Norway is to heighten awareness of language itself. The Scandinavians are among the best and most natural linguists in the world. Belonging to small nations, they understand the necessity of communicating in other languages and with other cultures. They have long known that there is no tension between being local, national and international. That is another lesson we Scots could learn to our advantage.

10

The Dialects of Scots

Because Scots does not have a recognised standard spoken form today, many believe that the various dialects spoken in Scotland are dialects of English. They are in fact dialects of Scots and form an unbroken continuum with the language which was the national tongue of the Middle Ages. The speech of someone from a conservative Scots-speaking area such as West Angus for example, has not changed a great deal in the intervening centuries; if time travel were feasible, a courtier speaking the Standard Lothian Scots of the fifteenth century would have little difficulty communicating with a contemporary Angus chield. The major dialect divisions of Scots have existed since the days when it was the national tongue, but these divisions were rarely reflected in the writing of the period. Writers wrote in a standard literary Scots, even if this did not reflect exactly the way they spoke. For example, by the sixteenth century, people in the North-east already pronounced the sound 'wh' as in 'what' with an 'f', giving the modern dialect spelling 'fat' or 'fit' in the area; but at that time, writers in the region used the standard Scots spelling 'quh' or 'wh', giving 'quhat', or 'quhair'. The reason we know that the 'f' was already in the spoken tongue of the North-east lies in the fact that in a few rare instances in the records the scribe 'slips up' and represents the sound in his writing – the exception proving the rule. In Walter Cullen's *Chronicle of Aberdeen*, he describes seeing James VI in 1580: 'I paist to Dunnottar, fair I beheld his graice.' Normally, the different spoken dialects were not reflected in the writing and the literary standard was in use all over Scotland – a standard written language which everyone could understand.

Nowadays, of course, things are very different. With the decline of Scots as the national language, a sign of its fragmentation is the fact that for many Scots speakers and writers the local dialect is more important and more clearly defined as an entity than something called Scots. This has had the beneficial effect of giving people pride in local culture and history, and encouraging writers to compose in a local form of Scots. But it has also produced the erroneous idea that the vernaculars of Buchan, Shetland or Dundee, for example, are unrelated, isolated in their own locality and different from all others, when in fact they are all regional dialects of the same Scots tongue.

This phenomenon is illustrated by the plethora of articles and books that have been published to satisfy local interest in the dialects but which obscure the national dimension of the language. In the Aberdeen *Press and Journal* on 27 March 1986, for example, an article on North-east speech had the following under the title 'North-east Sayings': 'aul' farrant, fair fleggit, fair forfochen, sleekit, scunnert, trauchelt'. Now, every one of these is common Scots and would be known by most Scots speakers. I have seen the same thing in lists of Dundonese vocabulary which include words like 'hirple', 'humff', 'halikit' and 'hurdies'; in *The Shetland Dictionary*, with words such as 'bide', 'birl' and 'ben'; in Glasgow glossaries, with 'Glaswegian' words such as 'neb', 'neeps' and 'noak'. In almost every one of these, the fact that 90 per cent of the words are common Scots is played down and the uniqueness of the local dialect played up. That is not to say that every dialect does not have its unique vocabulary, as we shall see, but genuinely local words are the exceptions rather than the rule. Even in Shetland, where Scots replaced the Scandinavian tongue Norn, the core vocabulary of the dialect is still general Scots with an admixture of Scandinavian words which are particular to the dialects of the Northern Isles.

The identity with the Doric in the North-east is particularly strong. 'Doric' was originally the name given to a dialect of ancient Greek, whose rustic strength contrasted with the sophistication of the literary language of Athens. In the eighteenth century, Scots writers like Allan Ramsay justified using Scots by comparing it to the use of the Doric by Theocritus. Since then, the term has been interchangeable with Scots and has been applied to all Scots dialects. Writing to MacDiarmid in 1931 anent his bairn rhymes, William Soutar wrote, 'if the Doric is to come back alive, it will come first on a cock horse.' Older speakers all over the country will refer to their language as 'Scotch' or 'the Doric', knowing they are one and the same thing.

In the North-east, however, Doric has become almost an exclusive term for the Scots spoken in the area and as such has enjoyed substantial backing from august bodies like the North East of Scotland Heritage Trust. According to the Business Plan for the Heritage Trust in the late 1990s, the area's 'most unique feature is the Doric, the local dialect and one of Europe's neglected languages'. My main misgiving about this otherwise promising development was that there was no mention of the Doric's relationship with other Scots-speaking areas or with the Scots language at all. It was simply something called Doric and appeared to have made a unilateral declaration of independence from Scots. Given the ignorance concerning Scots, this emphasis on the local at the expense of the national can only serve to diminish the case for national and international backing for the language, which is the direction in which we should all be heading together, as one voice. As discussed in the previous chapter dealing with the foreign parallels with Scots, the energy of the Catalan movement has been deliberately dissipated in Valencia by the authorities there refusing to admit that the regional variation Valencian is in fact Catalan.

Again through ignorance of the historic national language and national literature in the language, speakers of local dialects today presume that theirs and theirs only is the genuine article. The first Aberdonian I ever met was in Munich's Hofbräuhaus when I was 17. When I spiered, 'Hou ur ye gettin oan?' an he replied, 'Nae bad,' I thocht tae masel, 'He cannae be a richt Scots speaker, awbody that kens ocht aboot Scots says 'no bad', he must be pittin it oan!' Nae dout monie fowk fae different airts hes thocht the same aboot ma Scots. Indeed, because of the controversy surrounding literary Lallans, there are those in the North-east that gar things gae badly agley and presume that all Scots spoken south of the Dee is an ersatz kiddie on.

This intense local focus and loyalty to the dialect is also determined by social factors. People are conditioned to switch to English in formal situations, so that Scots-speaking strangers will naturally communicate, at least initially, in English. The isolation of the dialects is also heightened by lack of exposure in the media – if people became accustomed to hearing the different dialects, they would quickly realise the similarities rather than fear the differences. The myth that Scots is only intelligible within a short radius and that one dialect speaker cannot communicate with another one from a different area has also resulted in a reduction in the use of Scots and a reinforcing of speakers' identification with the local rather than the national tongue. All of this is a sign of a language in retreat and similar manifestations have occurred within every deposed language in Europe. Listen to the echoes for Scots here in Pierre-Jakez Hélias's description of his native parish in Brittany in the book *The Horse of Pride*:

> Today most grandmothers know nothing but Breton, their
> children are fluent in both languages, and their grandchildren
> speak only French. That's why mass is celebrated in French,
> and too bad for the grandmothers. However, under ordinary
> circumstances, the parishes of Plozévet and Plonéour still speak
> Breton. It will take a long time to die out and will last as long
> as the people need it to express precisely what they are and
> what they want. Moreover it is such a strictly private matter
> that some Bretons claim that the language they speak is not the
> same as that spoken by the people of Plozévet or Plonéour.
> Indeed, you often hear them say: 'That bunch doesn't speak the
> same Breton that we do.' It's somewhat true and also
> completely false. But the difference between that 'somewhat'
> and that 'completely' is enough to make Breton-speaking
> people from two different districts speak French when they
> meet.

Similarly, I have heard many Scots speakers say that they are only
comfortable talking Scots to someone from the same locality. We
ourselves, in other words, contribute to the decline in use of our
language. With everyone conditioned to some extent by official
disdain for the tongue, it takes a strong person to speak Scots in a
formal situation, where people may classify them according to one or
other stereotype as coarse or uneducated; it is so much simpler to
speak English and save yourself the hassle.

Today, with mass communication influencing speech in every part
of the country, the dialect differences are not nearly as great as they
were even 50 years ago. Then, towns a few miles apart, such as
Galston and Darvel in my own area, spoke with recognisably different
twangs. Nowadays, accents that are frequently broadcast, such as
Glaswegian, can influence children's speech in Lerwick and Fort
William, not to mention places nearer by. The distinctions are slowly
becoming blurred but the major dialect divisions still prevail and can
be detected immediately when you move from one area to another.
The alert football fan, for example, will notice a result of 2–1 given as
'twaw-wan' in Glasgow, 'twa-ane' in Dundee and 'twae-yin' in
Lothian.

According to the *Scottish National Dictionary*, the main dialect
divisions are Insular Scots (Orkney and Shetland), Northern Scots,
Mid or Central Scots and Southern Scots. Within these major

divisions, there are many regional variations and dialect subdivisions, as we shall see when we outline the features of the individual dialects more closely. For the sake of geographic precision, I have used the same county references as the *Scottish National Dictionary* to pinpoint the dialect boundaries rather than relate the dialects to the regions which came into being in 1975. With over two-thirds of the population of Scotland living in its area, and being the dialect from which the standard literary language derives, Central Scots deserves first place in any discussion on the dialects of Scots.

CENTRAL SCOTS

The Central dialect of Scots stretches from West Angus and North-east Perthshire in the north, to Galloway and Ulster in the South-west and the River Tweed in the South-east. Thus, apart from the small Southern Scots area in the counties of Roxburgh, Selkirk and East Dumfriesshire, Central Scots is spoken all over the Lowlands south and west of the Tay. It can be subdivided into South Central, West Central and East Central Scots – with the latter showing differences north and south of the Forth – but the differences tend to be in accent rather than dialect. I can confirm that from personal experience. I was brought up in the West Central area but spent summer holidays in Fife, in the East Central area. The Fifers kidded me on about the elongated vowel sounds of Ayrshire Scots – 'Ye come fae near Kilmaaarnock!' – and I imitated their singsong twang, but we spoke the same language. The difference was in accent. I recall an old worthy in Bowhill called Grace who used to visit my grandmother, acting as newsbearer and Greek chorus for the pit village. She invariably entered the house and with a suitably portentous pause, announced, 'Ye kain Mrs Bruce that bides alang the road . . . well, she's daid.' In Ayrshire, we would have said 'ken' and 'deid' but I always felt 'daid' conveyed the mystery of death better than the stark finality of 'deid'.

With the medieval Scottish court in session at Edinburgh, Linlithgow and Dunfermline, the dialect of East Central Scotland is the nearest we can approach to imagining the Scots spoken by the likes of William Dunbar or James IV back in the language's golden age. North of the Forth, the language retains its older forms, with the area of West Angus and East Perthshire being more conservative in its retention of certain forms than Fife. For example, that area retains the older *ae*, *ane* and *aince*, against the *yae*, *yin* and *yince* south of the Tay. Similarly, the 'oo' sound in *mune*, *spune* and *gude* is retained in Angus, while to the south it has become *muin*, *spuin* and *guid*, pronounced as in Scottish Standard English 'bid'. It was of course the spoken Scots of this area which proved such a rich source for Professor Lorimer when he began his mammoth translation of the New Testament into Scots. It has also proved to be a fertile source of poetry in the language, with William Soutar, Violet Jacob and Helen B. Cruickshank just a few of the writers who hail from this heartland of Scots.

The speech of the cities, of course, is farthest removed from the more classical rural dialects but Perth and Dundee are still broadly Scots in speech, though the English accents of the 'county set' and the incomers can be heard frequently in Perth. Dundee's unique feature is the 'eh' sound for 'I', as in 'Eh hud meh eh on a peh' – 'I had my eye on a pie'. Theories such as the common one that it developed out of jute spinners having to mouth their words so that their fellow workers could lip-read above the clack of the mills are good stories but little else. As in Glasgow, the local dialect of Scots was influenced by immigrants from further north in Scotland, but more especially by thousands of people from Ireland. Most of the latter came from Ulster and you can hear a sound close to the 'eh' in some parts of the north of Ireland.

Edinburgh is Scotland's most anglicised city, at least in matters of speech. The reasons for this are many: the university, the high percentage of children who attend fee-paying schools, and the old professional institutions such as the law, whose members have changed considerably from Cockburn's day, when they spoke Scots. The huge Edinburgh middle class tends to speak Standard English or Scottish Standard English. Scots is there too; a friend who was born and bred in the Southside speaks good Scots, so much so that people presume she is not a native of the city. Edinburgh is so dominated by the values of the middle classes, that working-class culture and speech had very low prestige even among the working class. This has changed in recent years due to the phenomenal success of Irvine Welsh's brilliant novel *Trainspotting* and the movie that emerged from it. The Edinburgh dialect now had street cred, but that is something the weejies of the west have always had in abundance.

West Central Scots
Whereas in Edinburgh the working class are defined by the predominant middle-class culture, in Glasgow the opposite prevails and the professional classes have some of the street wisdom and gallusness of the predominant working-class ethos of the city. The result of this is that almost everyone from Glasgow is recognisably

Scottish in speech. In Edinburgh, it is sometimes difficult to tell if someone is Scottish or English by their accent; in Glasgow, that confusion rarely exists. The middle classes may not like the Glasgow dialect but they are influenced by it. Years ago, when I lived in South Carolina, I often heard elderly white gentlemen apologise for the fact that their speech had been influenced by their close associations with the blacks. The inhabitants of Glasgow's leafy suburbs are in a similar relationship with the speech of the masses. Glaswegian has enormous internal prestige.

The vitality of the dialect there lies in the strength of a working-class identity which is basic to people from the western industrial belt. Also, through the media, working-class heroes such as footballers or characters from popular television series like *Chewin' the Fat* have given Glaswegian 'underground' prestige in the rest of Scotland, so that its influence is extending well beyond Glasgow – much to the horror of English and Scots purists alike. For both groups, Glaswegian expressions such as 'a'm urnae gaun' and the plural 'youz' are abhorrent shibboleths. 'Youz', of course, fills an important gap in English – most of the major European languages have a singular and plural 'you'. The Glaswegian financier Angus Grossart tells the story of an interminable business meeting in London to discuss the wording of a multi-million-pound transaction. Present were his client (fellow Scot James Gulliver) and 40 advisers, most of whom were English. Deeved by the inability of the lawyers to decide whether a mutual obligation was to fall on 'you both' or 'both of you' and anxious not to miss the last shuttle home, Grossart perplexed the English and delighted the Scots by suggesting that the obvious solution to the problem was to ditch both and settle for 'youz'!

Michael Munro's books on the Glasgow patter reveal that the dialect is constantly coining new terms. It is particularly rich in terms of abuse. Recent expressions collected by Michael Munro include 'You've got a face lik a meltit wellie' and 'You've got a face like a horse in a huff.' My own favourite is still the put-down voiced memorably by a cleaning lady in the BBC engaged in a rammy with one of her colleagues: 'Hey, whit'll you dae for a face when King Kong asks for his erse back?' The ultimate test of a dialect's worth is its ability to communicate, and there are few more extrovert communicators than Glaswegians.

There are big differences between the speech of Glasgow and its Lanarkshire and Ayrshire hinterland, especially in the smaller industrial towns, such as those in the Irvine Valley, and of course the country. Because most people with a west-of-Scotland accent live in

Glasgow, Glaswegians are often surprised to hear Ayrshire people, for example, use Scots words and sounds which have been lost in the city dialect: *ye ken* for *ye know*, *seiven* for *seven*, *brocht* for *brought*, etc. Other features of the western dialect of Scots include the 'aw' vowel giving *snaw*, *baw*, *braw*, whereas, say, Angus would have *snaa*, *baa*, *braa*; the 'oo' or 'ui' vowel in *do*, *muir*, *puir*, *teuch* and *eneuch* are pronounced *dae*, *mair*, *pair*, *tyuch* and *inyuch*; the Fife 'a' vowel sound in *parritch* or *bannet* are pronounced *purritch* and *bunnet* in Ayrshire.

South Central Scots

In South Ayrshire, West Dumfriesshire and Galloway, you enter another subdivision of the Central or Mid Scots dialect area, South Central Scots. It retains a few more conservative features that have changed in North Ayrshire, for example the words for tough and enough mentioned above still retain the older forms of *teuch* and *eneuch* with the 'oo' sound rather than the altered *tyuch* and *inyuch* of the West Central dialect. However, the West Central dialect appears to be spreading into this area and older people can point out the differences between the Scots of the older and younger generations. Western Galloway has also long been influenced by communication with and settlement by Irish people.

Wigtownshire is set apart for this reason from the neighbouring county of Kirkcudbright. There the people talk about going 'over the Cree and into the Irish' – the Cree being the river marking the linguistic boundary. Ironically, though, some of the features people think of as Irish in Wigtownshire are possibly older forms of Scots brought back to Scotland in more recent times by the descendants of Scots speaking participants in the seventeenth-century Plantation of Ulster.

Ulster Scots

Ulster Scots is derived from the West and South Central Scots of the thousands of Scots who emigrated to Ireland before, during and after James VI's Plantation of the province. As the only major contemporary Scots-speaking area outwith the borders of Scotland, it deserves more detailed consideration.

The official Plantation of Ulster in the reign of James VI took place only in the counties west of the River Bann. There, English and Scottish 'undertakers' settled with their countrymen on lands granted by the Crown. The result is an ethnic and linguistic patchwork which is still discernible; the localities which the Scots settled in East Donegal, Derry and Tyrone are still Scots in speech. The Revd John

Graham of Maghera in County Londonderry described the situation as it pertained in the early nineteenth century:

> In reporting the language and customs peculiar to this neighbourhood, attention must be paid to the usual division of the inhabitants into English, Irish and Scotch. The dialect and customs of these distinct races are as different from each other as their respective creeds . . . The Dissenters speak broad Scotch, and are in the habit of using terms and expressions long since obsolete, even in Scotland, and which are only to be found in the glossary annexed to the Bishop of Dunkeld's translation of Virgil.

The reference to the poetry of Gavin Douglas is apt, not only because Ulster Scots, being more remote from the anglicising influences which swept Scotland, preserves older forms of the language but also because the Scots 'ower the sheugh', as they call it, continued to have a passion for literature in Scots. But whereas Scots settlement west of the Bann is interspersed with English and Irish communities, Antrim, North Down and the Ards Peninsula are almost entirely Scots in culture and language, with the native Irish community speaking a form of Ulster Scots as well. When Irish-speaking seasonal labourers travelled from West Donegal to help in the harvest in the rich farmlands of lowland Ulster, they made reference to 'lifting the Scotch' – picking up the language of the farmers. These areas of East Ulster began to be settled before the official Plantation and continued to attract immigrants from Scotland long after the scheme had ended.

Inspired by the success of Burns, the area produced a prolific Scots poetic tradition, particularly among the hand-loom weavers; the same men were in the vanguard of the United Irishmen and their efforts to create Home Rule for Ireland in the 1790s. Then, Presbyterian dissenters and Catholics were united in the same cause. When the movement was quelled, many left Ulster for the religious freedom of America, the 'Scotch Irish', as they are called there, forming 15 per cent of the population at the beginning of the nineteenth century. James Orr of Ballycarry, County Antrim, described their departure in 'The Passengers':

> How calm an' cozie is the wight,
> Frae cares an' conflicts clear ay,
> Whase settled headpiece never made,
> His heels or han's be weary!

Perplex'd is he whase anxious schemes
Pursue applause, or siller,
Success nor sates, nor failure tames;
Bandied frae post to pillar
Is he, ilk day.

As we were, Comrades, at the time
We mov't frae Ballycarry,
To wan'er thro' the woody clime
Burgoyne gied oure to harrie:
Wi' frien's consent we prie't a gill,
An' monie a house did call at,
Shook han's, an' smil't; tho ilk fareweel
Strak, like a weighty mallet,
Our hearts, that day.

That stanza form of course is very common in Scots verse and is used by both Fergusson in 'Leith Races' and Burns in 'The Holy Fair'. The weaver poets were aware of the tradition to which they belonged and proud of it as an expression of community. Hugh Porter of Down writes:

And thirdly, in the style appears
The accent o' my earlier years
Which is not Scotch, nor English either,
But part o' baith mixed up thegither.
Yet it's the sort my neighbours use,
Wha think 'shoon' prettier far than 'shoes'.

Since the days of the United Irishmen, the pressures against Ulster Scots have been similar to those against Scots in Scotland, with the dialects there classified as 'provincial and barbaric'. That the professional classes were adopting Standard English and creating a division between themselves and the common people is revealed in James Orr's poem 'The Irish Cottier's Death and Burial', which is based on Burns' *The Cotter's Saturday Night*. Here, the local minister visits the home of a dying cottar:

The minister comes in, wha' to the poor,
Without a fee performs the doctor's part:
An' while wi' hope he soothes the suff'rer's heart,
An' gies a cheap, safe recipe, they try

To quat braid Scotch, a task that foils their art;
For while they join his converse, vain though shy,
They monie a lang learn'd word misca' an' misapply.

Today, the dialect is still widely spoken and the tradition of writing folk poetry in it prevails, as Alex McAllister from Larne humorously demonstrated in *The Mother Tongue*. Until recently, it had suffered from the same lack of status as in Scotland and, as here, the prevailing feeling was that it was dying. As is the case here, though, it has a long time to go yet. The following extract from *The Humours of Druids Island* by Archibald McIlroy gives the flavour of the Antrim dialect at the turn of the twentieth century. It concerns some ladies gathering for tea:

> No yin o' the ithers had the guid manners tae tak' aff their gloves, which made it very awkward for me, – for on account of my rheumatics, a wear knitted wool gloves a' the year roon. A didna daur tak' them aff, an' no a haet could a dae wi them on; for while a was fummlin an tryin tae get a haud o the wee bit cup han'le the half o the tay got jebbled intae the saucer.
>
> The slice o' breid fell in pieces in my lap; for a couldna bring mysel' tae rowl it up like a lettuce as the ithers were daein', havin' always been teach't that it's the worst o' manners tae dooble up yer piece; an a was that much put aboot that a could nether eat nor drink; so a slipped oot my han'kerchie', gathered up the breid in't an stuffed it in my pocket; an what was left o the tay a emp'ied intae a floerpot that was sittin' on the table; an dae ye know, they wur a' that busy gossipin' intae ithers lugs that no yin o' them saw me.

In recent years, the promotion of Ulster Scots has received a dramatic boost through the language being tied in to political changes brought about by the Good Friday Agreement. Today, people driving into the town of Ards, south of Belfast, are regaled with the welcoming sign 'Fair Fa Ye Tae the Airds', while nearby in Greyabbey, street signs like 'Hard Breid Raa' proclaim the area's linguistic identity. In North Belfast, bilingual signs announce both 'Silverstream Park' and 'Sillerburn Pairk', and if the Ulster-Scots Culture Group in the area has its way, the Shankill Road – a name of Irish origin – will soon acknowledge the Lowland Scots roots of some of its people with signs reading 'Auld Kirk Raa'. In stark contrast to our own parliament, the Northern Ireland Assembly will employ someone to keep records in Ulster Scots. All of these are manifestations of a remarkable process of cultural rediscovery by a people who until recently were thirled to the twin monoliths of British and Irish identities within the province.

Like Monsieur Jourdain in Molière's *Le Bourgeois Gentilhomme*, who is astonished to find out that he has been speaking prose all his life without realising it, the Ulster Scots community is becoming increasingly aware of a hitherto suppressed and despised linguistic identity. In seeking parity for Scots with Irish, the Scots activists have stirred up a bee's byke of varied reactions – not surprising when they provocatively point out that the 100,000-plus speakers of Scots in the province are native speakers, while the 100,000-plus speakers of Irish are learners from the current revival – the last indigenous Irish speakers having died out early in the twentieth century. The republican newspaper the *Andersonstown News* dismissed Ulster Scots as a 'Do-It-Yourself language for Orangemen', while unionist reaction varies from totally supportive to totally dismissive. The latter regret the 'waste' of so much money being devoted to Irish and have no desire to see it repeated with Scots. Its unionist supporters, on the other hand, see the massive sums of money given to Irish cultural activities in the nationalist community and want similar resources to be made available to what they see as their ain folk.

As with any hauden doun tongue surviving only as an oral medium, then seeking status as a written language, the sight of an Ulster Scots hoatchin wi neologisms in official statements such as 'New Graith Officer for Ulstèr-Scotch Heirskip Cooncil' has provoked hostility and ridicule. The fact that the vigorous pro-Scots lobby has been active only since the early 1990s has entrenched the view that it is merely an invented and artificial unionist front created to deprive nationalists of the cultural funding they have successfully fought for. With £1,000 of public funding spent on Irish to every £1 spent on Ulster Scots, protagonists in the Irish lobby may well be looking over their shoulders with a mixture of guilt and trepidation. What they should not do, however, is dismiss a culture with such deep, lasting and tangible roots in Ireland.

Throughout the eighteenth century, editions of Barbour's epic *The Brus* and Blin Hary's *The Wallace*, and the poetry of Sir David Lyndsay and Alexander Montgomerie, were available in chapbook form or in Belfast editions. When the new Scots poetry of the eighteenth-century vernacular revival reached Ulster, not only was it a huge popular success – children could recite whole sections of Ramsay's *Gentle Shepherd* – but it also sparked off a vibrant Ulster Scots poetic revival, especially among the region's radical weavers, many of whom took part in the United Irishmen rebellion of 1798. Much of the excellent poetry produced then remained underground until it was revived by the respected poet John Hewitt in his seminal book *Rhyming Weavers* of 1974.

One of the first encouraging signs of the current wave of interest was the formation of the Ulster-Scots Language Society in 1992 and the publication of a series of fine volumes called *The Folk Poets of Ulster*, which included writers such as Samuel Thomson, James Orr and Hugh Porter. This Scots tradition in literature is still ingrained in the character of East Ulster writing today, with work by poets such as John Clifford, Oonagh McClean and the comic performance verse of the late lamented Alec McAllister providing an unbroken link with the revival of the eighteenth century. The novels of the late Sam Hanna Bell are also graced with a native felicity in the use of Scots vernacular. Born in Glasgow, Bell moved back to the County Down home of his maternal grandmother when he was a child and lived there the rest of his life. I still recall Sam's face lighting up when he told me the story of a Ballymena man discussing the birth of a neighbouring Englishman's son. 'Whit are ye gaun tae cry him?' said the Ballymena man. 'Well, we were thinking of calling him Nathan,' replied the Englishman. 'Get awa oot o that,' said the Ballymena man, 'ye'll hae tae cry him somethin!'

Given the speed with which Scottish colonists have divested themselves of their native tongues elsewhere in the world in more recent times – a process which has its roots in the colonised mentality of the Scots since the Union of 1707 – the most remarkable feature of the Ulster communities is their retention of Scots in their everyday speech. Many of the areas have not had a fresh influx of Scots settlers for more than 300 years and have been exposed to the anglicising 'improvers' as much as any place in Scotland, yet their Scots is thrang with words you rarely come across in Scotland: *ferntickles* (freckles), *gowpinfu* (two handfuls), *forenenst* (opposite), *wale* (select) and *couter* (ploughhead) are a few of the words I have recorded folk using, all set in a dialect as rich as anything in my native Ayrshire. Indeed, native Scots from an urban background often comment on how they have extended their own knowledge of Scots through living in Ulster.

Adding piquancy to the current debate is the fact that one of the strongest Scots-speaking areas actually lies in the Irish Republic, with the Scots lobby there demanding the rights of a linguistic minority. The marked Lowland Scots strand in the English spoken in the *Gaeltacht* of West Donegal came from seasonal migration to both

Scotland and the fertile east of the county. One West Donegal harvester in the nineteenth century addressed a traveller in his home area thus: 'It's the Irish we speak among wursels, but we hae eneuch Scotch to speak till yer honer.' The Ulster-Scots Heritage Council has targeted the Donegal Scots issue as one which will raise awareness and gain publicity for the Scots language cause.

Inclusiveness, however, must always be an ideal and a priority in Ulster if the old divisions are to be healed. That process is already taking place and one of the joys about continuing contact with the region is the number of times the stereotypes only too prevalent outwith Ulster are shattered by what is happening in the community itself. A few years ago, I spoke at a conference about Ireland and Scotland in Wigtown. Among the entertainers for the evening ceilidh were an exhilarating Irish dance group. In the recent past, they would have been exclusively Roman Catholic, but all these girls were from the heart of Protestant East Belfast. Similarly, I once attended a ceilidh in East Antrim and presumed that the hilarious folk poetry in the local Scots dialect was being performed by a member of the local Protestant majority. It was not, and the warmth of feeling was devoted to Alec McAllister, a Catholic from Larne. In most of the country areas, of course, overt sectarian hostility was and still is a rarity. Nevertheless, it is fine to see culture being used to bridge the divide. One of the courses planned for Scots language learners in the province will take place in a predominantly Catholic area of Armagh. With an egalitarian tradition ingrained in Scots, it is encouraging to see this positive force for good again at work in one of the language's traditional heartlands. However, it is hard to accept the fact that Ulster Scots in Ireland receives more recognition and, crucially, more government support than Scots in Scotland. What a strange country we belong to.

SOUTHERN SCOTS

Southern Scots, or Border Scots, as it is sometimes called, is the dialect spoken in the counties of Roxburgh, Selkirk and East Dumfriesshire. Apart from a stretch of land between Carlisle and Gretna where Scots and the Cumbrian dialect mix and merge – a linguistic parallel to the old 'Debatable Grund' between the two kingdoms – the dialects spoken on either side of the border are markedly different. The *Scottish National Dictionary* affirms this: 'For all practical purposes the political and linguistic boundaries may be considered to coincide.'

The most noticeable feature of this dialect to Scots speakers from other areas is the lack of what we think of as the characteristically

Scots sounds of 'oo' in *doon*, *coo* and *broon*, and 'ee' in *wee*, *bree* and *gie*, and their replacement with the diphthongs 'ow' and 'ey', which sound English to us. For this reason, it is often known as the 'yow an mey' dialect, a feature emphasised by local rhymes:

> Yow an' meyee, an the bern dor keyee,
> The sow an' the threyee weyee pigs.

> Yow an mey'll gang out an pow a pey
> (you and me will go out and pull a pea)

Diphthongs are fairly rare in Scots, so the prevalence of them within a rich dialect of the language strikes the outsider as unusual. Another vowel which is diphthongised is the 'ai' sound in *baith*, *braid* and *claes*, which here becomes something like *beeath*, *breead* and *cleeaz*. Another feature of the dialect which closely resembles English is their use of a vowel sound similar to the southern Standard English 'back', 'bad' and 'bat'. Other dialect speakers used to send up the Borderers 'posh' accent by pronouncing Nellie as *Nallie*, bed as *bad*, and pen as *pan*. The people who speak 'the saft lawland tongue o the Border' take all this in their stride; pushed up against the border, they have an intense national pride in their Scottishness, an identity enhanced by being tied in with the fierce local loyalties you can feel in ancient burghs like Selkirk, and not only at Common Riding time. Walter Elliot of Selkirk writes articles on Border Scots for the *Southern Reporter* and also publishes local poetry in Scots. The poem that begins *The clash-ma-clavers Chap Book* makes wry comment on the changeover from Scots to English in his native Ettrick:

> Ah only sterted writin
> Tae preserve ma mither tongue
> An the language that was spoken
> In the days when Ah was young.

> Noo there's fewer folk in Ettrick,
> It's maistly aa wee trees
> An Dykers are ootnumbered
> Bie Liberal MPs.

> Then there's the Ettrick English
> (An they're really aa nice folk)
> Bit they didnae ken oor faithers
> Or the language that they spoke.

Ah hope ye'll like the efforts
In this wee book o rhyme.
The verse is often rotten
Bit the language is sublime.

Much of the beautiful Border country has been settled by retired people from England, another phenomenon affecting the linguistic balance in the region. The Borderers tend to 'gang thegither' when their culture is threatened, and their innate thrawnness makes them hold on to their Scots and no be blate to use it in every social circumstance. They are aware that the Border ballads are among the finest composed in any language; the language happens to be Border Scots and they see no reason why they should give it up.

Another unique feature of Southern Scots is the large number of words which have entered the Scots of the area from the Romany language of the gypsies who were always associated with Yetholm in Roxburghshire. Words like *barry*, meaning good, or *radge*, meaning enraged or excited, spread into the mixed Scots/English speech of Berwick nearby and, more recently, have become part of the colloquial vocabulary of urban teenagers elsewhere in Scotland. This verse by Thomas Grey, published in the *Berwick Advertiser* in 1910, gives a flavour of the Romany words:

A 'Gadgie' when he is a 'Chor'
A 'Jugal' always fears,
For 'Jugals' as a rule are kept
By 'Gadgies' with big 'keirs'.

(*gadgie* man; *chor* thief; *jugal* dog; *keir* house)

Although the characteristics mentioned make this dialect unique, it is still one which in its intonation and pronunciation is not unlike the Central Scots dialects lying to the east and west, and north to West Angus and Perthshire. It is only there, north-east of Dundee, that we enter the dialects of Northern Scots, which are so different and distinct from Central Scots that some regard, for example, the Buchan dialect almost as a separate language; it is not, and once the lugs have adjusted to the radically different intonation, pronunciation and sounds of these dialects, you soon realise that they are simply beautiful, richly textured dialects of the same language that is spoken in the south of the country.

NORTHERN SCOTS

Northern Scots stretches from East Angus and the Mearns in the south to Caithness in the north and includes the great bulge of fertile land between the Moray Firth and the North Sea known as the North-east, an area which has strong claims to be the heartland of spoken Scots in our day. Coastal Angus and the Mearns appears to be a transitional area from Central Scots to North-east Scots. It has some but not all of the distinguishing features of the North-east. Here, as further north, Central Scots 'aw' in *braw* and *baw* becomes *braa* and *baa*; *bane* and *stane* become *been* and *steen*; and *wha* and *whit* become *fa* and *fit*.

But once you are north of Stonehaven and beyond the Dee, the sound-changes from Central Scots become more numerous and distinctive. While the Mearns has the 'f' sound only in the words who, where, what and when, in Aberdeenshire and Buchan the 'f' replaces 'wh' in almost every instance: whistle and whippet become *fussle* and *fuppet*. Central and North-east Scots differ radically in their vowel sounds: *muin* and *spuin* become *meen* and *speen*; *guid* and *schuil* become *gweed* and *skweel*; the vowel in *wey* is pronounced almost like the 'oy' in 'boy', Central Scots *Whit wey?* becoming North-east *Fit woi?*; Central Scots *wame* becomes *wyme*; the 'ea' sound in *speik* or *sweit* becomes *spyke* and *swyte*; and *naikit* and *caird* become *nyakit* and *cyard*. In the Buchan dialect, there are consonant changes as well: *faither*, *mither* and *brither* become *fader*, *midder* and *bridder*; *wrocht* and *wricht* become *vrocht* and *vricht*; and the unsounded 'k' in *knie* or *knock* is sounded in the North-east, as it is in German. This is a sound that is dying out of the dialect now. Similarly, the 'gn' of *gnaw* used to be sounded and still is in the word *gnap*; *gnappin* or *gneppin* is the derogatory term people in the Northern Scots area use for folk who affect English, or talk posh. The strength and vitality of Scots in the area is such that even those who gnap take an interest in the Doric as an expression of the strong regional identity. That identity has been seen by outsiders as a parochial one and sent up in apocryphal stories such as the mythical (I hope) headline in Aberdeen's *Press and Journal*, 'North-east Man Drowned', with in smaller letters beneath, '*Titanic* sinks'.

The identity is undoubtedly a source of the strength of traditional Scots culture in the area and other regions of Scotland could be doing with a bit of it. But it is an identity produced by very different social circumstances from those which pertained in, for example, the central Lowlands. There, industrialisation and the resultant influx of immigrants changed the local language and culture dramatically. In the North-east, farming and fishing were the mainstays of the economy until very recently – activities which encouraged local culture and speech to thrive isolated from outside influences. Indeed, the North-east is home to a series of local cultures and dialects rather than a monolithic, homogeneous one. The fishing communities were traditionally cut off from the farming hinterland and you can hear the result of that in the local variations of the dialect. Lossiemouth and Hopeman on the Morayshire coast differ from each other considerably but they share features which do not prevail in the rural dialects inland. Again, Hopeman is different from Burghead a mile or so along the coast; the linguistic line separating Scots and Highland English appears to pass between the towns, creating markedly different ways of speaking in the two commmunities. Moray and Nairn generally differ from the rest of the North-east area in that they do not have the Buchan *meer* and *peer* sound but the more common Scots *muir* and *puir*.

The self-contained nature and comparative isolation of the fishing and farming communities mean that the Scots of the region is conservative and auld farrant, preserving a wealth of vocabulary which has been lost in other areas. The spoken dialects are strong and it is just as well; the rapid social change in the area precipitated by the discovery of oil has produced the same kind of challenge to the local culture as that posed by industrialisation to the south of the country in the late eighteenth and early nineteenth centuries. The romantic image of rangy chieldes like Long Rob and Chae in *Sunset Song* speaking pure Doric in a remote howe somewhere ayont Alford I am afraid is becoming less and less based on reality. Such has been the effect of the arrival of people from outwith the area that the old certainties of this unique dialect surviving unaided are having to be reassessed.

In some airts, incoming children are picking up the local dialect and, like the locals, becoming bilingual. In other areas, the dialect is redundant. A teacher in a town north of Aberdeen said that he could point exactly to the age group which had stopped using it. Thus he had older pupils whose lingua franca was Scots but younger ones who had ceased using it actively and whose mother tongue appeared to be Scottish Standard English. I say 'appeared', because the same younger pupils may still use it in the home or their passive knowledge of the Doric may be activated in later life. But in public, it has gone and they call country children who still speak it 'cheuchters'.

This process is happening despite the fact that Scottish literature traditionally appears to have been given higher status by education authorities in the North-east than elsewhere in the country. From Alexander Ross at the end of the eighteenth century through till the present day, the North-east has been the most vital area in regional literature in Scots, with poets like David Rorie, Charles Murray, J.C. Milne and Flora Garry contributing important work. This is an example, Flora Garry's poem 'Bennygoak':

It was jist a skelp of the muckle furth,
A skylter o roch grun,
Fin grandfadder's fadder bruke it in
Fae the hedder an the funn.
Granfadder sklatit barn an byre,
Brocht water to the closs,
Pat fail-dykes ben the bare brae face
An a cairt road tull the moss.

Bit wir fadder sottert i the yard
An skeppit amo' bees
An keepit fancy dyeuks an doos
'at warna muckle eese.
He bocht aul' wizzent horse an kye
An scrimpit muck an seed;
Syne, clocherin wi a craichly hoast,
He dwine't awa, an deed.

I look far ower by Ythanside
To Fyvie's laich, lythe lan's,
To Auchterless an Bennachie
An the mist-blue Grampians.
Sair't o the hull o Bennygoak
An scunnert o the ferm,
Gin I bit daar't, gin I bit daar't,
I'd flit the comin' term.

(*funn* whin; *closs* farmyard; *fail-dyke* sod wall; *sottert* idled; *skeppit amo' bees* kept bees; *dyeuks an doos* ducks and doves; *craichly hoast* wheezing cough; *dwine* fade; *laich* low)

The test, I suppose, is whether the Doric can adapt to the new economy of the area. The fact that Aberdeen city is still, in general, healthily Scots in speech is a sign that it may do. Outsiders used to smile when Aberdeen shop assistants said, 'Hae a braa day' – the translation of the ubiquitous Americanism 'Have a nice day' – but it is nevertheless a sign of adaptation to outside influence rather than renunciation of the local language. The culture clash is being exploited by the writers. This is a verse from Donald Gordon's poem 'Cultural Revolution':

> As I gaed by the College Croon
> I spied a braw-like carriage.
> A denty lass wis steppin doon,
> Aa buskit for her marriage.
> Quo I: 'Ye tak a Buchan lad?
> For o but they are gallus!'
> Quo she: 'You must be joking, Dad,
> My luve was born in Dallas.'

More than any other Scottish city, Aberdeen maintains close links with its hinterland. That is another reason why North-east literature enjoys such popularity and credence within education, for there is little of the notion of two cultures – the urban versus rural conflict which bedevils attitudes to Scots in Glasgow, for example. One of the finest poets writing in Scots to emerge in recent years is Sheena Blackhall. In her poetry, she celebrates both her country roots on Deeside and present day life in a scheme in Aberdeen. This is her 'Delinquent's Sang':

> I am o Clootie's kin,
> I am the rib o Cain,
> I gaed tae ma mither fur breid,
> Fur breid, an she gied me a stane.
>
> I am the scud and the skelp,
> The heid bang, the snot on the face.
> I am the slash. I'm the whelp,
> Shunted frae ilkie place.
>
> I am the spit on the slab,
> King o the strut. Haud ower!
> I gaed tae ma da fur a kiss,
> A kiss, an he gied me a cloor.
>
> Write me doon on the waa,
> Doon as a snappin breet,
> Doon as a hoodie craw,

Doon as a mushroom geet.
Crucified, I will bleed
Reid, as the hunger o hate.
Fa will unlock my nieve?
Polis, or shrink, or state?

See me, in gutter or gang,
Ootlinned in ilkie toon.
I am the scapegoat o aa,
Weirin the thorned croon.
I am yer brither. Haud me.
Haud me, or cut me doon.

That poem is recognisably North-east but is written in a Scots accessible to all who read or speak the language. In the past, it was much more of a dialect literature, with the spellings often reflecting local forms rather than following the more classical spelling conventions of literary Scots. This is how William Alexander opens his novel *Johnny Gibb of Gushetneuk*; the orra loon Tam Meerison is helping Johnny to yoke the cairt. As with the Burns letter earlier, ye'll hae tae consult the dictionary for the vocabulary:

'Heely, heely, Tam, ye glaiket stirk – ye hinna on the hin shelvin' o' the cairt. Fat hae ye been haiverin at, min? That cauf saick'll be tint owre the back door afore we win a mile fae hame. See't yer belly-ban' be ticht aneuch noo. Woo, lassie! man, ye been makin' a hantle mair adee aboot blaikin that graith o' yours, an' kaimin the mear's tail, nor balancin' yer cairt, an' gettin' the things packit in till't.'

'Sang, that's nae vera easy deen, I can tell ye, wi' sic a mengyie o' them. Faur'll aw pit the puckle girss to the mear?'

'Ou, fat's the eese o' that lang stoups ahin, aw wud like tae ken? Lay that bit bauk across, an' syne tak' the aul' pleuch ryn there, an wup it ticht atween the stays; we canna hae the beast's maet trachel't amo' their feet. Foo muckle corn pat ye in?'

'Four lippies – gweed-mizzour – will that dee?'

'We'se lat it be deein. Is their trock a' in noo, I won'er?'

'Nyod, seerly it is.'

The last branch of Northern Scots is spoken in a few coastal settlements in Easter Ross, Inverness-shire and Sutherland, and more substantially in the populous lowland east of Caithness. Caithness apart, this area has been Gaelic speaking until comparatively recently in its linguistic history; when Gaelic has waned, it has tended to be replaced with Highland English rather than Scots. Communities like Avoch in the Black Isle, however, have been Scots-speaking plantations in the *Gaidhealtachd* since the seventeenth century. Surrounded by Gaelic and separated from other Scots-speaking communities until recently, Avoch preserves older forms of Scots which have died out elsewhere and which appear 'foreign' to other Scots speakers. These examples of the old Avoch dialect from the *Scottish National Dictionary* illustrate the point well: 'Twuz a braa knap o' a sheelie an' no a dymock' – 'it was a fine knap of a boy and not a girl'; 'Al keyme thee dossan for thee' – 'I'll comb your hair for you.'

The Black Isle and Caithness dialects share the same features which distinguish this dialect area from the North-east. The diphthong 'ow' is common: *dowg* for dog, *cowld* for cold, *bowld* for bold. These remind one of Irish English. Curiously, the same sound occurs in Kintyre, a similar Scots-speaking island surrounded by a sea of Gaelic. It is possibly a Gaelic influence on the speech, for the Caithness dialect includes many Gaelic as well as Norse words in its vocabulary. Other noticeable features in the speech of people from Caithness are the use of 'sh' for 'ch', making cheese and chimney in the dialect *sheeze* and *shumley*; and the replacement of the initial 'j' sound in judge and jury with 'ch', giving *chudge* and *chury*. The 'th' at the beginning of the, that, they, there, etc. is dropped, giving *ee*, *at*, *ey* and *ere*, for example, 'Fas at ere?' – 'Who's that there?' Often in Caithness dialect, in the, on the, at the, of the are reduced to the sound 'e', giving, for example, 'He bides 'e centre 'e toon' – 'He lives in the centre of the town.' Caithness and Sutherland were at one time part of the Norse sphere of influence and the John o' Groats area is particularly close to Orkney in speech. The Scandinavian linguistic heritage is even more clearly evident in the dialects of Orkney and Shetland.

INSULAR SCOTS

The dialects of the Northern Isles differ from the Scots of mainland Scotland as a result of the more recent and profound influence that the Norse language exercised there. Scots already has a strong Scandinavian legacy: *to flit*, *to big* (build), *loof* (palm) and *nieve* (fist) are just a few everyday examples in the language. Some of these words have been in Scots since the settlers from the English Danelaw established themselves in the new burghs in the eleventh century. In Orkney and Shetland, however, the Norse influence was much more direct because of the Norse occupation of these islands from the eighth to the fifteenth century. The islands were transferred from Danish to Scottish jurisdiction in 1468. Only then did the Scandinavian language of the islands, Norn, come into constant contact with Scots. Through the political power enjoyed by the Scots, the Norn language was gradually eroded and replaced by Scots over the following centuries. There was a period of bilingualism; in 1680, a minister reported of the people of Cunningsburgh in Shetland: '[They] seldom speak other [than Norn] among themselves, yet all of them speak the Scots tongue more promptly and more properly than generally they do in Scotland.' The similarities between Scots and Norn, and the number of shared words, facilitated the transition from Norn to Scots, as it facilitated the transition from Scots to English more recently. Dr Hugh Marwick, in the introduction to his book *The Orkney Norn*, states:

> Before it ultimately died, the Norn tongue must have been increasingly impregnated with words from Scots. Yet the change was something more than a steady inflation of Norn with Scots words, until it became more Scots than Norn. What probably happened was that the common everyday phraseology of Norn ceased and was replaced by the corresponding Scots terms of speech.

Although Scots and eventually English replaced Norn, there remained many words from the older language which continued in everyday use by the people of the islands. When the Faeroese scholar Jakob Jakobsen researched the Norn influence on the Shetland dialect at the end of the nineteenth century, he found that 10,000 words of Norn origin were still extant, though half of them were only remembered by older folk. Many of the words were intimately bound to the local way of life and the sensitivity to the natural environment required of fishermen and crofters: *pirr*, *laar*, *flan*, *bat*, *gouster* and *vaelensi* are different strengths and kinds of wind. Some of these words are still in common use, though in the introduction to *The Shetland Dictionary* John J. Graham points out that of the 720 words beginning with 'h' in Jakobsen's dictionary, approximately 65 could be identified by a young Shetlander today. The dialects of the Northern Isles also preserve older forms of Scots and vocabulary like *owsen*, *thrawart* and *grice* which has disappeared from most mainland dialects.

Because of the isolated nature of the many island communities in both Orkney and Shetland, there are many locally distinct features in the various dialects. The following are a few of the more general

195

features of Insular Scots. Voiced 'th' is replaced by 'd', so the becomes *da*; thy, thee and thine are all still current in Shetland, pronounced *dy*, *dee* and *dine*, as in the following example from *The Shetland Dictionary*: 'I hoop dy bairn is as göd ta dee is my ane has bön ta me.' The unvoiced 'th' in, for example, thin, thick or thrapple becomes *tin*, *tick* or *trapple*. The personal pronoun has two forms, *du* and *you*, used like the French *tu* and *vous*. A Shetland girl I once knew used to greet me with the delightful, 'Foo is du, my chewel?', which is almost as nice in English: 'How are you, my jewel?' The auxiliary verb 'to be' is used in places where English has 'to have'; instead of 'I have written', 'I'm written' would be used.

The Shetland dialect in particular has undergone a revival of interest in recent years. The threat to the way of life posed by the oil industry has galvanised the people into action for their culture and a more enlightened attitude to the dialect exists in the local radio station and the local education authority than that which prevails in most parts of Scotland. The dialect's prestige is also helped with the growth of a strong literature, which has modern exponents like Rhoda Bulter and Robert Alan Jamieson. One of the most famous Shetland poems is 'Aald Maunsie's Crö' by Basil Anderson; the end of Maunsie ends my chapter on the dialects of Scots and provides an example of Shetland poetry:

> Time booed his rigg and shore his tap
> An laid his crö in mony a slap;
> Snug-shorded by his ain hert-steyn
> He lost his senses een by een,
> Till lyin helpless laek a paet
> Nor kail nor mutton he could aet,
> Sae deed, as what we au maun dö,
> Hae we or hae we no a crö.

(*crö* an enclosure for growing cabbages; *booed his rigg* bowed his backbone; *shore his tap* sheared his top; *slap* ditch; *shorded* propped, supported; *hert-steyn* hearthstone)

11

The Future Oors?

Back in my home town in Ayrshire recently, a local electrician came up to me in the pub and recounted for me an incident that had happened the day before: 'It wes gey nearhaun fower o clock, Billy, sae I says, "Richt, boys, redd up and gaither aw yer graith thegither, it's lowsin time." Juist then a bit came on the wireless aboot the daith o Scots an the expert lamented the fact that "once common words like 'graith' and 'redd' were no longer in currency". Me an the boys juist luiked at wan anither an speired whit kinna planet we wes leivin on!'

I think of such 'expertise' when I see anti-Scots harangues by such as Michael Fry in *The Sunday Times*. Mr Fry says that Scots does not exist but, like him, monie o thaim that threaps on aboot Scots wuidnae ken a Scots word gin it lowped up an skelped thaim on the puss! In recent years, we have seen the publication of L. Colin Wilson's *Luath Scots Language Learner*, the completion of the *Dictionary of the Older Scottish Tongue*, the launch of a plethora of Scots websites and the expansion of a series of highly successful children's books by the Itchy Coo project. And every time there is a wave of Scots creativity, as sure as night follows day, there will be a spate of newspaper articles saying what a waste of time it all is, as Scots is a dead or dying language. The detractors are obviously in serious denial, for in the past few years or so we have had novels by James Robertson, Matthew Fitt, Janet Paisley and Irvine Welsh, plays by David Greig and Liz Lochhead, festivals, music shows, poetry and performance, all in varieties of a very much living language which the General Register Office survey of 1996 estimated to have 1.5 million speakers – by far the greatest number of speakers of any indigenous minority language in the United Kingdom.

Many of those speakers, like me, experienced a Scottish education system which considered itelf successful if each generation was less Scottish than the one before and tholed bizarre anomalies such as being given a prize for reciting the Bard's poetry on Burns Day then getting belted for speaking his language every other day of the year. Despite such incongruities, Scots remained a crucial part of my family's identity, enriching every part of our lives, from the joy of a niece's wedding, where my daughter sang the Scots love song 'The Lea Rig', to the sadness of my father's funeral, when he joined my mother under a heidstane inscribed with the words 'Till a' the seas gang dry.'

Yet for most Scottish people, feelings about their native culture *are* fraught with powerful dichotomies which pull individuals in different directions. Pride and prejudice, love and hatred, reverence and contempt – Scots tend to react with extremes of feeling to different aspects of their culture. You may well say that is the right of the individual in every free nation, and I would agree. But the extreme reactions in Scotland are a direct result of the lack of Scottish content in the educational system and, to a lesser extent, the shortage of it in the all-pervasive media which helps form ideas in the twenty-first century. When Scottish history or literature is not taught, the implication for many is that it is not worth teaching. Many in fact draw the conclusion that it does not exist. With no grounding in their culture, objective assessment of its worth is well-nigh impossible and frequently people react with a passion which astonishes outsiders. The frequent eruption of letters discussing the minutiae of Scottish speech in *The Herald* and *The Scotsman*, for example, and the intensity of the debate provoked, is apparently a uniquely Scottish phenomenon.

This passion for things Scottish is often an instinctive gut reaction to the culture being put down by the authorities, the reaction against it often the product of derived irrational prejudice. Like Pavlov's slaiverin dugs, many Scots are conditioned to react to any aspect of their culture with the word 'parochial' or 'tartan' or 'couthy', no matter how universal the content may be. By doing programmes which have posed questions about people's cultural identity, I have often provoked strong reactions. The ratio is in the region of seven love letters to every three hostile letters. Into the latter category fell a lady from Alloway who wrote in high dudgeon, asserting that Scots did not exist and that my guests and I on Scottish Television's *Kay's Originals* series were all putting it on. We were a disgrace to Scotland

and what would the English think! An example of our putting it on was our use of the place name Glesca. The lady had not, she assured me, heard it pronounced thus since she attended the music halls in the 1940s. In my reply, I asked her which institution she had been locked up in during the intervening years. Many Scots do not want to believe Scots exists and steik their lugs accordingly – I refuse to hear it, therefore it does not exist!

Yet hers is not an uncommon reaction. Lacking the objectivity education in the culture would give, the typical Scottish reaction is intensely personal rather than considered and objective. George Gordon, Lord Byron's autobiographical lines in the poem *Don Juan* sum up the dichotomy perfectly:

> But I am half a Scot by birth, and bred
> A whole one, and my heart flies to my head.

Being educated as an Englishman yet having folk-pride in being Scottish without knowing exactly why you should be proud is again a typical Scottish experience and has interesting social consequences. Every Scot will assert that he belongs to a nation rather than a region or a province. Ask the same person, however, whether the national history, literature and language should be integrated into the educational system and you will get a very different, possibly uncomfortable response. For this type of question demands a lot more of the person's Scottishness than supporting the fitba team and most have not had the training to help formulate a considered reply.

At the core of all this is the complex question of language. It is a veritable tinderbox of a subject, for although only a tiny group of people have had the opportunity to study it, everyone has very strong opinions on the matter. This is not surprising, as language is central to people's being and, as I have shown, Scotland has long been a linguistic battlefield. For many folk, the local dialect of Scots is literally the mither tongue and is held dear as an integral part of their identity, even though they are conditioned to speak it only in certain social situations. The heart and head division among native speakers of Scots is beautifully expressed by Lewis Grassic Gibbon in this famous passage from *Sunset Song:*

> So that was Chris and her reading and schooling, two Chrisses
> there were that fought for her heart and tormented her. You
> hated the land and the coarse speak of the folk and learning was
> brave and fine one day and the next you'd waken with the

peewits crying across the hills, deep and deep, crying in the heart of you and the smell of the earth in your face, almost you'd cry for that, the beauty of it and the sweetness of the Scottish land and skies. You saw their faces in firelight, father's and mother's and the neighbours', before the lamps lit up, tired and kind, faces dear and close to you, you wanted the words they'd known and used, forgotten in the far-off youngness of their lives, Scots words to tell to your heart, how they wrung it and held it, the toil of their days and unendingly their fight. And the next minute that passed from you, you were English, back to the English words so sharp and clean and true – for a while, for a while, till they slid so smooth from your throat you knew they could never say anything that was worth the saying at all.

If a little sentimental and very much based on the rural experience, passages like that were powerful enough to hook this 15-year-old town-dweller on literature when he was given the book as a school prize. It was the first time I realised that literature could be about me and mine, and the effect had the force of revelation. Gibbon's depiction of the Scots/English dichotomy of language fitted my own experience perfectly and made me understand it better.

Yet many make, I feel, false divisions between town and country speech, making evaluations based on class prejudice rather than linguistic truth. The 'peasant' of the country is regarded by the middle classes as an admirable character, while the 'keelie' of the city working class is despicable. It is a fallacy which goes back to the Romantic age; the German folklorist Johann Gottfried Herder encapsulated the belief in this statement about the urban masses: 'The mob in the streets which never sings or composes but shrieks and mutilates, is not the people.' I have had a few backhanders in print myself because of this prejudice. The television page of Glasgow's *Evening Times* printed beneath the billing for an *Odyssey* programme the words, 'Billy Kay, the man with the broadest accent in broadcasting, mouths gutteral [*sic*] noises about the Temperance Movement.' They did, however, have the courage to publish my reply which suggested that they were insulting not only me but 90 per cent of their readers who make the same 'guttural noises'.

Tragically, the urban versus rural division is a live and divisive issue among those who actually know something about the history of Scots and frequently use the language to excellent effect in poetry and prose. Many Glasgow writers will have nothing to do with Scots and relegate it as the irrelevant dialect of an idealised rural past. Its advocates are regarded as retrogressive nationalists. Much of this, however, is a perhaps understandable reaction against the dismissal of the Glasgow dialect by both English and Scots linguistic purists in the past. Fuelling the controversy is the unfortunate remark made in the introduction to the *Scottish National Dictionary* of 1929: 'Owing to the influx of Irish and foreign immigrants in the industrial area near Glasgow the dialect has become hopelessly corrupt.' The disenfranchisement of the huge immigrant population, which is now completely Scottish in culture, is implicit in that statement and is naturally a source of resentment.

However, the Lallans purists who dismiss urban speech as corrupt Scots and the urban writers who in turn dismiss Scots as an irrelevancy to modern industrial society are equally far off the mark. Scots is spoken in the cities and the urban dialects are every bit as vigorous and racy as the rural ones. Scots is also the language of people who live in towns and worked in mines and mills, a language of gusty realism and a lifestyle quite removed from the rural idyll. Scots is also the language of the ethnic groups who have added their distinctive contributions to Scottish society. The immigrants learned the language of the people and the people's language was and is a form of Scots. I was never able to record the Scots/Yiddish dialect of the Jewish commercial travellers recalled lovingly by David Daiches in his autobiography *Two Worlds: An Edinburgh Jewish Childhood*, where a common barmitzvah saying was 'Wull ye hae a drap o the bramfen' – the Yiddish for whisky! I have, however, recorded for *Odyssey* the rich mell of Scots spoken by first-generation Lithuanians, Italians and Spaniards in different parts of Scotland. The last group settled in the iron and coal area of Logan, near Cumnock in South Ayrshire. I remember beginning an interview with an old man born in Seville, both of us speaking our Ayrshire Scots. Shortly into the interview, however, Mr Esquierdo gradually switched to English and would have continued in the same vein had his wife not intervened, 'Talk Scoatch, you, stoap pittin it oan.' She too was born in Spain but, like the people around her, had absorbed Scots as the language closest to her adopted community – a source of identity for her and her family.

The artificial divisions that have arisen between Scots purists on the one side and Glasgow writers on the other is one in which reaction against what one side has said prevails over logic. Entrenched positions have been established which are untenable because there are no hard-and-fast rules in language – it is fluid, flexible and ever-changing. Besides, the pressures against local speech forms are exactly the same in rural Buchan and urban Glasgow, and it is time the different factions realised this and called for acceptance of all speech forms indigenous to the country. In doing that, a national focus would be a lot more powerful than a local one based on the Doric or Glaswegian.

One of the fundamental problems facing the continuation of Scots and all the facets of Scottish culture which make the country distinctive is the conflict between regional and national identities within Scotland, and the country's definition as a region in the rest of the UK. The desire to encourage Scottish culture often runs up against the fear of upsetting the monolithic British status quo, the values of which the majority of Scots are conditioned to adhere to. J. Derrick McClure examines the phenomenon in detail in *Chapman* 41, where he quotes the following responses from teachers asked to consider the feasibility and desirability of expanding Scottish studies in the schools and introducing a separate SED paper on Scottish literature and language:

> Scottish studies have a place in education, but I'm suspicious of the intentions behind the movement. All children should be encouraged to take an interest in their cultural heritage as a means of aiding the discovery of their own identity, both local and national – this, however, shouldn't simply become a means of instilling political values.

> Where do we draw the line in defining national heritage? The implications may be too far-reaching, especially in the political sense.

Now, there is nothing inherently political in wanting to teach a country's heritage – the opportunity of learning about one's own culture and history should be the birthright of all humankind. But Scots culture has been suppressed or remained on the periphery for so long that the thought of giving it status provokes feelings of unease and insecurity. This reaction is provoked both by guilt feelings about ignorance of things Scottish and fear of the responsibility of having to teach them on the part of teachers who have not themselves been educated in the subject. Fear of political implications – claymores under the bed – the dismissal of Scots literature as 'difficult' or 'parochial', or 'not as good as Shakespeare' are all expressions of the same syndrome: the conflict between the national and the provincial in the Scottish mentality.

THE FUTURE OORS?

Fionn MacColla went to the root of the conflict in his book *At the Sign of the Clenched Fist:* 'Scottish education regards itself as successful, as having fulfilled its objective, in proportion as each generation is less Scottish than the last, in language, knowledge, culture, and consciousness.' Although the situation has improved dramatically, MacColla's statement still rings true to the experience of most Scots alive today. The Portuguese colonists in Africa gave the name *assimilado* to members of the native population who adopted not only the language and the culture of Portugal but also the Portuguese contempt for the native culture. To some extent, Scotland is a country of *assimilados*, with everyone educated here inheriting this ambivalence about the Scottish/English balance within themselves and their culture. Some refer to it as the Scottish cringe, and it affects every individual and every institution.

BBC Scotland, for example, is defined within the Corporation as a 'national region'. It is constantly trying to work out whether it is 'regional' or 'national' and quite often finds it difficult to ride both horses at once. The BBC Charter states that its aim is to reflect the distinctive features of Scottish culture. A sign of its having achieved that goal will be when Scots, along with Scottish English and Gaelic, is accepted as a natural medium of communication. A few years ago, when Radio Scotland encouragingly broadcast *Amang Guid Companie*, a series of six interviews by me in Scots, the reaction within the BBC was the usual mixture of approval and disapproval. The disapprovers' main plank is the inappropriateness of 'coorse' Scots and the need for one constant broadcasting register – Standard English, of course. One producer was heard to say: 'My mother didn't allow me to speak that way, so why are we broadcasting in it?' In response, a Gael said that the level of debate reminded her of the sterility of the 'tinker Gaelic' stushie within the Gaelic media in the 1960s, when the Lewis dialect used by the majority of speakers was not considered fit for broadcast.

As you have seen, it is a problem confronted by all lesser-used languages, from Gaeldom to Galicia, the problem of 'normalising' a language for broadcast which has hitherto been deemed unsuitable. 'Artificial' is the accusation frequently levelled at me for using my mither tongue in formal, public situations where Scots speakers are expected to and conditioned to defer to English. The accusation generally comes from monoglot English speakers. The greatest vitriol, however, is thrown by bourgeois aspirants from working-class backgrounds like my own. Having been conditioned to lose their Scots and ditch the culture of their people, they naturally harbour deep-seated guilt complexes about the whole matter. They cannot thole seeing someone who has rejected the socialisation they are thirled to being himself, and successful forbye! By speaking Scots in the media, what I am doing is both totally natural – a native speaker using his mother tongue – and totally artificial – native speakers of my mother tongue have never previously had the opportunity or confidence in their ability to use their language as the medium for serious discussion. It is the scenario which is artificial, with many people so conditioned to expect English there that anything else comes across as strange.

Even generally supportive critics, who at the very least have a knowledge of Scots as a literary language and should know better, are drawn into the trap and have used words like 'synthetic' and 'artificial' when discussing the programmes. Everyone I know who shares my conviction about the need to extend the use of Scots in the public domain and has the strength of character to go against their socialisation and use their Scots in public has experienced similar stounds to their sensibilities. The poet Ellie McDonald was criticised by a family friend for demeaning herself and using 'coorse' Dundee Scots in one broadcast. 'How dae ye explain tae an auld bodie that ye're makin a political statement?' said Ellie. Sadly, she is correct. There should be nothing more natural in the world than using our first language in our national media, but the majority of us are so uneducated in our own culture that to use the native language of what I would still consider to be the majority of Scots can indeed be regarded as making a political statement. For the language to break out of the cycle of ignorance, confusion and erosion that besets it, however, a lot more people are going to have to start making that same 'political statement'. Fortunately, for the native speakers of the language and the vast majority of the listeners and viewers, this political dimension does not intrude. Programmes in Scots are simply a breath of caller air, confirming for them the power and beauty of their mither tongue.

Politics, in support or suppression, are central to the fate of languages. Yet political support at a given time is not in itself enough to guarantee a language's survival if the historical process which has eroded it has been unrelenting over centuries and has pushed the language to a geographical and psychological periphery in the nation's consciousness. That is certainly the case with Irish and until recently was certainly the case with Gaelic. The principal reason why Welsh is in a much stronger position than Scottish Gaelic today is that the Welsh had not posed a political threat to the British state for hundreds of years, while Gaelic was the language of the Jacobite forces which almost overthrew the state in the rebellions of the eighteenth century. The attempts at linguistic genocide foisted on the Gaels stem from this period and this fact. In modern times, both languages were expected to die slowly by neglect. It was when the Welsh again became a threat through burnings, hunger strikes and political lobbying that they forced the Government to recognise the language and create S4C, the Welsh television channel, which is one of the major focuses for the language's survival. Many Gaels believe that the Welsh kicked the door open for them to walk through. The Gaels did not need to be militant. Their recent success in gaining massive funding for Gaelic television has been achieved through sustainedly brilliant lobbying by professionals working in the field of promoting the language. They have used economic and cultural arguments, deliberately avoiding becoming embroiled in politics, especially party politics.

Just as the Gaels learned and gained from the Welsh, the Scots language movement can act on the experience of the Gaels. Our problem is that, as yet, there is no full-time professional working to lobby support for Scots at government level, though there are many volunteers working hard at local level in the fields of culture and education. In the media, a lot of hard work is necessary to convince television especially of its responsibility towards Scots. The BBC has produced good educational programmes on language and in oral-history-based documentaries has shown that Scots can be an effective and popularly acclaimed medium. Scottish Television has sporadically produced stimulating series in Scots and on Scots. Border and Grampian's contribution has been negligible. All of their attitudes would change, boy, would they change, if Scots, like Gaelic, had 9 million pounds per annum to invest in programmes.

Certainly, the spread of Gaelic in the media, in the schools and in playgroups has meant a higher profile for the culture and greater recognition in the rest of Scotland. But the recent optimism must be tempered with an awareness of the huge forces working against the language. Starkly put, if the native speakers of a minority language all speak the majority language of state, the native tongue ceases to be regarded as useful. Arguments about tradition, poetry, history and song, tragically, do not count. This, then, is the worry for proponents of both Scots and Gaelic. Both are under threat from the most useful language in the world. Unlike Scots, Gaelic is at least perceived as a distinctive language. Ironically, the similarity of Scots to English has contributed to the ignorant view that it is a mere dialect of English and the erosion of the tongue has fed on the accompanying lack of status.

But it is this similarity that would make the recovery of the language comparatively easy if the political will existed. In the Iberian context, the Catalans and Galicians are restoring languages related closely to Spanish; both are aware that their fellow-travellers in Euzkadi face a much more difficult task in the restoration and extension of the Basque language. Both Scots and Gaelic should survive and thrive as an integral part of our national identity and as unique elements in European civilisation. Whether they do will depend on time – and a lot of infighting in the realm of cultural politics.

The political climate in Europe has never been more sympathetic to the myriad cultures it harbours. For 30 years now, the European Bureau for Lesser-Used Languages has been working effectively at EU level to promote and protect the languages and cultures of over 40 million Europeans. In the past, European nation states regarded cultural diversity within their borders as a threat to be put down. Now, the European Union accepts the concept of unity in diversity and actively promotes regional and minority languages and cultures. In 1992, the Council of Europe adopted a Charter for Regional or Minority Languages – the first ever international legal instrument for the protection of languages like Scots and Gaelic. Significantly, when the Council of Europe voted on the Charter, it received overwhelming support. The only major European states to abstain were France and the United Kingdom, the last bastions of the centralist mentality. Finally, the UK was embarrassed into signing, and the outcome of that was detailed earlier in this book.

Based in Dublin and Brussels, the Bureau does an excellent job in pooling the resources and experiences of the peoples who make up Europe's linguistic mosaic, making them realise that together they form an important and substantial group which is an essential component of European civilisation. Active support for these languages and their rights will undoubtedly be consolidated in the coming years. The concept of a Europe of the Regions is now becoming embedded in the psyche of politicians who previously regarded the monolithic centralised nation state as political perfection. As power is gained, it generally goes hand in hand with increased confidence in and promotion of the regional or national culture. Policies of positive discrimination in favour of the native languages are instigated to counter years of positive discrimination in favour of the language of state.

All of this may come through our involvement with a changing Europe but many people believe that the tension can only be resolved when Scotland achieves political independence. Only then will Scottish culture be central to our education, our media and our life. Political change may be necessary – but it should not be. The case for the Scots language and the culture it has expressed is watertight by whatever cultural criterion you care to draw upon, be it in a Scottish, British, European, or world context. For we Scots, the language is fundamental to our present identity and essential to an understanding of our history and literary tradition. We are heirs to this tradition, and our linguistic and cultural inheritance makes us more sensitive to its genius than other people.

It is our duty to our children's children to ensure that Scots never becomes an alien tongue, or they will be strangers to the traditions that have nurtured us and that give us a unique place in the world. In that world, there are over 25 million people of Scots descent. We are guardians of their tradition as well. The survival and revival of Scots is of vital importance to British and European culture – a vivid part of the multicultural tapestry of European life. For example, Provençal and Scots were the media of Europe's greatest literature at different periods of the Middle Ages, so knowledge of such languages is essential for recall of important phases in European life. The greatest literature written in Britain between Chaucer and Spenser was produced in Scots by the Makars. When the English break out of their philistine, parochial and debilitating attitude of superiority towards the other cultures of Britain, they will recognise the brilliant alternative and complement to their own glittering literary tradition, here on their very doorstep.

Scottish culture is important nationally and internationally. The irony or tragedy of its lack of status in its homeland is one that only fully strikes home when it is seen in a world context. In the 'new' countries of the English-speaking world, American, Canadian and Australian literature are taught as a matter of course in schools and universities. In the American South, a part of the world whose landscape I know well and whose literature was practically derived from Walter Scott, Southern literature is naturally taught in all her universities. In Scotland, whose literature goes back centuries before that of any of these countries and is in most cases superior to them, there is only one department of Scottish literature in a Scottish university. Pupils can actually go through the whole of the Scottish educational system without reading a single Scottish novel. When you try to explain as best you can to intelligent foreigners why this is the case, you meet with astonished incomprehension. It is impossible for any civilised being to comprehend why one of the oldest and richest literatures in Europe is not taught in its native country. We Scots are so used to the situation that most of us are unconscious that an anomaly exists. Foreign scholars, however, who specialise in Scottish literature are highly aware of the culture's lack of prestige in its homeland.

In 1984, the Fourth International Conference on Scottish Language and Literature – Medieval and Renaissance was held at the Scottish Studies Centre on the Germersheim Campus of the University of Mainz in Germany. Here is part of an open letter, sometimes known as the Germersheim Declaration, signed by distinguished scholars from all over the world:

> The undersigned members of the Germersheim conference believe that young Scots deserve to have far more opportunity than they are now given to learn about the history and present situation of the native languages of Scotland and to acquire some understanding of their own patterns of speech and tolerance for those of other members of the Scottish community. We believe that the Scottish Education Department and other educational bodies should now take positive action to this end, and also that the press and the broadcasting media should now seriously consider whether their treatment and exposure of native varieties of Scots is fair and adequate; we ourselves believe it falls far short of this. It is particularly important that the potential of Scots as a means of communication in Scotland beyond the conveying of the humorous, the sentimental, the nostalgic and the trivial should be actively developed. This potential is amply illustrated by 600 years of distinguished literature in Scots, access to which is the right of every Scot.

One of the stock Scottish media replies to such statements is that you cannot broadcast braid Buchan, for example, because people in Glasgow will not understand it. Many Scots broadcasters have reneged on their responsibility and used this as an excuse not to broadcast the dialect. If they went ahead and allowed the native language on the airwaves, braid Buchan would be as easily grasped by the Glaswegian as the dialects of Dallas, Lancashire or the West Indies! Once the ear is attuned, all the dialects of Scots are immediately accessible and if broadcast regularly would become as familiar as Oxford English.

One of the standard teachers' responses or excuses for not allowing the use of Scots in class is that their duty is to teach Standard English and that to encourage the dialects would be to sow seeds of confusion in the children. Nonsense! This is part of the monolingual world picture refuted by the experience of multilingual communities such as Switzerland or Sweden. It is the attempt to eradicate the children's home language that has created the confusion. But the belief that there is only one acceptable speech form is so all pervasive, so ingrained and all consuming, the counter argument so rarely voiced, that an alternative bilingual policy is literally unimaginable, even to people who are themselves bilingual.

Yet an active bilingual policy whereby both Scots and English are fostered and encouraged is surely the only logical way forward. Scots will not go away, the death-wish curse that has been upon it since the eighteenth century has gone unfulfilled. For the raucle tongue is a thrawn craitur that will bide on an on, tholan ilka dint fowk hes thrown at it. Even Scots who were not raised to speak it are affected by it and frequently prove their fascination for it. Thus we have the huge popularity in the theatre of plays in forms of Scots. People care about their language.

They will continue to care about it, because they realise how central it is to our continuation as a distinctive people. At a conference for writers in lesser-used languages in Luxembourg, which I attended, someone asked provocatively, 'Why do you choose to write in these languages when you are all bilingual and could write in the principal languages of Europe?' Pierre-Jakez Hélias replied for us all when he said that it was not a matter of choice, he was *enceinte*, pregnant, with Breton and his creativity had to be given birth in that language. Many monoglots think you can simply translate one language into another and nothing is lost in translation. They do not realise the nature of language, that each one is a different window to the world. What is under threat is the treasure of a people's experience expressed through their native tongue, their unique way of seeing the world. A Welsh philosopher, J.R. Jones, eloquently expresses the potential loss:

> It is said of one experience that it is one of the most agonising possible . . . that of leaving the soil of your native country forever, of turning your back on your heritage, being torn away by the roots from your familiar land. I have not suffered that experience. But I know of an experience equally agonising, and more irreversible (for you could return to your home) and that is the experience of knowing, not that you are leaving your country, but that your country is leaving you, is ceasing to exist

under your very feet, being sucked away from you as it were by a consuming, swallowing wind, into the hands and the possession of another country and civilisation.

There should be no tension between English and Scots. They are branches of the same tree and with some effort and good will are mutually intelligible and complementary to one another. Yet they are keys to radically different world pictures. I am delighted that I am a native speaker of a national variety of English, the most powerful, prestigious and useful language in the world. But as English has become the world's lingua franca, it has become rootless and impersonal. For some Scots, it has always been that. But its role as the medium of international dialogue has made it more alien as it has been twisted to conceal, rather than tell the truth. For the Pentagon during the Vietnam war, the term 'de-escalation' often meant bombing densely populated areas and napalming children. Nearer home, words such as rationalisation are used as a smokescreen behind which shareholders and politicians can hide as their victims are condemned to the misery of long-term unemployment. In contrast, the power of Scots is its lack of duplicity, its vigorous directness, its ability to see through the false and the phony – the language reflecting the perspective of the kinds of people who have been using it for the past century.

Also, because language itself helps form the thoughts we have about our environment, Scots has a unique role as the tongue that is rooted deeply in the physical landscape we inhabit and has expressed our relationship with it for many hundreds of years. In *Haud Yer Tongue*, the schools series broadcast on Channel 4, foreign learners of Scots gave me their favourite words. For an American, it was the ability of the language to describe our weather which appealed. Her word was 'feechie, which is even worse than dreich'. The Swedish girl who followed elaborated: 'Ma favourite word is loons . . . cos they keep me warm whan it's feechie!' The students knew what everyone brought up in the Scots-speaking tradition knows: that Scots is rooted in the landscape, people, culture and history of the country, and preserves a unique way of looking at the world. Along with words like *Gemütlichkeit* in German or *saudade* in Portuguese, words like scunner, shuilpit, sonsie and nyaff are impossible to translate accurately, and any attempt will be peelie-wallie compared to the original. So if Scots were to disappear, we would lose part of our sensitivity to the environment, because no other language can describe it with the same 'feel': a snell founeran wind that wad gar yer banes chitter, a dreich haar happin aa thing alang the coast, a douce simmer's gloaming that's saft an bonnie, a thrang city street wi fowk breengin aboot an joukin atween ane anither. It is also the language that describes perfectly the human types that inhabit this landscape: a wice-like bodie . . . a sleekit scunner . . . a braw, sonsie lassie . . . a gleg wean . . . a sapsie muckle-hertit sumph . . . a thrawn besom . . . a shuilpit wee nyaff . . . a bachle wi no eneuch sough tae sprachle oot a sheugh . . . a fushionless craitur . . . a kenspeckle chield . . . a gallus chancer . . . in fact, the haill jingbang o sister an brither Scots frae Maidenkirk tae John O' Groats.

What will happen to it in the twenty-first century? To begin with, we shall see a continuation of the process of recent decades: rapid erosion in some airts, thrawn survival in other airts. In aw the airts, the structure of the dialects of Scots survives and can thrive again if the political, cultural and financial will is there to normalise the language. First, though, we have to get rid of the Scottish cringe – for many Scots are the unwitting victims and agents of a process of cultural colonisation which has been endemic for centuries. Recently, a newspaper columnist criticised the leader of the Scottish National Party, Alex Salmond, for his increasing 'affectation' of using Scots expressions such as 'I'm kent the better' in public. Only in Scotland can it be an 'affectation' for a person to use their native idiom – even if it is from a pedigree literary source! Burnsians among you will recognise the Bard's marvellous lines referring to gossipmongers:

> The mair they talk I'm kenn'd the better,
> E'en let them clash!
> An auld wife's tongue's a feckless matter
> Tae gie ane fash.

Such ignorance will surely disappear as Scotland becomes a normal country, where her culture is increasingly taught in her schools and where her native tongues are increasingly used in prestigious public forums like the Parliament. And I am convinced that Scots will be used increasingly in parliamentary debate itself as we throw off the linguistic shackles imposed by almost three centuries of adapting to English norms; statements like that from the classic sook Boswell expressed a colonised mindset shared by far too many: 'I do indeed come from Scotland, but I cannot help it.'

As Scot speaks unto Scot, the inverted commas will gradually fall away from the use of Scots words and the language's genius for both invective and affection will come into its own. The maisters of soundbite will realise that the bite will be deeper an hae mair grip gin it's couched in direct Scots terms. As newspapers report the increasingly vigorous oral medium, Scots will appear in the headlines and they too will loosen up in their attitude to the written language. Scots will gradually be validated and its use will increase and extend. The old shibboleths will brek doun and, within a generation or two of such normalisation, even the formal English spoken in Scotland will have a much higher Scots content. Seeing the language used with effect in public forums, Scots speakers will cease to regard its use as an underground activity practised by consenting adults in the privacy o their ain hame, but rather as one to be savoured openly for the sheer expressive joy of it. By 'coming out' linguistically, the native dialect speakers will in turn influence the rest to broaden their range and speech patterns. Eventually, we could even have a confident people at home with the way everyone speaks, not just a select few.

Developments in education will also be crucial. For Scotland to move towards the ideal of an inclusive society it has traditionally prided itself on, it will be necessary for generations of ingrained prejudice to be overcome and a culture of tolerance to prevail. A friend doing teaching practice recently decided to conduct the lessons in Scots. In one class, he was told that he would get problems from a group of disruptive boys and a terrific response from a group of conscientious girls. In the beginning, it was just so. Gradually, however, as the language of the boys was validated for the first time, they began to produce brilliant work. The girls, meanwhile, felt culturally excluded and their behaviour deteriorated accordingly. Imagine if all those in the past who were mocked for retaining the language at the core of their identity had been similarly praised, validated and included. That is what our education system, through our parliament, should be working towards in the future.

Ultimately, it will also demand changes in you, my brither an sister Scots! Oral retentiveness leads to strange and unhealthy complexes and fixations. Go on, break every grammatical rule in your mental straitjacket and sing out, 'A'm urnae like that – for gin I'm no pairt o the solution, I'm pairt o the problem.' Liberating, isn't it? All you middle-aged and now middle-class folk who once were patted on the heid by teachers and mammies as you divested yourself of your local dialect in order to get on in life and who now find it difficult and artificial to go back – regress now! Regain your lost heritage! Knit thy divided self back thegither again. Efter a while, ye'll no notice the jeyn. Mammies that checked their weans wi thon war cry in appalling English 'Talk proper!' – stop it. As far as the bairns gettin on is concerned, the future is Scottish. Speakers of received pronunciation

– dinnae be feart, there will aye be a wee totie Establishment for ye ti belang tae gin ye finnd it necessair. But fredome is a nobill thing. Cut your crystall vowels first with safe words like kenspeckle and clanjamfry before walking on the wild side with swally, chib, gadgie and likesae!

This inclusiveness will also need to extend to the highly effective Gaelic lobby. Aince upon a time, we were aw suppressed minorities thegither and supported ane anither, but since you climbed a bittie higher, I fear yer leaders hae kicked the ladder awa. When they speak of Scotland as a bilingual country, they mean Gaelic and English, an deil tak the hindmaist – Scots bein by far the hindmaist in the linguistic pecking order. Jeyn the process of liberation, o Gaels! All the estimated 1.5 million Scots speakers seek is parity with you 60,000 Gaelic speakers. Jeyn us, all you have to lose is your monopoly on ethnic Scottishness in our media, and a few suits!

And to you, the vast majority of Scots who still have a Scots tongue in yer heids, thank you for keeping the faith and retaining the tongue as a cherished living entity for future generations. Keep it, extend it and teach it to those linguistic less fortunates. Aye mind, though – tak tent or it's tint. Over two centuries ago, Burns was advised not to write in Scots, as it was a dying tongue which no one would understand within a generation or two. Yet here we are, still speaking, writing, singing and celebrating in this our ain raucle mither tongue. Gin we're ocht ava as a fowk, we'll still be daein the same come the twenty-saicond century! For Scots is a mirror of Scotland's soul. That is why it, and the values it expresses, will endure for aye . . . an it is comin yet for a that . . .

> For we hae faith in Scotland's hidden poo'ers
> The present's theirs, but a' the past and future's oors.

Further Reading and Bibliography

Aitken, A.J., ed., *The Dictionary of the Older Scottish Tongue* (Aberdeen University Press)

Aitken, A.J., ed., *Lowland Scots* (Association for Scottish Literary Studies, Occasional Papers No. 2, Edinburgh, 1973)

Aitken, A.J., and McArthur, Tom, eds, *Languages of Scotland* (W&R Chambers, Edinburgh, 1979)

Akenson, D.H. and Crawford, W.H., *Local Poets and Social History: James Orr, Bard of Ballycarry* (Public Record Office of Northern Ireland, 1977)

Blackhall, Sheena, *Fite Doo/Black Crow* (Keith Murray Publications, Aberdeen, 1989)

Blackhall, Sheena, *Loon*, in *Double Heider: Twa Novellas in Scots* (Itchy Coo, Edinburgh, 2003)

Buchan, N. and Hall, P., eds, *The Scottish Folksinger* (Collins, Glasgow and London, 1973)

Burton, J.H., ed., *The Autobiography of Dr Alexander Carlyle of Inveresk* (Foulis, Edinburgh, 1910)

Caa Doon the Mune (Angus Libraries and Museums, 1992)

Connolly, Linde, 'Spoken English in Ulster in the 18th and 19th Centuries', in *Ulster Folk Life*, Vol. 28, 1982

Corbett, John and Findlay, Bill, eds, *Serving Twa Maisters: Five Classic Plays in Scots Translation* (The Association for Scottish Literary Studies, Glasgow, 2005)

Daiches, David, *Literature and Gentility in Scotland* (Edinburgh University Press, 1982)

Daiches, David, ed., *A Companion to Scottish Culture* (Edward Arnold, London, 1981)

Davie, George Elder, *The Democratic Intellect* (Edinburgh University Press, 1961)

Dillon, Des, *Me and Ma Gal* (Review, London, 2001)

Elliott, Charles, ed., *Robert Henryson Poems* (Oxford University Press, 1963)

Fitt, Matthew, *But n Ben A-Go-Go* (Luath Press, Edinburgh, 2000)

Gibbon, Lewis Grassic, *A Scots Quair,* (Hutchinson, London, 1946)

Görlach, Manfred, ed., *Focus On: Scotland* (John Benjamins Publishing Company, Amsterdam and Philadelphia, 1985)

Gordon, Donald, *The Low Road Hame* (Aberdeen University Press, 1987)

Glauser, Beat, *The Scottish-English Linguistic Border* (Francke Verlag, Bern, 1974)

Graham, H.G., *Scottish Men of Letters in the Eighteenth Century* (London, 1901)

Graham, John J., *The Shetland Dictionary* (Shetland Publishing Company, Lerwick, 1984)

Graham, William, *The Handy Guide to Scots* (Ramsay Head Press, Edinburgh, 1991)

Graham, William, *The Scots Word Book* (Ramsay Head Press, Edinburgh, 1977)

Grant, W. and Dixon, J.M., eds, *Manual of Modern Scots* (Cambridge, 1921)

Grieve, Michael and Scott, Alexander, eds, *The Hugh MacDiarmid Anthology* (Routledge and Kegan Paul, London, 1972)

Haugen, E., McClure, J.D. and Thomson, D.S., eds, *Minority Languages Today* (Edinburgh University Press, 1981)

Hélias, Pierre-Jakez, *The Horse of Pride* (Yale University Press, New Haven and London, 1978)

Hubbard, Tom, ed., *The New Makars* (Mercat Press [James Thin], Edinburgh, 1991)

Jack, R.D.S., ed., *Scottish Prose 1550–1700* (Calder & Boyars, London, 1971)

Jones, Richard Foster, *The Triumph of the English Language* (Oxford University Press, 1953)

Kratzmann, Gregory, *Anglo-Scottish Literary Relations 1430–1530* (Cambridge University Press, 1980)

Leonard, Tom, *Intimate Voices: Selected Works 1965–1983* (Galloping Dog Press, Glasgow, 1984)

Macafee, Caroline, *Glasgow*, Varieties of English Around the World series (John Benjamins Publishing Company, Amsterdam, 1983)

Mackenzie, W. Mackay, ed., *The Poems of William Dunbar* (Faber & Faber, London, 1932)

MacQueen, J. and Scott, T., eds, *The Oxford Book of Scottish Verse* (Oxford University Press, 1965)

McClure, J.D., *Why Scots Matters* (Saltire Society, 1988)

McClure, J.D., ed., *Scotland and the Lowland Tongue* (Aberdeen University Press, 1983)

McClure, J.D, Aitken, A.J. and Low, J.T., eds, *The Scots Language: Planning for Modern Usage* (Ramsay Head Press, Edinburgh, 1980)

McDiarmid, M.P., ed., *The Poems of Robert Fergusson* (Scottish Text Society, Edinburgh, 1954)

MacDonald, Hamish, *The Girnin Gates*, in *Double Heider: Twa Novellas in Scots* (Itchy Coo, Edinburgh, 2003)

McGugan, I., 'Inquiry into the role of educational and cultural policy in supporting and developing Gaelic, Scots and minority languages in Scotland, 2nd Report (2003)' (The Scottish Parliament Education Culture and Sport Committee, Edinburgh, 2003) Scots translation available. English and Scots versions can be accessed via the Scottish Parliament website, www.scottish.parliament.uk.

McIlvanney, William, *Docherty* (Mainstream Publishing, Edinburgh, 1983)

McIlvanney, William, *Strange Loyalties* (Hodder & Stoughton, London, 1991)

McNeill, P. and Nicholson, R., eds, *An Historical Atlas of Scotland c.400–c.1600* (St Andrews, 1975)

Marr, Andrew, *The Battle for Scotland* (Penguin Books, London, 1992)

Mather, James Y. and Speitel, H.H., eds, *The Linguistic Atlas of Scotland, Scots Section*, Vols 1 and 2 (Croom Helm, London, 1975/1977)

Millar, J.H., *A Literary History of Scotland* (London, 1903)

Morgan, Edwin, *Essays* (Carcanet Press, 1974)

Munro, Michael, *The Patter* (Glasgow City Libraries, 1992)

Munro, Michael, *The Patter: Another Blast* (Canongate, Edinburgh, 1988)

Niven, Liz and Fortune, Pete, eds, *A Braw Brew: Stories in Scots for Young Folk* (Watergaw, Newton Stewart, 1997)

Niven, Liz and Jackson, Robin, eds, *The Scots Language: Its Place in Education* (Dundee, 1998)

Murison, David, *The Guid Scots Tongue* (Blackwood, Edinburgh, 1977)

Murison, David, ed., *The Scottish National Dictionary* (Edinburgh, 1931–76)

Nicolaisen, W.F.H., *Scottish Place Names* (B.T. Batsford, London, 1976)

Paisley, Janet, *Not for Glory* (Canongate, Edinburgh, 2001)

Price, Glanville, *The Languages of Britain* (Edward Arnold, 1984)

Robinson, Mairi, ed., *The Concise Scots Dictionary* (Aberdeen University Press, 1985)

Robertson, James, *The Fanatic* (Fourth Estate, London, 2000)

Robertson, James, ed., *A Tongue in Yer Heid* (Black & White Publishing, Edinburgh, 1994)

Royle, Trevor, *The Macmillan Companion to Scottish Literature* (Macmillan, London, 1983)

The Scots Pairlament Cross Pairty Group on the Scots Leid, *Scots: A Statement o Principles* (Edinburgh, 2003)

Scott, P.H., *In Bed With an Elephant: The Scottish Experience* (Saltire Pamphlets, The Saltire Society, Edinburgh, 1984)

Shreeves, W.P., *A Study in the Language of Scottish Prose Before 1600* (John Murphy & Co., Baltimore, 1893)

Smith, G. Gregory, *Specimens of Middle Scots* (Blackwood, Edinburgh, 1902)

Stephens, Meic, *Linguistic Minorities in Western Europe* (Gomer Press, Llandysul, 1976)

Telfer, Glenn, *Robert the Bruce: A Scots Life* (Argyll Publishing, 1996)

Trudgill, Peter, ed., *Language in the British Isles* (Cambridge University Press, 1984)

Ulster Folk Museum, *Ulster Dialects: An Introductory Symposium* (Hollywood, County Down, 1964)

Watson, Roderick, *The Literature of Scotland* (Macmillan, London, 1984)

Wheeler, Leslie W., ed., *Ten Northeast Poets* (Aberdeen University Press, 1985)

Williams, Gordon, *From Scenes Like These* (London, 1968)

Williamson, A.H., *Scottish National Consciousness in the Age of James VI* (John Donald, Edinburgh, 1979)

Wilson, Sir J., *The Dialects of Central Scotland* (Oxford, 1926)

Wilson, L. Colin, *Luath Scots Language Learner* (Luath Press, Edinburgh, 2002)

Wolfe, J.N., ed., *Government and Nationalism in Scotland* (Edinburgh University Press, 1969)

PERIODICALS

Cairn: The Historie Jurnal in the Scots Leid, AUSLQ, 1997

Lallans, John Law, ed., The Scots Language Society (quarterly)

Scottish Language, J. Derrick McClure, ed., Association for Scottish Literary Studies (annually)

Ullans, Ulster-Scots Language Society (bi-annually)

Resources

Association for Scottish Literary Studies
Department of Scottish History
9 University Gardens
University of Glasgow
Glasgow
G12 8QH
www.asls.org.co.uk

European Bureau for Lesser-Used Languages
Sr. Chill Dara   Kildare Street 46
Baile Átha Cliath   Dublin 2
Eire   Ireland

Scots Language Resource Centre (SLRC)
A.K. Bell Library
York Place
Perth
PH2 8EP
Phone (44) (0) 1738 440199
Fax (44) (0) 1738 477010
Email: office@scotsyett.com

Scots Language Society
Blackford Lodge
Blackford
Perthshire
PH4 1QP

Phone: (44) (0) 1764 682315
Fax: (44) (0) 870 428 5086

Scottish Language Dictionaries
27 George Square
Edinburgh
EH8 9LD
Phone/Fax: 0131 650 4149
Dictionary of the Scots Language: www.dsl.ac.uk

The Ulster-Scots Agency	**Tha Boord o Ulstèr-Scotch**
Franklin House	Franklin Haw
5th Floor	5t Flare
10–12 Brunswick Street	10–12 Brunswick Raa
Belfast	Bilfawst
BT2 7GE	BT2 7GE
Phone: 028 9023 113	
Fax: 028 9023 1898	

The Ulster-Scots Language Society
218 York Street (2nd Floor)
Belfast
BT15 1GY
Phone: 00 44 28 9075 8985

SCOTS ON THE WAB
The following list came from Scots Tung's website: http://uk.geocities.com/rfairnie@btinternet.com. Many thanks to Bob Fairnie.

www.scotsyett.com
Scots Language Resource Centre, the high heid yin o aw the Scots language organisations. Distributer o *Lallans* magazine.

www.scuilwab.org.uk
Scottish Language Dictionaries' interactive Scuil Wab for bairns at the scuil, wi rowth o Scots language teachin graith for teachers.

www.scots-online.org
Andy Eagle's Scots wabsteid. A comprehensive guidal tae the Scots language, comin oot o Germany.

www.scotstext.org
Sandy Fleemin's Scotstext: traditional Scots texts, poetry, sangs, plays, novels, essays an owersettins.

http://myweb.tiscali.co.uk/wirhoose/but
John M. Tait's wabsite, wi an innin tae Shetlandic an maitter baith in an aboot Scots.

www.mithertongue.co.uk
Mither Tongue's new wabsite. Production o cairds, gifts an stationery, waddin an celebration stationery, maistly in the Scots language.

www.scottish.parliament.uk/vli/language/scots/index.htm
Hame page o the Scots Pairlament's new wabsite owerset intae Scots.

www.scotlandsculture.org
The wabsite for aw strinds o Scots culture pitten oot jyntly bi the Scots Executive an the Scots Library an Information Cooncil.

www.lallans.co.uk
The auldest an senior o aw the Scots language upsteerer groups, the Scots Leid Associe is the furthsetter o *Lallans* magazine an co-foonder o the SLRC.

www.itchy-coo.com
Scots language buiks for bairns o aw ages, giein them an inlat tae readin an writin in Scots an learnin them a sight mair aboot their ain culture.

www.rampantscotland.com/gaelic.htm
The Rampant Scotland Directory that gies ye aw the cleeks ye'll ever want for kennin aboot baith the Gaelic an Scots languages, an a yett tae the culture o the Celts forbye.

www.mcott.freeserve.co.uk/BerryBush
Plain, easy unnerstuid Scots, juist the wey it's spoken the day athoot ony literary fur coat an nae drawers.

www.scottishcorpus.ac.uk
SCOTS, The Scottish Corpus Of Texts & Speech, providin an important, valuable an sindry resource for linguistic an cultural research intae Scots an Scottish English.

www.scotsgate.com
A treisure kist o Scots graith. Juist aboot awthin ye ever wantit tae ken aboot the Scots language aw rowed intae the ae wabsite.

Index